# REYNER BANHAM REVISITED

RICHARD J. **WILLIAMS**

# REYNER BANHAM
# REVISITED

**REAKTION** BOOKS

*For my children, Abby and Alex*

Published by Reaktion Books Ltd
Unit 32, Waterside
44–48 Wharf Road
London N1 7UX, UK
www.reaktionbooks.co.uk

First published 2021
Copyright © Richard J. Williams 2021

All rights reserved

No part of this publication may be reproduced, stored in a retrieval
system, or transmitted, in any form or by any means, electronic,
mechanical, photocopying, recording or otherwise, without the
prior permission of the publishers

Printed and bound in Great Britain by TJ Books Ltd, Padstow, Cornwall

A catalogue record for this book is available from the British Library

ISBN  978 1 78914 417 8

# CONTENTS

Banham adjusts the rear-view mirror of his rental car.
From *Reyner Banham Loves Los Angeles*, dir. Julian Cooper (1972).

# PREFACE

Reyner Banham's extraordinary work first got my attention in
1988 when his mischievous and provocative film on Los Angeles
was re-broadcast by the BBC as a memorial tribute. I was a
Goldsmiths art student at the time and the film, although it
was by then seventeen years old, made a powerful impression.
Banham was earthy and grounded, and seemed to consume
the same things as ordinary viewers: hamburgers, cars,
advertising. But it was also the fact that these ordinary things
obviously *were* for him as much art history as anything else,
so his riffs on Los Angeles's genuine achievements in modern
architecture coexisted with his reflections on freeway driving,
surfboard design or simply the experience of the beach. There
was something refreshingly unjudgmental about it all, as if to
say that art was, and could be, anywhere, and that a hamburger
was as important in its way as a Hockney. I had a discussion not
long after that with Jon Thompson, then Goldsmiths' head of
art, and a few others. Thompson, who liked to talk to students
about anything, was unconvinced by Banham. He belonged to
a simpler, more optimistic time, Thompson thought, pre-oil
crisis, more trusting of technology and authority. The world was
nastier and art needed to be tougher and more critical; Banham
was an anachronism.

I wasn't so sure. Banham's LA film raised questions about
what culture was, and who was entitled to pronounce on that
didn't seem to me to be simplistic at all; certainly not after
the 1980s art boom, which as much as it saw an increase in
art's popularity, also saw its prejudices and power structures
intensify. I continued reading Banham and then much
later started teaching him, starting with an essay he wrote

collaboratively with Paul Barker and others for *New Society* in 1969, 'Non-plan'. The essay asked difficult questions about the built environment that couldn't be labelled traditionally right- or left-wing, and it revealed prejudices that cut across both. Its embrace of the consumer society saw its promise taken up by the right in the 1980s in the form of the development corporations that took charge of failed industrial zones, but its thoroughly liberal, even hedonistic approach to the city was at odds with the social conservatism emanating from government at the same time. These contractions were both unsettling and appealing, and consequently great to teach.

Banham's work started to seem prescient. He was not the first to think about social class and art history, but he did so from the point of view of lived experience, which was unusual; aspects of his take on popular culture could seem more in sync with the 'new' art-history of the 1980s. His 1955 essay on the Cadillac Eldorado was as provocative in its implications for the study of culture as the essays Roland Barthes published as *Mythologies*; his understanding of energy consumption in architecture in *The Architecture of the Well-tempered Environment* suggested an architectural history written from the perspective of environmental controls; *A Concrete Atlantis* was an account of the taste for industrial architecture well in advance of its becoming mainstream; he took Silicon Valley seriously years before most, perhaps even any, architectural historians did. And in common with colleagues at the *Architectural Review*, his work was shot through with an understanding of ruins and the picturesque, themes that powerfully re-emerged throughout the humanities in the 1990s. Banham's own position seemed to get more, not less interesting. As a working-class scholar in a uniquely privileged field, he was well placed to see prejudice and taste for what they were. And in a manner reminiscent of contemporary media figures, his career was a series of performances contingent on the audience: overlapping, contradictory, often inconsistent. I make no attempt to rescue Banham from those contradictions here, because they seem to me to be the point.

Banham's status is less certain than you might imagine. For historians of post-war British architecture he is inescapable, especially when those histories touch on Brutalism, about which he wrote a manifesto in 1955. His *Los Angeles: The Architecture of Four Ecologies* is, whatever kind of a book it is, one of the most widely read accounts of that city. He is a historical figure himself, one of the key members of the Independent Group that met at London's ICA, a group that is one of the founding myths of Pop art. He was an accomplished media performer too, and the theatre of his appearance, with its assorted props – beard, glasses, small-wheeled bicycle, cowboy hat – was both loved and caricatured. That media presence, along with the colossal volume of his journalism, meant that he thought he was not taken as seriously as an academic as he would have liked. There were eight, perhaps nine, major books, depending on how you account for them, and they loosely structure my account of Banham's life here, but they were only a fraction of the overall output. The seriousness with which he undertook paid writing was partly a function of needing the money, but partly also resulted from a sensibility that understood public communication as part of the job – and his writing and speaking were lucid in ways that academic writing and speaking is often not. That sensibility may have sometimes played against him. There was also a contradictory approach to what we would now call theory. Part of the time, his theory – and it came closest to being stated in the inaugural professorial lecture he never gave at NYU – was 'being there'. Presence, physical presence and experience was what gave you the right to talk about anything. He had been there, and the contact with the thing in real life gave him the evidence to talk about it. At the same time, his writing is full of high-flown concepts: 'image', 'structure', 'aformalism', 'ecology', 'environment' – there are countless examples.

Banham didn't necessarily use the same words, but his work repeatedly touched on concerns that were central to the way the humanities and social sciences rethought themselves at the end of the twentieth century. His interdisciplinarity is critical: it is telling in many ways that many of his articles appeared under the bylines 'Not Quite Architecture' (for the *Architects' Journal*) and 'Arts in Society' (for *New Society*). The operation of social class was also a repeated concern, as was the encounter with consumer society and its effect on politics, the canon of art and the politics of desire. He never wrote at length in a psychoanalytical mode, but he often invoked psychoanalytical language, and showed how desire might complicate architecture. In rewriting modernism through the prism of Futurism, Banham made a good case for the irrational, and he retained a taste for it throughout his career. He was largely unconcerned with issues that later troubled the humanities, for example gender and race. His imagination was a stereotypically masculine one by contemporary standards, and as the design historian Gillian Naylor has pointed out, women designers or writers scarcely featured. They were 'dolly birds' for the most part, as they were for 1960s man in general. But the fact is that so many of Banham's objects – Futurist cities, hamburgers, aircraft, outrageous cars – remain troubling in myriad ways, and it is precisely because they do that I think his work is worth returning to. Writing the book has been an attempt to make sense of Banham now, to make the interpretative leap that in some ways he didn't. It is a history of ideas, only some of which are architectural. Critically, those ideas were embodied by

Banham himself: often the best way to understand his thinking is to see it as essentially performative, acted out in public, and sometimes quite literally involving dressing up.

In the final stages of writing the book, the world plunged into the coronavirus pandemic. The effect on the richest parts of the world was, temporarily, catastrophic, calling into question technologies, and forms of urbanization and architecture, in the most unprecedented way. I couldn't help thinking how much Banham, had he still been alive, would have been captivated by it all – by the apocalyptic images of empty cities, by the sudden shift of the world economy online, and the appearance of new medical technologies. It was hard not to look at the enormous field hospital created in London's Excel Arena and not think of Banham, for it was a big shed, an architectural type-form he had often written about, here given a rather morbid twist. It is not difficult to imagine him writing about it, or – on a smaller scale – the ventilator, the technology about which there was so much anxiety in the early stages of the pandemic. Banham might have been a product of a particular time and place, but many of his interests were transhistorical and interdisciplinary and remain relevant. Certainly still relevant is his vision of the human world as a fragile, thin technological layer in which design is at best contingent – that is worth returning to, repeatedly and often.

Banham at Silurian Dry Lake, 1980.
Photograph by Tim Street-Porter.

# 1 MULTIPLE BANHAMS

If there is an image that embodies something of the complexity of the architectural historian and critic Peter 'Reyner' Banham, it is this one. Taken in 1980 through a long lens by the Los Angeles-based English photographer Tim Street-Porter, it shows Banham, then aged 58, riding a small-wheeled Moulton bicycle along the base of a dried-up lake bed.[1] It was one result of an epic three-day shoot with Street-Porter for the 1982 book *Scenes in America Deserta*. The bicycle was Banham's idea: he had adopted the Moulton in the middle of the 1960s to get around Bloomsbury.[2] The location is Silurian Lake, some 20 miles north of Baker in the middle of the Mojave Desert, about three hours by car inland from Los Angeles. It is one of the more extraordinary images of Banham's career, a career not lacking in such images. Banham, a transplanted Englishman from Norwich, was in full Western mode by that stage: Stetson hat, cowboy boots, bolo tie, his spectacular beard now a resplendent grey. The lake bed shimmers; rugged mountains project in relief in the background. Banham's imposing frame makes the bicycle look faintly ridiculous, more so here because the tiny wheels are so indicative of the urban context this is so obviously not. Where you expect a horse you get a bike made for inner London.

A funny, surreal, otherworldly image, it says a great deal about its subject. Banham was a mass of contradictions, and most of them can be found here. He was as central to the project of the Modern Movement as many architects, and his career-long commitment to it is there in the design of the Moulton bike, a paragon of function defining form. But that coexists with the kitsch of the cowboy outfit, and beyond that, a lifelong passion for popular American culture. And if you could have

been there listening to him, you would have been startled
by the contrast between the Western garb and the wearer's
rich, Norfolk-accented voice, a signal from a much older,
and very different civilization 6,000 miles to the east.
Banham's contradictions were, as this book argues, his
strength. If you revisit his work now, whether in his mode
as an architectural historian, cultural critic, essayist or travel
writer, you find someone at ease with the complexity of the
contemporary world.

Banham is not easy to categorize. He was born in Norwich,
Norfolk, in 1922 to working-class parents in a suburb of small
brick terraced houses. His father was a gas engineer and a
practical man, good with machines. Banham was a clever
school pupil, talented at languages, whose teachers saw him
pursuing an academic career. But he took an apprenticeship
with the Bristol Aeroplane Company instead, where he trained
and worked as an engineer during the Second World War.[3]

Banham, c. 1926, with toy crane.

Wedding of Banham and Mary Mullett, 1946.

Banham returned to Norwich thereafter, working briefly at the Maddermarket Theatre in the city, and writing art criticism for local newspapers including the *Evening News*, the *Eastern Daily Press* and the *Norfolk Magazine*. In 1946 he married Mary Mullett, a schoolteacher and subsequently an accomplished artist, curator and writer.[4] Her contribution to Banham's career would be immense, in the first instance letting him know of the existence of the Courtauld Institute of Art in London, where he enrolled on an art history degree programme in 1949 aged 27.[5] He finished this first degree in 1952, staying on at the Courtauld to study part-time for a PhD supervised by the architectural historian Nikolaus Pevsner, who although based at Birkbeck was permitted to supervise through the University of London's federal structure. The PhD subsequently became Banham's first book, *Theory and Design in the First Machine Age*.[6] Banham's class background was relatively unusual in this context; in addition to this, he was one of a tiny, albeit growing, number of students

Banham family, Christmas 1956.

in England to have done a PhD in art history at this point. He
had some rarity value from the start.[7] The same year he started
the PhD, 1952, he joined the *Architectural Review*, also part-time,
as 'literary editor'. At the same time he became involved with
the much-discussed Independent Group that met at London's
Institute of Contemporary Arts (ICA) (see Chapter Three). In the
middle of all this professional production, he and Mary also
produced a family: Debby, born in 1953, and Ben, born in 1955.

Banham lectured widely as well as working at the
*Architectural Review* before eventually securing a lectureship
in architectural history at University College London's Bartlett
School of Architecture in 1965, a position he held until 1976.
A lifelong Americanophile, he then crossed the Atlantic to
the department of architecture at SUNY Buffalo, and then in
1980 the University of California, Santa Cruz. He was appointed
Sheldon H. Solow Chair of Architectural History at New York
University (NYU) in 1988, a post he was unable to take up because

of the cancer from which he was then suffering. He returned
to England, gravely ill, and died at the Royal Free Hospital in
London in March 1988, aged 66.

It was an extraordinarily prolific career, so much so that it is
hard to know how much output there was. Banham published
anywhere between 750 and 1,000 articles, depending on whose
account you read, and up to sixteen books, made many radio
broadcasts for the BBC and several documentary films, and
held a number of prestigious consultancies, including the
selection of architect Richard Meier for the new Getty Center
in Los Angeles in 1984.[8] There is also no question of Banham's
importance at some key moments in the history of the Modern
Movement: his involvement with the Independent Group, for
example, saw him in a dialogue with some of the most radical
architects and artists then working in England, including Peter
and Alison Smithson. He was subsequently one of the key
supporters of the group Archigram, led by Peter Cook. Banham's
doctoral work on architectural modernism contained not only
the first serious analysis of Le Corbusier's writings in English,
but the first detailed re-evaluation of Futurism in English.
Banham's career as an architectural critic found him the chief
advocate of Brutalism. By the mid-1960s, when he took up the
post at the Bartlett, Banham was an inescapable part of the
London architectural scene.

If you care about the architecture of the modern movement,
or Brutalism, or Pop art, or post-war industrial design, you will
undoubtedly have read fragments of Banham: he is ubiquitous
in the literature on those things. But these really are only
fragments given the volume of his output, and the more you
look at it, the more complex and contradictory it can seem.
Sometimes it seems he wrote on anything, from the familiar
architectural topics to fast food, desert landscapes, aircraft
design and crash-test dummies. Some of it was extremely

scholarly, some of it really not, especially after the first book, *Theory and Design in the First Machine Age*, was out of the way. The architectural critic Robert Maxwell wrote that he was 'relatively careless' of his scholarly reputation, his later books 'directed towards a view of life he believed in rather than the fulfilment of a scholarly career'.[9]

Banham often seems prescient now. Many of our contemporary anxieties he had already seemingly anticipated. What happens when advances in technology threaten architecture's relevance, even existence? What do we do with the ruins of industrial civilization? What happens when culture really becomes mass culture? What becomes of our cities, when mobility displaces place as a core value? What do hamburgers mean? An inveterate traveller, he was in Silicon Valley decades before the technology boom, and he was poking around the ruins of post-industrial Buffalo years before such ruins became the default form for museums of contemporary art. He was concerned too with the environmental aspects of architecture in the late 1960s, and asked questions about the politics of energy use that have only become more pertinent. He wasn't always right. His Silicon Valley, visited in 1987 for the Italian magazine *Casabella*, is a de facto ruin, all broken dreams and abandoned buildings – he thought, mistakenly, it was finished.[10] But he was there, and everywhere, and the questions he asked remain, in large part, our questions too.

In person he was as complex as his output. The name, to begin with: Peter to friends and colleagues. 'Reyner' was an invention he adopted for professional work as soon as he started writing art criticism in Norwich just after the war. Apparently a family name, Reyner had a gravitas and distinctiveness that would mark him out; it provided an identity and a shell for someone who was, despite appearances to the contrary, quite shy.[11] The adoption of a stage name was a theatrical device of a piece with his dressing up. In the 1950s at the ICA, as part of the Independent Group, he affected a top hat and tails; in the early 1960s he devised an inimitable look of flat cap, bow tie, small-wheeled Moulton bike and huge, Old Testament-style beard.[12] In 1976 he could be found lecturing in a Superman T-shirt and faux-military jacket, an ironic pseudo-revolutionary pose.[13] His life in the United States saw him become, superficially at least, a cowboy. He liked dressing up, because he regarded public life as inherently performative, and we ought to regard his writing in the same way, varying significantly according to the mode and the audience. Others have recognized something of this. Todd Gannon has written of different Banhams emerging at different periods of his career, according to who is doing the history: an anti-establishment Banham emerges in Panayotis Tournikiotis's work, a Futurist in Anthony Vidler's account, and a pragmatist in Nigel Whiteley's 2002 book. All of these things seem to me more or less true, but I argue here that he was

Banham family Christmas card, 1967.

Reyner Banham riding a Moulton bicycle along Carteret Street, Westminster, London, c. 1965.

capable of being all of them, and others, simultaneously. It just depended on the audience.[14] There were in some respects as many Banhams as there were audiences, and this performative complexity is one of the reasons why his work is worth revisiting: his performativity shows he understood something fundamental about the modern world. His inconsistency certainly doesn't make him any less important, or compelling.[15]

Certain aspects of Banham and his work were, however, consistent: in terms of writing, a taste for plain speech, facts and jokes, and in architecture, a commitment to the project of the Modern Movement. He was firmly opposed to postmodernism, for example, a tendency he thought reactionary and silly – see his review of the second edition of Charles Jencks's *The Language of Post-modern Architecture*.[16] Yet his treatment of the architecture of Los Angeles in his 1971 book is surely, even if the term was not yet widely in use, postmodern in spirit. It is a city of surfaces, where kitsch is elevated to an art form, and the city's modernist experiments relegated to supporting acts. His tribute to American car design in the 1955 article 'Vehicles of Desire' is an earlier example of the same thing: the car in this essay is no longer a functional device but 'a thick stream of loaded symbols'.[17] His discussion of the car, in that case a Cadillac Eldorado, has a great deal in common with the French structuralist critic Roland Barthes's famous discussion of the Citroën DS. In both cases the world has been in effect replaced by its representation, a position indistinguishable in retrospect from the postmodern.[18]

Banham's multiplicity in fact had origins in English class politics. You can see this in a photograph published in the *Journal of the Royal Institute of British Architects* in May 1961. The picture was taken on 7 February of that year on the occasion of Banham's lecture to the RIBA, titled 'The History of the Immediate Future'. [19] It shows Banham after the talk with Pevsner and another eminent architectural historian, John Summerson, then curator of the Sir John Soane's Museum. He stands a little to the left of the others, looking on while they engage in intimate conversation. There's nearly a generation between them, Banham 39 and the others nearly in their sixties. And how awkward he looks in the poor-quality photograph of the occasion, published in the RIBA *Journal*, gripping his wine glass with both hands. Despite their diverse origins in Scotland and Germany, Summerson and Pevsner were born to rule and look it. Banham wasn't, and also looks it, standing on the periphery of their conversation in a way that could be both figurative and literal. That is maybe an over-interpretation of what is not much more than a snapshot, and there could be any number of reasons for Banham's seeming edginess. At the same time, the responses to the talk, published at length in the RIBA *Journal*, give some weight to that interpretation: full of put-downs and point-scoring, they're all about keeping an outsider in his place. His entry to the RIBA was on the grounds of being part of the editorial team of the *Architectural Review*, a position he had held since 1952, but institutionally he was an outsider, as he would be, one way or another, his whole life. That position, played up for effect in Banham's media work, meant a particular alertness to class. Banham was far from alone in that, either with friends emerging from the Independent Group or in terms of broader cultural trends, but it was something distinctive in the architectural area, and discernable right the way through his career.[20]

The RIBA picture perhaps shows something of that class consciousness. Three years later he gave a talk in London that elaborated this further.[21] This was 'The Atavism of the Short-distance Mini-cyclist', given in 1964 as a memorial lecture to Terry Hamilton, Richard Hamilton's first wife.[22] Here he made clear that if you were, like him, of working-class origins but playing in a middle-class field, you were already operating in multiple registers depending on with whom you were speaking. More specifically, Banham identified a class-based political contradiction. He was caught between two things, he said: an adherence to mainstream Labour politics, with its somewhat censorious and utilitarian view of culture; and a genuine love of mass-produced, particularly American, culture, which

Banham, Pevsner and Summerson at Banham's 1961 RIBA lecture, 'The History of the Immediate Future'.

he developed as a child in Norwich. The latter, if not exactly proscribed by the left, was regarded with suspicion or worse (this was certainly true of Herbert Read, ICA director during the Independent Group period; Read's anti-Americanism was explicit).[23] Banham's childhood culture, he liked to say, only partly for effect, was Hollywood.[24] American culture was the dominant culture, displacing anything mainstream left intellectuals like Richard Hoggart regarded as either authentic or appropriate.[25] For Banham, the authentic popular culture celebrated by Hoggart and the intellectual left was not much more than a comforting myth.[26] The 1964 talk is as clear as anything on that problem of being both left-leaning and America-consuming. It wasn't only the political left that represented a problem for Banham, but architects, certainly the younger modernists, many of whom represented a subset of the left (the overlap was structural in post-war England in any case, given the importance of the state as a client, and the fact that the country's biggest firm was the architects' department of the London County Council). Banham's position was a difficult one. The architects' response to popular culture was 'continually fascinating, frustrating and in the end disappointing', and they cited the way former collaborators such as Peter and Alison Smithson had increasingly distanced themselves from their previous enthusiasm for it. For Banham, the architectural difficulties were illustrated by an unbuilt Tecton scheme in Finsbury, London:

> The whole proposition still called for a carefully framed working class still life. It kept such firm quotation marks round the inhabitants that they were not deciding the aesthetic of their own dwelling or anything of the sort, the big frame dominated and the working class was simply allowed to peep out through little carefully-framed holes on every floor.[27]

That architectural observation pointed to a larger one about culture, that in the Banham universe it was entirely possible to have agency as a consumer. To like Hollywood movies did not mean one also bought into American politics, a position he shared with his Independent Group friends. One could be left-leaning and also a moviegoer; one could simultaneously inhabit different universes, as any working-class intellectual routinely had to do anyway. One way Banham dealt with that was to turn consumer passions into respectable academic ones. He was, for example, a motor racing fan, and the interest in Futurism was certainly in part a way to give respectable form to what was otherwise straightforward autophilia.[28] Banham's identities

were multiple, as they are for any intellectual; his were arguably
more multiple than most.

One consistency in Banham, however, was humour: he
consistently looked for (and found) the absurd and the perverse;
the writing is strewn with wordplay, giving much of the
journalism a comic tone. He was a Monty Python fan and there
is something in their characteristic sketch format that is also
his, especially in the journalism.[29] It appealed a great deal to his
visionary editor at *New Society*, Paul Barker, who also saw that
the jokes were ways to more serious matters. 'He was very witty,'
Barker said. 'That was always one of the attractions about him.
He realized you could conduct serious arguments while making
jokes.'[30]

They could also be deflections, as Barker also realized.
Banham joked only 'when there something that was serious
enough to be funny about', and there is no question that
Banham's work was accompanied by a set of traumas, never
fully acknowledged or alluded to, but which have a presence.[31]
Banham's war experience at the Bristol Aeroplane Company,
for example, when a single air raid in 1943 involved the
instantaneous loss of perhaps two hundred friends and
colleagues, was compressed into a joke after the war – Banham
declared, 'I decided to recycle myself as an intellectual' – but
that left out not only the death and destruction but the effect
on its writer's own mental health.[32] There were domestic
traumas too: in 1956 Mary Banham had a leg amputated after
cancer was diagnosed, resulting in a stay of several months in
hospital, with no contact with the young children, and a long
period of convalescence while she recovered.[33] Professionally,
his career looks like one of consistent success, but the Banhams'
move to the United States in 1976, initially to the school of
architecture at SUNY Buffalo, was difficult, throwing into
question many of their hopes about the country. Banham's

public presence, whatever hat he was wearing at the time, was sunny positivism for the most part, and that is how he was often received. The reality was more complex.

This more complex Banham emerges once you try to look at the career as a whole. The many historical treatments of the Independent Group show a youngish critic-provocateur, in the right place at the right time. London in 1955 was a landscape of opportunity for an historian of modernism; Banham was, and remains, essential to it. However, the later phases of Banham's career find someone often enough out of both time and place, as, for example, when he seemed to abandon writing about architecture altogether to engage with the experience of the high desert (*Scenes in America Deserta*).[34] Things could also go wrong for this most accomplished of intellectual performers, when, for example, in his involvement with the design in business organization IDCA (International Design Conference Aspen) in 1970, he misjudged the intervention of the French delegation, which included the young sociologist Jean Baudrillard. Banham's optimism about technology in this context was out of step with a post-1968 left increasingly critical of these things; he was roundly criticized in the French remarks.[35]

Banham's timing was off again in relation to what is arguably his most innovative book, *The Architecture of the Well-tempered Environment*, originally published in 1969. It was the first architectural history since Sigfried Giedion's *Mechanization Takes Command* to be oriented about building services and, unlike Giedion, it was written by a one-time engineer.[36] The reception to the book at the time of its publication was sometimes negative, however; a book that cast architecture in an environmental context, it didn't sit well with the emergent environmental consciousness in architecture, which (post-*Silent Spring*) sought limits on human activity.[37] As Banham noted, acerbically, in the introduction to the second edition of the book, some reviewers had interpreted it as a manifesto in favour of 'wasting energy'.[38] It wasn't, but Banham's complaints about the technologically regressive qualities of contemporary environmentalism and his aversion to vernacular architecture did not endear him to mainstream environmentalists. But Banham's use of the term 'environment' was more subtle and inclusive than it might at first appear.

Even Banham's take on Los Angeles, although probably his best-known work, was oddly out of time. His first forays into the city took place in the mid-1960s, and it was for the BBC Third Programme (the forerunner of today's Radio 3) in 1968 that Banham first developed his argument about the city's ecologies (his use of the term was very much his own).[39] By the time it appeared as a book, in 1971, the city's poor air quality was perhaps the dominant theme in the popular perception of the city, and the film he made the following year for the BBC with Julian Cooper, *Reyner Banham Loves Los Angeles*, makes this clear enough: even in the original 35mm print, which is rarely seen these days, the city's skies are thick with yellow smog, with little of the famous sunshine.[40] Banham's defence was to note, probably correctly, that the experience was no worse than that of the London he had left behind. But to celebrate Los Angeles at the moment at which it had started to think of itself as an environmental disaster was, in retrospect, perverse. A savage review of the book by the LA-based artist Peter Plagens characterized the city as of 'The Ecology of Evil', a place of environmental and moral pollution that Banham, 'the fashionable sonofabitch', could enjoy because he didn't have to live there. It was, he thought, the classic fantasy of a middle-aged Englishman abroad.[41] Whatever the validity of Plagens's judgement, after the October 1973 oil crisis a city organized around the prolific use of energy could certainly seem anachronistic.

Banham's later books have an elegiac quality about them. No longer was he writing about cultures that were vigorously alive (as the Modern Movement had been in 1950s London); instead his subjects were frequently dead or dying. His *Megastructure* was a lament for a future that for the most part had never arrived, 'urban futures of the recent past' the vaguely mournful subtitle.[42] *Scenes in America Deserta* explored the ruins of abandoned settlements in the high desert. *A Concrete Atlantis* was nearly an elegy for the author himself as he narrated the perils of what would nowadays be called urban exploration.[43] What he has to say about contemporary architecture arguably mattered less as he went on. In 1988, at the moment of his death, Banham wasn't one of the figures you turned to when you wanted to know more about the then rising tendency of postmodernism; if anyone had taken it on, it was Banham's former doctoral student Charles Jencks. At his death, in terms of architecture at least, Banham had become uncharacteristically rearguard.

When I show *Reyner Banham Loves Los Angeles* to students, as I have done countless times, the anachronisms intrigue them first of all: the beard, his hats, his leather jackets, his distinctive speech patterns and vocabulary. The cars are as profligate and sprawling as the landscape, the quality of the air visibly dreadful, the casual sexism occasionally grating. The treatment of race is unsteady to say the least: the film opens with Watts, the 1966 riots that profoundly destabilized the city, and drew attention to the fact that perhaps not all was well. But Banham's LA is for the most part a city of relative privilege and entitlement, and mostly white, where Hispanics exist for colour and entertainment. If these things are now puzzling for students, they are nevertheless generally drawn to something in Banham that has to do with the fact that as an art historian he had found a way to deal with a whole city, not only in terms of images as art historians generally

Banham gives the viewer a lesson in driving LA's freeways.
From *Reyner Banham Loves Los Angeles*, dir. Julian Cooper (1972).

do, but as a set of complex and multi-dimensional experiences.
For them, as much as for Banham, it makes art history bigger
– and it's not just freeways, but hamburgers and strip malls and
beaches, all things that have profoundly aesthetic dimensions,
but are not normally recuperable to the realm of art. Suddenly
a lot of things that normally reside outside the discourse of art
history are included – and that links Banham to the utopianism
of early twentieth-century art movements such as Futurism that
actively sought the aestheticization of the everyday. Banham
identified with Futurism and remained excited by its possibilities
throughout his career. In a work such as *Los Angeles*, life in
some ways had fulfilled the promise of Futurism and become
aesthetic spectacle; a mixture of opportunities as well as threats,
it was to be explored with enthusiasm.

That world Banham explored mainly through the medium of
journalism. Banham divided his work into historical scholarship

and other writing that he did to 'pay the bills', but in reality the distinction is harder to call.[44] Much of the sharpest writing is not to be found in the academic books, but in his journalism, especially the work he did for Paul Barker at *New Society*.[45] (A selection of this can be found in the posthumous anthology *A Critic Writes*.[46]) Barker's magazine was left-leaning, but unaligned to any party, and he found in Banham an open-minded and energetic writer prepared to investigate any aspect of the emergent consumer society, and one who was at least alert to the possibility that some of the more interesting cultural solutions might come from the USA. The byline was 'Arts in Society', giving Banham free rein to discuss anything. His journalistic concerns were typically expansive: freeway driving, Italy, the planning system, Los Angeles. But they could also be small and everyday. He wrote reasonably often about food, for example, not because his tastes were anything out of the ordinary (they were not) but because food represented in microcosm the modern world. There was also a residual legacy of post-war austerity, as he pointed out in the 1979 BBC film *Fathers of Pop*: food was of perpetual interest because his generation had simply been hungry so often.[47] His 1970 article 'The Crisp at the Crossroads', for *New Society*, is a way of describing how a well-developed consumer society has democratized and industrialized the production of food, to the point at which it is not really food at all.[48] It was Barker's favourite Banham piece.[49] Trivial at first sight, it started out as a series of light-hearted reflections on the history of the crisp, its aural and tactile qualities, its nutritional value (zero) and its increasingly baroque variations in flavour. Its packaging, Banham wrote, was peculiar: the crisp, once wrapped up, was necessarily more air than product. There was some social history involving women and pubs, and crisps as a means to keep them there respectably. And then there was a discourse

on engineering. English crisps were no good in an advanced
civilization, he argued, because they disintegrated in dips ('have
a good look at the contents of the bowl of dip. The chances are
that you will see a surface so pocked over by the shards of
wrecked crisps that it looks like the Goodwin Sands during
the Battle of Britain.')[50] Far superior was the American 'taco
chip', which he had lately discovered. Superior because of its
engineering, it was more robust while still being edible, entirely
outperforming the crisp. Everything important in Banham's
cultural criticism is here: technology, advanced manufacturing,
American pragmatism vs English traditionalism, the
displacement of function by image, the War.

Food plays a crucial role in the chapter on roadside
architecture in *Los Angeles*, where Banham described the
ever more fantastic forms roadside buildings would take,
especially those associated with food. The chapter's opening
image, on the left-hand side of the double-page spread, was a
photograph of the ludicrous Jack-in-the-Box hamburger stall,
which clearly appealed to Banham for its complete disregard
for function.[51] It was (although he did not use their term)
the acme of what Robert Venturi and Denise Scott Brown
would call the Decorated Shed, designed to grab the driver's
attention at 50 mph and draw him or her in. The hamburger,
he wrote, 'is a non-Californian invention that has achieved a
kind of symbolic apotheosis in California'. He didn't mean the
'functional hamburger', he quickly elaborated, for that burger
was a straightforward piece of engineering. The hamburger-
eater was likely to be in motion, and as a structure the burger
was a secure armature for a balanced meal: 'not only the
ground beef, but all the sauce, cheese, shredded lettuce and
other garnishes are firmly gripped between the two halves of
the bun.' The functional hamburger is the modernist burger,
whose every element has a purpose, and whose structure has

tectonic integrity. It was also by 1972 the out-of-date burger; the Californian apotheosis is a postmodern deconstruction in which convenience and structural integrity have been thrown out of the window. No longer was this a structural unit, but an array, or as Banham put it, 'an assemblage of functional and symbolic elements, or alternatively a fantasia on functional themes'. He continued:

> the two halves of the bun lie face up with the ground beef on the one and sometimes the cheese on the other. Around and alongside on the platter are the lettuce leaves, gherkins, onion rings, coleslaw, pineapple rings and much more besides, because the invention of new varieties of hamburger is a major Angeleno culinary art.[52]

Functional elements have become symbols, and the purpose is play. 'It must be considered a visual art first and foremost', Banham noted; 'the seemingly mandatory ring of red-dyed apple . . . does a lot for the eye as a foil to the general greenery of the salads but precious little for the palate.'[53]

Here and elsewhere in Banham, the ethics are somewhat muddy. His analyses of popular culture overlapped repeatedly with those of the French structuralist Roland Barthes, who also wrote about food, cars and architecture at much the same time as Banham. But Barthes' project – whatever its intellectual complexities – was inherently critical of consumer culture, his observations in *Mythologies* shot through with irony and sometimes disdain.[54] Barthes never drove the Citroën DS that he wrote about in 1955, because he couldn't drive, but it's hard to imagine him ever feeling the need to enact such an ordinary desire.[55] Banham's relationship with his objects was much more engaged, his identity as a consumer more straightforward, his desires more openly declared. At the same time he retained a distance by virtue of being more often than not a tourist. This was certainly true of the work on America, where his carefully developed subject position is that of a latter-day Grand Tourist, the splendours of Southern California having displaced Rome (California has a mythical status all of its own).[56] His ethical position takes on something of the dilettante, enthusiastic but also removed and uncommitted, for as a tourist he can enjoy the spectacle and leave. So in relation to the postmodern hamburger, we never entirely understand what it represented.

Jack-in-the-Box hamburger restaurant, Los Angeles, CA.

Was this food-become-Pop art any good? What purpose did
it serve? Was its profligate form something to be celebrated?
Did it matter to Banham any more as an object than it did
as another thing that would annoy the English cultural
establishment, interchangeable in that purpose with the
Cadillac Eldorado, or the bag of crisps? These and other
similar questions are not completely answered in *Los Angeles*,
and never really anywhere else, which is an observation more
than a criticism. He was as much a cultural theorist as Barthes
in his own way, although, characteristically, what he never
produced in relation to that part of his work was an overarching
method. His career in cultural theory is rather like the first
half of Barthes's *Mythologies*, which is to say the journalistic
observations of contemporary cultural life first published in
*Les Lettres nouvelles*, without the structuralism of the second,
the essay 'Myth Today' with its diagrams and principled exegesis
on *Paris Match*. In Banham's writings on culture, theory tends
to be implied.

According to the architectural historian Barbara Penner,
Banham was the 'man who wrote too well', quoting his
sometimes exasperated supervisor, Pevsner. His rhetorical
abilities in some ways obscured the need to fully develop a
position, or to put it another way, his positions were always
contingent, for there was always another fascinating object
to write about, be it a car, a desert or a Frank Lloyd Wright
house.[57] He also changed his mind a good deal, rationalizing
it as, 'the only way to prove you have a mind is to change it.'[58]
His changes of mind, and more generally, his ambiguous ethics
could occasionally trip him up – as was made clear in 1970 by
Baudrillard, whose provocations revealed Banham's position
there, to that audience at least, to be fragile. His positivism –
for that is what his position was at IDCA, a conference of design
professionals – could seem naive in 1970 and Baudrillard's

takedown of it was unsparing (Banham, ever the liberal, generously included it in his volume of edited papers, with a commentary explaining what he thought had happened).[59] To engage with Banham is to engage with a writer for whom politics was rarely an explicit object, and certainly not political theory. In one respect, however, he was always political: in his choice of objects, and what he said about them, there was always the politics of class, and that underpinned his involvement in one of the most provocative urban theories of the 1960s, 'Non-plan'.[60]

## Writing on Banham

Writing about Banham presents a number of problems. There is the sheer volume of writing itself – those 750 (or is it a thousand?) articles, and all the books. Then there is the range of types of output: television and radio broadcasts, lectures, consultancies. There is a lot to write about, and its forms are much more varied than usual, along with the subjects that extend vastly beyond architectural history to almost any kinds of art and design, and, as we have seen, food. Most of it is easily accessible in the public domain, although some of the original sources – journals such as *Art*, the venue for the 1955 essay 'Vehicles of Desire' – are hard to come by.[61] But it is mostly there in published books and journals, television programmes, archived radio broadcasts and filmed lectures, many of them available online. It is the scale of the output and its range that are the initial problems for the biographer, rather like dealing with three or four careers simultaneously, instead of one.

At the time of writing there are no especially significant archival sources, no interpretative key to the whole career, no private commentary in any significant form. Go to the Getty Research Institute collections in Los Angeles, where Banham's papers are located, and the initial excitement at finding 140 boxes of material is tempered by the contents, with very little pre-dating 1976 and Banham's move to the United States. There are drafts of the last two books, *Scenes in America Deserta* and *A Concrete Atlantis*, both of which are remarkably close to the finished product. It is not clear whether Banham's thoughts emerged fully formed on the page, or he simply destroyed his drafts, or a bit of both. At any rate there is little to be gained by going through these drafts (his handwriting is remarkably legible, it has to be said). You might have expected something on *Los Angeles* given the location, but there is only a set of photographs from which the final selection was made for the book, no correspondence or draft material.[62] There are notes towards what would have been Banham's last book, provisionally titled *Making Architecture: The Paradoxes of High Tech*, including the draft of an introductory chapter, and this part of the collection has produced the one significant archivally based project on Banham, Todd Gannon's *Reyner Banham and the Paradoxes of High Tech*, which reproduces that text along with an extended commentary on Banham's approach to the topic.[63] You could not reconstruct anything much from this fragmentary collection, least of all the prolific journalistic career. Banham's attitude to the past was unsentimental. 'He burned everything', according to Debby Banham, 'he just liked having bonfires. And there wasn't a sense at that point that he was an important figure and that he ought to leave a legacy.'[64] But it is important to know this: there is nothing much outside the published texts, and apart from what Gannon brought to light in 2017, so far nothing much to uncover through archival work, and nothing from the family to indicate otherwise. There are a few items at the Architectural Association in London, including some slide collections, but other elements that might help the writer on Banham are missing: his library, for example, apart from a few items that remain in the family, was broken up and sold long before this project started out.[65] What you have to work with is largely what exists in the public domain.

The challenges of writing about Banham have led to a rather fragmentary approach to him, selecting phases or aspects in the service of a larger argument. Studies of Banham are unavoidable in relation to both Brutalism and the Independent Group, both of which have been of enduring academic interest. For the American art journal *October*, both tendencies were worth reviving (in 2000 and 2011, respectively) because they had been overlooked from the American perspective, and more importantly, they were ways of giving new life to the project of Modernism, the journal's *raison d'être*.[66] Banham was prominent in both revivals for obvious reasons, and his 1955 text was reproduced in the issue on the New Brutalism, along with critical essays that explored aspects of it. But somehow he was a supporting figure here, rather than a central one, perhaps because his politics were so hard to read, certainly in comparison with his contemporary Kenneth Frampton, who was much more *October*-friendly. Of other attempts to write directly about Banham, Vidler's treatment of him in *Histories of the Immediate Present* is one of the pithiest and most important, tracing Banham's interest in Futurism and the way that informs a reaction to the picturesque theories that were then taking root in the English architectural mainstream. Focused on two case studies, *Theory and Design* and *Los Angeles*, it has range but also limits it to only small elements of the whole career: this is Banham simply as a theorist of architecture. This version of Banham can present him as a distinctly *arrière-garde* figure, as he is, briefly, in Felicity Scott's analysis of architecture and technology in *Architecture and Techno-utopia*, where he exists as a positivist foil against which more radical characters can be seen. She is by no means wrong, but the representation of Banham here is, as almost everywhere, fragmentary.[67] 'Almost' because one comprehensive, large-scale account of Banham does already exist, the colossal *Reyner Banham: Historian of the Immediate Future* by the design historian Nigel Whiteley, published in 2002.[68] Whiteley's book is likely to be the only survey that will be written that will attempt anything like comprehensiveness. Its scale means it is inescapable as a reference point here, but it remains a book focused on Banham as an academic architectural historian, and its preoccupations are what Banham's work has to say about that world.

This book is different. It draws on the promise of two much shorter, but rather more suggestive accounts of Banham by Barbara Penner and Adrian Forty, respectively, both of which indicate a more complex and perhaps more literary figure than the academic architectural historian who tends to be at the centre of most accounts.[69] It would not be too much of a stretch to say that Banham was principally a writer who also happened to be an academic (that was certainly Robert Maxwell's view). In Banham's work there is no distinction between style and content; the work is all rhetoric, and like the best rhetoric it constantly flips between modes, between the grand and the intimate, the public and the personal.

To take on Banham as a subject is really to take on a writer, with all that implies. Some works seem like writing experiments, not least *Scenes in America Deserta*, which draws on and develops a 1918 art-historical project by John C. Van Dyke; both books were in large part attempts to describe the ineffable simply to see if it could be done. Writing about Banham is to write about writing. His working methods were distinctive. Forty, who worked with him as a PhD student between 1973 and 1976, wondered how he worked at all given his capacity to talk. But he came to realize that it was through talking, rather than academic modes of collecting information, that a perfectly formed seven-hundred-word article would emerge, usually in not much more than half an hour's concentrated effort.[70] That sense of a writer, rather than an academic per se, is central to the anthology *A Critic Writes*, published in 1999, which brings together a cross-section of journalism from Banham's whole career, with a foreword by the planner Peter Hall, a friend and occasional collaborator.[71] Hall's introduction makes clear how singular he was too: 'a most unusual person; the most unusual that many of us will have had the privilege of knowing'. Hall, along with Penner and Forty, and the many former colleagues, students and family members I talked with for the purposes of this book, suggest a more humanistic project on Banham than the ones that already exist. To treat Banham only as an academic is to describe a fragmentary version of him: he was someone with immense capacities to provoke, to disturb and to move beyond the sphere of his ostensible academic research. In writing this book I wanted to recover this larger Banham. I also wanted to make his work available beyond architecture. He was more than Brutalism, or megastructures, or a revisionist approach to modernism, or industrial structures, or environmental services – although those interests alone describe a very valuable contribution. His work is also, although it paradoxically sometimes pretends not to be, a serious body of cultural theory that in its choice of objects alone has the capacity to destabilize and question thinking across the humanities. That body of writing about culture, and more widely the work of the Independent Group, did arguably open up possibilities in cultural studies, an area that Banham might not have latterly recognized. And our starting point in this introduction – the idea that Banham had multiple and overlapping identities –

is more pertinent than ever in a world that tends to require identities to be singular and fixed.

The book is ordered around a series of episodes that explore those identities, and by naming them, I emphasize the complexity of Banham's career. It is by no means comprehensive, nor intended to be. 'The Futurist' explores Banham's early academic career and the publication of and critical response to *Theory and Design in the First Machine Age*. 'The New Brutalist' concerns both the iconic essay on Brutalism, and the provocations of the Independent Group that it embodied. 'The Autophile' considers the question of Banham's autophilia, starting with the seminal essay 'Vehicles of Desire'. 'The Environmentalist' deals with Banham's most radical work, *The Architecture of the Well-tempered Environment* (1969), and his singular approach to environmentalism in general. 'The Angeleno' explores the enduring appeal of Los Angeles for Banham, and what it meant. 'The Desert Freak' considers Banham's most problematical book, and the appeal of deserts in general, while 'The Connoisseur of Ruins' situates his history of u.s. industrial buildings in the context of his unsettling encounter with the country as a new resident. The final chapter, 'Reyner Banham Revisited', considers Banham's return to architectural history at the end of his career, along with his peculiar legacy.

# 2 THE FUTURIST

Banham was a Futurist. Not literally, because he was too young
to have been a witness to the creation of the movement in
Milan, or to have read Filippo Tommaso Marinetti's incendiary
manifesto when it was published in *Le Figaro* in 1909, or to have
been connected, socially or otherwise, with its authors. But
he was Futurist in sensibility, certainly as soon as he knew of
the manifestos, and the alignment was part of his early public
identity: the architect Colin St John Wilson said Marinetti was
Banham's 'muse'.[1] To be a Futurist in this sense meant several
things, all of which certainly applied to Banham: frustration
with tradition; an associated frustration with institutions,
and a desire, at least rhetorically, to overturn them; a love of
modernity; a love of technology; a belief in modernity as an
aesthetic project; and an understanding that it was fundamentally irrational, and libidinal. Futurism in its best-known,
Italian version was a rhetorical project as much as anything.
Its grand gestures existed mainly in its manifestos, which
were gestural and declarative, unconcerned with details or the
possible consequences of their ideas. Futurism also signified a
complex and uneasy politics, even if that was rarely recognized
in architectural circles at the time. The author of the 1909
manifesto, the poet Filippo Tommaso Marinetti, gave the
movement the gloss of violence from the start, declaring that
they would 'glorify war – the world's only hygiene – militarism,
patriotism, the destructive gesture of freedom-bringers,
beautiful ideas worth dying for, and scorn for woman'.[2] He
founded the Partito Politico Futurista in 1918, absorbed by
Mussolini's Fascists two years later; Marinetti's relationship
with them was fractious but he remained, like many Futurists,

aligned with them until the end of his life. Futurism was certainly ethically uncertain and something of that would have appealed to Banham in relation to the architectural establishment. Futurism was also arguably a way of coming to terms with the reality of the Second World War and its effect on the built environment. Banham was a key member of the Independent Group, the loose collective that met at the ICA in the early 1950s, overlapping with his work on Futurism. All of their careers had been in different ways 'impaired by war', as Anne Massey has written: it conditioned what they did, and Futurism was a natural part of their cultural landscape.[3]

Banham recalled his first proper encounter with Futurism as being in Milan in September 1951 when he found a collection of manifestos in a bookshop. It piqued his interest at a point when almost nothing had been translated into English, but he didn't buy it straight off: 'I picked it up, looked at it, and walked off without enquiring the price. I must have been mad – or rather, I should say that I cannot possibly now reconstruct the frame of mind in which I could do such a thing.'[4] Typically, he later attributed its appeal to a concrete experience. Having read the manifestos, he didn't really 'get' Futurism, he recalled in a 1976 interview, until standing one night on a North London railway platform in the early 1950s: 'at a certain point the Flying Scot or something used to hurtle through underneath and the whole building would shake and steam would come up through the platform. And at the same time an electric would come through at the high level, bursting through the steam.'[5] It is a compelling story because the experience it describes is so physical: noisy, atmospheric, at some level libidinal. The story recounted in 1976 was no doubt something of a post hoc rationalization, and one can't be entirely sure of its veracity – but it was significant in connecting a body of theory to lived experience. It is tempting to see this as a projection of Gino

Severini's *Suburban Train Arriving in Paris*, purchased by the
Tate Gallery in 1968, back onto humdrum suburban North
London, a modern city bifurcated by a fast-moving train in a
dynamic, smoky tableau. Precisely what Banham would have
known of Futurism's enigmatic art in the 1950s is not clear,
although he may have seen the exhibition *Modern Italian Art*,
staged by the Amici de Brera and the Italian Institute and held
at the Tate Gallery in 1950, which included a good selection of
key Futurists.[6] Having read the manifestos in 1951 he would
certainly have seen *Modern Italian Art from the Estorick Collection*
in late 1956, which showed major works by Balla, Boccion, Carrà,
Severini and others.[7] What he would have known of Sant'Elia
would have come from limited sources, as he described in a 1955
article for the *Architectural Review*: six pages of Bruno Zevi's
*Storia dell'architettura moderna*, and a further seven items, none
substantial – in fact he asked the reader for help finding more.[8]
In English there were just a footnote by Pevsner and a page of
Giedion's *Space, Time and Architecture*. A student in London at
the time (which is to say, Banham) would likely have seen only
ten images of the architect's work, and no photographs of the
only building he ever erected, a war memorial in Como.[9]

Banham became an enthusiast for, and advocate of, Futurist
ideas and images, and the article on Sant'Elia was likely the first
proper account of the architect in English. In the PhD thesis he
wrote at the Courtauld Institute, and in the book that emerged
from it in 1960, *Theory and Design in the First Machine Age*, he
was instrumental in bringing Futurism to the proper attention
of an Anglophone readership.[10] (The audience for his advocacy
of Futurism was broad, too: he made a radio programme about
it for the BBC in 1959, which among other things insisted on
its contemporary relevance.[11]) Others have made something
of this: the architectural historian Anthony Vidler's account
of Banham in *Histories of the Immediate Present* is all about

Banham's use of Futurism to antagonize the English architectural establishment, a way of attacking their residual picturesque.[12] That instrumental use of Futurism was also a way of trumping the historical consensus emerging around primacy. Pevsner gave Futurism no more than a footnote, but Banham found in Sant'Elia a set of destabilizing precedents: 'anti-monumentalism twenty years before Mumford, the house/machine equation

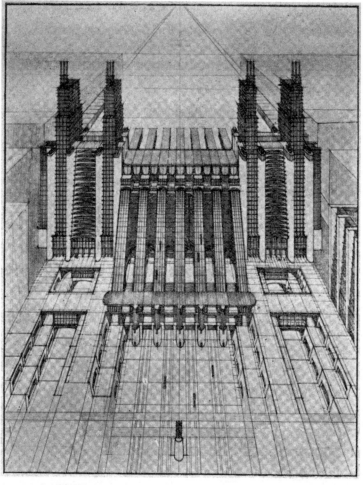

Antonio Sant'Elia, reconstruction of Milan Central Station (1914).

eight years before Le Corbusier, mechanistic Brutalism nearly
forty years before Hunstanton'.[13]

Futurism had a strange politics if one was concerned with
its evolution beyond 1914, which may partially explain its
marginalization by earlier historians of the Modern Movement,
perhaps especially Pevsner, who had after all run from fascism.[14]
In a 1957 article for the *Architects' Journal* Banham noted the
tendency of contemporary architectural historians to disassociate
Sant'Elia from Futurism, and to downplay Futurism altogether
in the context of a re-democratizing Italy. 'That apparently settled
situation has blown apart like an art historical time bomb,' he
wrote, noting the discovery of 150 or so new drawings by Sant'
Elia, as well as evidence for the existence of at least two other
architects who might be considered Futurists (Mario Chiattone
and Virgilio Marchi).[15] 'As a democrat I feel for them,' he went
on. 'As an art-historian nurtured however ungratefully in the
tradition of Pevsner, Blunt and Wittkower, I must disagree with
them.' That bomb, needless to say, was not a timed device, but
one detonated by Banham.[16]

Beyond that generational dispute, for Banham what mattered
most was the interpretation of technology, and technology
trumped any uneasiness about fascism.[17] Futurism was the one
Modern Movement tendency unequivocally to celebrate modern
technology, especially (as evidenced by the 1909 manifesto) that
of the car. Architecturally it was most visible in the drawings
of Sant'Elia. His architecture, and Futurism more generally,
signified a 'complete acceptance of the machine world with
an ability to realize and symbolize that acceptance in terms of
powerful and simple geometrical form. The acceptance is more
complete than Le Corbusier's, the forms more powerful than
those of Gropius.'[18] The city was quite literally a machine,
most legibly so on the studies for the reconstructed Milan
Central Station with its multilevel canyon bearing different

Banham in Bristol,
c. 1939, wearing ARP
Warden badge.

transportation functions. It was an enormously exciting image for someone drawn to machines as much as Banham, a chunk of city built in technology's image.[19]

Technology was in the Banham family. Banham's father had been a gas engineer in Norwich and during the First World War an aircraft engineer, which explains some of the family obsession.[20] Banham himself started training as an aeronautical engineer aged seventeen at the Bristol Technical College in 1939, having apparently chosen this aeronautical route against the advice of his school, King Edward VI Grammar in Norwich, who wanted him to study French at Cambridge.[21] A bright student, Banham was awarded a Society of British Aircraft Constructors scholarship, having achieved the second-highest mark in the country for the competition.[22] The training combined study at the Technical College with a placement at the Bristol Aeroplane

Company's Engine Division at Filton airfield (at this point, like many aerospace companies, Bristol made both airframes and power plants). The war effort meant the work with the Bristol company soon took over, and Banham remained at Filton for the duration.

The Bristol company manufactured and serviced three types of aircraft in 1939, all twin-engine, low-wing monoplanes, and all derivations of the same basic design: the Beaufighter, a fighter-bomber used by RAF Coastal Command to provide aerial defence against seaborne attack; the Blenheim, a light bomber of a similar size; and the Beaufort, a torpedo-bomber. The best-known and most numerous of the three (nearly 6,000 were built), the Beaufighter was a two-seat, all-steel aircraft, capable of carrying a much heavier armament load than the more famous Spitfires and Hurricanes of the Battle of Britain. A ponderous and rather slow aircraft, it lacked the glamour that excited news reporters about the Spitfire fighter or, in a different way, the Avro Lancasters of RAF Bomber Command.

What Banham actually did at Filton has emerged subsequently only in fragments. He worked in the engine division as a fitter, unintentionally duplicating the role his father had

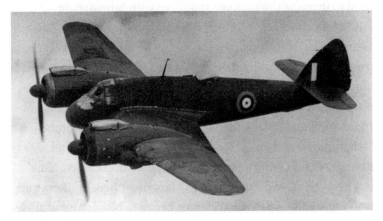

Bristol Beaufighter, c. 1940.

had in the First World War. He acquired unusual knowledge
of the Stromberg carburettor at one point, as he reported in an
aside to a 1966 article: he was for three days the only man in
Britain who understood it, and he briefly contemplated holding
the country's military-industrial complex to ransom. 'Then the
other handbook arrived.'[23] He probably also learned to drive
while at Filton, although his driving would have been confined
to airfield fire tenders, as he did not achieve an ordinary driving
licence until he was well into his forties.[24] Banham driving at
Filton was possibly a 'terrifying' prospect, although he would
certainly also have been excited by the prospect.[25]

Typically Banham 'reduced the whole period to a series
of amusing anecdotes'.[26] But Bristol had been a brutal
experience. Partly it was the tedium: the job simply entailed
engine maintenance, with no opportunity to fly or develop
any of the other skills Banham wanted. Partly it was the
maintenance regime itself, which at worst involved 72 hours
of inactivity followed by 72 hours without sleep.[27] Partly it
was the war itself. Servicing of the Beaufighters would have
brought Banham into repeated contact with the consequences
of military action; these were frontline machines and it is not
hard to imagine the cockpits spattered with human debris.[28]
Filton was also a key military target and was bombarded by
German aircraft throughout the war. In an unpublished account
from 2004 Mary Banham described an aerial attack on a shelter,
almost certainly the raid of 21 September 1940, the worst of the
war: 'they had these huge shelters underground and all his
[Banham's] mates were in that one time when it was bombed.
Two hundred of them.'[29] He was invalided out in 1945 and
discharged following a physical and mental breakdown. 'One
day he went off without warning,' Mary described, 'walking and
walking, and stopped when his feet began to bleed. And went
very sensibly into the local police station, because he didn't

know who he was. Went in and said "Who am I?", and they beat him up.'[30] He was hospitalized, and left Bristol unqualified, having failed to achieve the Higher National Diploma. Hence 'I decided to recycle myself as an intellectual.'[31] The period was marked by epic life events: leaving the family home, a failed engineering career, the outbreak of war, the mass killing of friends and colleagues. It was by any standards an intense set of experiences. *Theory and Design* was the work of someone who simultaneously loved technology and was also nearly killed by it.

If Banham said little subsequently about Bristol, he did say plenty about aircraft, and he could write authoritatively about them when called to do so: a piece for the *Architects' Journal* from 1962, for example, describes in some detail the relative merits of the design philosophies of the Boeing and Douglas companies.[32] In *Theory and Design* he could bring Le Corbusier up short for his understanding of the area, and also show off his own (he would argue, superior) knowledge of 1930s aircraft design.[33] Banham was already attentive to car design too, as both *Theory and Design* and the underpinning thesis showed. There is nowhere in either the book or the thesis to confirm that the war experience was a direct cause of the interest in Futurism, no rationalization of Futurism in those terms, no footnote or other explanation. What we do know, however, is that for five years during the war at Bristol, only seven years before starting the PhD, Banham was engaged in the most direct way with the technologies Futurism celebrated, along with the ambiguities of war, which it also celebrated. And we also know, looking at his whole career, how often Banham wrote about his own experience, used it as a starting point for an argument, or – as is likely the case here – sublimated it, turning feeling into something academically respectable.[34] In other words Banham's latter-day Futurism was an oblique way of writing about these early experiences. Regardless of the plausibility

of that connection, his Futurism in any case was that of one
who really knew the technology and its consequences.

## A History of Futurism

Banham's PhD thesis, 'The Theory of Modern Architecture,
1907–1927', was accepted in 1958 after six years of part-time
study. Its pithy abstract made clear its revisionism, taking
on the assumption of the importance of the writings of Le
Corbusier and the Bauhaus. It was only very lightly revised
to make its way into publication in 1960 as *Theory and Design
in the First Machine Age*; the publishers were Architectural Press,
whose main business was the *Architectural Review*. The book's
short concluding chapter, 'Functionalism and Technology', was
all new, and there were some minor changes to punctuation
and the titling of the sections. In all other respects the thesis
was the book. *Theory and Design* has since become an essential
text on architectural history programmes worldwide, and
its sales (although hard to estimate because of the multiple
editions) run into very likely hundreds of thousands. It has
been translated into at least seven languages beyond English.[35]
It is an inescapable part of the basic infrastructure of modern
architectural history, and its Constructivist-inspired cover
designs are a familiar sight on architectural bookshelves. It has
been a major influence on subsequent architectural theorists.[36]

A revisionist history of the Modern Movement, it took
on Pevsner, who along with Sigfried Giedion had written the
positivist history of modern design, steeped in rationalism
and science.[37] (Like other rationalist histories, Giedion's
*Mechanization Takes Command* contained some decidedly odd,
surreal images, but Banham's history made the irrational
central and explicit.) *Theory and Design* was largely free of any
commentary about politics.[38] The Weimar Republic, perhaps

the most turbulent period in Germany's modern history, was the literal and figurative context for half the book, but its politics were those of the architectural world, abstracted from everyday life. It says nothing about European geopolitics after the First World War, or hyperinflation, or mass unemployment, and only tangentially Fascism as a mass movement.[39]

If your introduction to Banham is the journalism, or the breezy travelogue of *Reyner Banham Loves Los Angeles*, *Theory and Design* is a surprise: dense, academic, serious, exactly like the PhD it largely is. It has none of the sense of physical presence that is so important to the later writings, the authority of 'being there'. The 'there' in this case was the university library, for the most part, for this was (as the title made clear) a book of theories about design rather than finished designs themselves: the buildings of the book were more often than not imaginary, or where they were not, quite often demolished, inaccessible or in a wretched state. Banham (often initially with Mary) was assiduous about visiting the sites of early architectural modernism, but this was far more a book of ideas.[40] The dense text is peppered (still) with typesetting errors and interspersed with 101 of some of the worst-quality images in a piece of published architectural history.[41]

It splits into five parts, the middle three of which were lifted from Banham's Courtauld dissertation.[42] It opens with perhaps the driest and most difficult part of the book, a discussion of what Banham called 'predisposing causes' for modern design, a set of seven academic traditions from the Ecole de Beaux-Arts in Paris to an extended treatment of Adolf Loos in secessionist Vienna. The book moves on through its emotional centre, Futurism through Berlage and De Stijl in the Netherlands, to Le Corbusier and Paris, and finally the Bauhaus and Germany and what Banham termed the 'victory of the new style'. It covers a short period of thirty years or so, a 'Zone of Silence' in the development of modern design, after which it emerged apparently fully formed, but full of the contradictions that led to its formation. In the introduction to the 1980 reprint of the book, Banham wrote of it as an attempt 'to understand what went wrong and what went right with the Modern Movement' and even 'to try to re-experience the revolution in sensibility', as well as understanding 'the irrational mechanistic urges that underlay the rationalist platitudes with which the Bauhaus has been justified to later generations; what romantic dreams of prismatic crystalline splendours, cathedrals of light and colour are imprisoned in the snug and inexpressive towers of glass that form our current downtown scenes.'[43]

It is a remarkable few lines, elevating the irrational. The reference to dreams and fantasies ('prismatic crystalline splendours, cathedrals of light and colour') puts it in the orbit of psychoanalysis, something that was an occasional, if overlooked, feature of Banham's writing. He flirted occasionally with its vocabulary, and that of psychology in general, as many contemporaries did, and he went further here than usual, alluding to a therapeutic process involving the recovery of feeling, and its confrontation. He was literate in a layperson's way in psychoanalysis, and the family did live at the time in Hampstead and moved in psychoanalytically adjacent circles (although, as his daughter Debby put it, 'on the wrong side of the Finchley Road').[44] It is not a psychoanalytically driven book, but it is a book that is open to the recovery of the senses and their elevation above rationalism, with Futurism enlisted as a tool to do it. Futurism, after all, was the most libidinal of Modernist movements and it would not be invoked unknowingly.[45] Banham was concerned enough with these things to preview the book in psychological terms for the *Architectural Review* in May 1960, in an article titled 'History and Psychiatry', which introduced, among other things, the concept of the 'Zone of Silence' around modern design.[46] The allusions to psychology and psychoanalysis were not by later standards especially developed, but they made clear just how important the irrational was for Banham's theory of modern design.

Reading *Theory and Design* now, it is a surprise how long it takes to get to the argument. The opening paragraph requires you to take on board seven named individuals, four artistic movements, one artistic institution, a historical trajectory with three 'predisposing causes', and a set of punctuating revolutionary 'moments'. It is a lot to hold in your head at once, in a section that is largely academic scene-setting, laying out what academicism was in architecture, which is to say the ideological theatre in which the Modern Movement acted.[47] A deliberative, dense start, it is unlike Banham's later writings. By the end of this first section, however, on the Viennese architect and theorist Adolf Loos, a sense develops of the singular quality of the book, what the architect and curator Philip Johnson would call (with reason) its 'perversity'.[48] The appeal of Loos lay partly in his multiplicity: he was, Banham wrote, in demand as a cultural critic, and apart from architecture wrote on almost anything, including 'clothing, manners, furniture, music'. This versatility must have in some way affirmed Banham's own, as well as representing something about his hopes for the Modern Movement itself.[49] Partly it was the drastic quality of the argument itself, that ornamentation was a sign of cultural degeneracy.[50] The hyperbolic tone took the modern well away from the rational. Partly, too, Loos's appeal was what ornamentation had to say about engineering: engineers, wrote Loos, had no need of it, so it was a means of attacking architecture. 'To build without decoration', wrote Banham, summarizing Loos, 'is to build like an engineer and thus in a manner proper to a Machine Age.'[51] Loos's rationality is that taken to the point at which it becomes irrational, its desire for order an obsession. It was an essential precursor to the attitude shown up by Futurism itself, which Banham discussed in three sections, based loosely about the 1909 manifesto, its subsequent development and, via the work of Antonio Sant'Elia, Futurist architecture.

Writing at a remove of sixty years, it is important to recover a moment when Futurism was *not* important to the history of modern design. It was generally hard to see Futurism in the 1950s in London: the Tate Gallery owned one work, *The Syphon* by Mario Sironi, donated by the Estoricks in 1952, and there were, as far as it is easy to tell, no other works by Futurists accessible in public collections; the Tate's exhibitions of Italian art in 1950 and 1956 were brief correctives.[52] Nor were there easy opportunities to see Futurist architecture in reproduction, as Banham had noted in 1955.[53]

Futurism was not only generally hard to see, but not easy to like. It had murky connections with a recently defeated Fascist government, its leader and chief theorist, Filippo Tommaso Marinetti, was an aristocratic dilettante fond of bellicose pronouncements, and its art was underwhelming compared with the manifestos. And in terms of architecture, Futurism built almost nothing, seemingly only (as described in Banham's 1955 piece on Sant'Elia) that Como war memorial.[54] Until the point Banham took an interest, very little of the manifestos had been translated into English. An interest in Futurism certainly had perverse aspects, as Philip Johnson noted. Johnson, of all architects, would have understood what perversity might mean for architecture, how it might embody contradictions between surface and depth, public and private, licit and illicit, how whatever one may have professed on the surface, one may have been drawn to the opposite. (Johnson certainly knew all about fascism too, having written approving, first-hand accounts

of the Nuremberg Rally and the Nazi invasion of Poland in 1939.[55])
*Theory and Design* is perverse in that way: on the face of it, a
critique of modern design's contradictions, it in fact celebrated
them. Johnson wrote, perceptively: 'The Italians like funny
shapes; I don't like them, but who am I? . . . we are going through
a foggy chaos. Let us enjoy the multiplicity of it all. Certainly
Reyner Banham's book will further the chaos by analysing away
the last beliefs (the lovely, helpful, beliefs) of the last generation.'[56]
Johnson was right: the book has a powerfully desublimatory
character, almost a punk sensibility. Banham's Futurism was a
position as much as a topic.

Banham started with the 1909 manifesto by Marinetti,
published on the front page of the Paris newspaper *Le Figaro*
on 20 February 1909.[57] *Le Figaro* had form in publishing artists'
manifestos; perhaps more importantly, Marinetti's lawyer father
was friendly with the newspaper's principal shareholder.[58]
Banham quoted from the manifesto at length and showed
evidence of having visited the sites in question. The manifesto
opens with an account of Marinetti and his friends at home:
through the decoration Banham identified this as the family's
Milan home, loaded with decoration from Marinetti's expatriate
Egyptian childhood ('mosque lamps . . . filigree copper bowls').[59]
There followed the famous episode in which Marinetti and
his friends decide spontaneously to go on a nocturnal drive.
(Banham correctly noted that for a group of young men to
locate any reliable cars, and drive themselves at this moment
in history, at 5 a.m., would have been extremely unlikely even
in the recent past. By this means, along with the detail about
the trams and the industry, the manifesto can be quite precisely
dated.[60]) The manifesto continued with the group roaring
around the streets of Milan, before encountering two cyclists
wobbling in the opposite direction. Swerving to avoid them,
Marinetti dumps his car into a ditch, where, drenched and

dirty, his mouth full of mud, he undergoes a quasi-religious awakening. The cult of Futurism is thus born. A rant against museums, museum cultures and Italy follows, and then comes the revolutionary eleven points of the manifesto itself, before its extraordinary conclusion in which the death of the movement is prefigured before it has even started ('they will rush to kill us, driven by hatred made more implacable by the extent to which their hearts are filled with love and admiration').[61]

For anyone coming to Futurism for the first time, this would have been an electrifying passage – and at this point Banham's book arguably comes alive, suddenly all violence, bodies and unchained libidos. Marinetti described, and Banham quoted, the moment of the car crash: 'O maternal ditch, brimming with muddy water – O factory drain! I gulped down your nourishing mud and remembered the black breasts of my Sudanese nurse. And yet when I emerged, ragged and dripping from under the capsized car, I felt the hot iron of delicious joy in my heart.'[62] Banham's interpretation is the now standard one, which is to say it is a pseudo-baptism, the ditch a modern River Jordan. Marinetti's text is also highly erotic, from the obvious (the memory of his wet nurse's breasts), to the allusion to St Teresa of Avila's orgasmic vision of Christ, immortalized by Bernini ('I felt the hot iron of delicious joy in my heart'), to the factory sludge with its coprophiliac connotations, to the mess of bodies and machinery that seems to anticipate J. G. Ballard and *Crash*.[63] Banham didn't comment directly on the erotics of this passage, but in selecting and foregrounding it he advocated a highly libidinal version of the Modern.[64]

These passages, thanks partly to Banham, are now extremely well known. The appeal lay in the poetry they made of the violent industrialization of northern Italy, faster, later and more brutal than in England, and Banham described the shock as the appearance of the towns changed drastically, trams rapidly displacing canals alongside revolutionary social change literally pushing out the aristocracy. It was a set of historical circumstances that showed the power of technology; this meant not only the physical changes in the urban environment described poetically by the 1909 manifesto, but an understanding that the technology was 'transience' and 'obsolescence'. To embrace those things was unfamiliar and new, but, Banham argued, it signified 'a positive orientation and a point of attachment with the world of fact'.[65] *Theory and Design* reads differently from Banham's later writings, but here, you could say, are core themes – demands, even – that run all the way through the career: technology is change; change should be embraced; embrace technological change and new sensibilities emerge.

Fail to embrace those things, by contrast, and you might end up with John Ruskin. Banham reported on a Marinetti talk of 1912, in which the poet described Ruskin as 'a man who in full maturity wants to sleep in his cot again and drink at the breasts of a nurse who has now grown old in order to regain the carefree state of infancy'.[66] It was a startlingly regressive image, worthy of a Freudian case study. Banham didn't reflect at length on this passage, but in reproducing it he reinforced the opposition between the new (vigorous, sexual) and the old (sick, decaying, unerotic) that ran all the way through the account of Futurism as a subtext. Banham clearly identified with the Futurists here, and it is hard not to see the selection and quotation of this passage as a commentary on the 1950s English architectural establishment: Ruskin, as it were, equals English architecture, desexualized and infantilized.

Banham's account of Futurist architecture in *Theory and Design* focused on Sant'Elia's unbuilt designs for the Città Nuova (New City) of 1914, and the appeal here was of a modernism that has not had to suffer the translation into reality. It existed in the form of a text, the *Messaggio*, subsequently published with minor alterations by Marinetti in 1914 as the Manifesto of Futurist Architecture, and the perspective drawings for Milan as imagined in the year 2000. Banham provided a translation of the *Messaggio* more or less in full; a preview of this had been published already in 1957, the meat of 'Futurism and Modern Architecture' in the *Architects' Journal*.[67] What stood out in both the text and Banham's interpretation of it is the rhetoric of circulation, which prefigured Banham's much later arguments about the displacement of architecture by technology.[68] In 'Futurism and Modern Architecture' Banham was open about the application of Futurism to the contemporary city, identifying a proposed freeway-oriented remodelling of New York's Times Square as Futurist, at least in spirit.[69] Those contemporary comparisons were absent from *Theory and Design*, but you sense that they were barely suppressed.

For Banham, the excitement of the Futurist city was in this displacement of the fixed city of buildings by the city of flows, a city based on the sublimation of transport, 'a city based in a complex network of transport services, in some drawings as much as seven levels deep'. The building designs were dominated by highly rhetorical lift shafts, inspired by existing structures on landing stages at Lake Como. 'Rising vertically', he wrote, they 'stand well clear of the upper floors to which they are connected by bridges of an ever-increasing length as one goes up'.[70] In the drawings this feature was clear enough, as was the rhetorical emphasis on circulation, vertical, horizontal, and aerial. This was a city through which one was to move at high speed simply for the physical pleasure of moving about, a city of vectors, not monuments. It might be dangerous too, Banham noted, pointing out the 'suicidal' landing strip for aircraft between the towers of the *Stazioni Aeroplani*, an idea that would reappear, scarcely modified, in Le Corbusier's plan for the Ville Contemporaine, a city for 3 million on Modernist lines. He was curiously able to accept this proposal, in spite of it conflicting with an engineering-driven sensibility – no one seriously involved with flying would have found it acceptable. It was perhaps just too exciting an idea for Banham to leave out, despite his aviator's reservations, for it was of a piece with this city of bold movements, of speed and danger. The Città Nuova was not a rational city, but one apparently organized around bodily sensation as much as anything. Neither was it troubled by reality, as literally nothing of this was built. But Futurism served a vital purpose in recasting the Modern Movement in new terms: as a movement that responded to precise historical conditions, to technology and to the irrational. It was also a statement of Banham's own position, since his foregrounding of Futurism was a sublimation of his own enthusiasms, a way of getting engineering to be taken seriously by art.

## A Futurist History

Section 2 of *Theory and Design* may have provided a history of Futurism; what it also did was suggest a way of doing history, a Futurist history as it were, reiterating the suggestion in Banham's BBC radio talk that Futurism was a way of accounting for the contemporary world.[71] His treatment of other aspects of the Modern Movement was strongly conditioned by Futurism and its concerns with technology and the irrational. Futurism particularly informed the treatment of Le Corbusier, for Banham had already established in 1958 in the PhD thesis that Le Corbusier's voice could be challenged, along with the Bauhaus: they were not the only sources of Modern thought.[72] The need for the challenge, Banham thought, had to do with the Bauhaus's substantial disregard for the world of technology, and in relation to Le Corbusier, his tendency in both theory and practice to seek continuity with the existing world.[73] On Le Corbusier, Banham

was writing at a moment when he had two versions of Le
Corbusier available to him, namely the superficially rational
figure of the 1920s and the contemporary Brutalist; the
historical frame of the book meant that it was the early
Corbusier who was the subject, but the knowledge of the
later one, an architect much more open to the emotional
and the irrational, would have coloured the critique.

On the 1920s Corbusier, Banham wrote of his anti-
revolutionary tendencies. Part of that was the sheer difficulty
of building anything new at scale in Paris in the 1920s. The
result was an inadvertent conservatism when it came to
modern design, with the few projects that did emerge being
small and highly individualistic, and contingent on the
existing environment – the opposite, in other words, of
revolution. They were nearly all artists' studios, a peculiar
type, 'twisted out of recognition by random or personal
factors'.[74] In Le Corbusier's case, at programme level, his
villas inevitably reinforced the bourgeois lives of the clients
for whom they were built. Modern design, in other words,
might have addressed the universal in theory, but at this
stage it was highly individualized in practice.

So much of Banham's critique of Le Corbusier concerned
his accommodation of the past, either intentionally or through
lack of attention to detail. The account of the manifesto-like
*Vers une architecture* (1923, published in English as *Towards a
New Architecture*, a compendium of essays already published in
*L'Esprit nouveau*) latched on to what appeared to be a mistake,
the double spread of cars and temples on pages 106 and 107.
Here Le Corbusier reproduced photographs of the second
Temple of Hera at Paestum on the left, dating from 450 BC, and
the slightly later Parthenon, Athens, from 438 BC, while directly
below were two cars, a British Humber of 1907, reproduced
directly underneath Paestum, and a French Delage of the early

1920s below the Parthenon.[75] As Banham described, the reader
was *supposed* to understand significant progress in a fifteen-year
period though the arrangement of the images, from Paestum
to Athens, and from Humber to Delage. And there is, on
inspection, refinement legible in this juxtaposition with (in the
lower set of images) the inference of evolution from something
like a Chesterfield sofa on wheels to a streamlined and enclosed
vehicle, suggestive of speed. But Banham noted, 'the immediate
response seems always to read down the page, thus producing
an image of contrast, like Marinetti's between a racing car and
the *Nike* of Samothrace'.[76] The car, in other words, might be
understood as a revolutionary image.

But, as Banham argued, the reading was likely downwards
here, an indication of a conservative position, desiring continuity between the classical and the modern. That impulse
suggested the opposite of revolution, the desire for transhistoric
continuity Banham found throughout *Vers une architecture*, no
more so than in the unintentionally funny 'Manual of the
Dwelling', with its prescription for the good (modernist) life:

> Demand a bathroom looking south, one of the largest rooms
> in the house. Demand bare walls, built in fittings to take the
> place of much of the furniture. If you can, put a kitchen on
> the top of the house to avoid smells . . . Demand a vacuum
> cleaner. Teach your children that a house is only habitable
> when it is full of light and air and when the walls are clear.[77]

At the moment he came to this passage in the thesis, Banham
was the father of two small children in a cramped Primrose
Hill flat: the strictures about economy, given his limited
circumstances, would have seemed at best amusing.[78] He
drew attention to it for its combination of pomposity, lack of
self-awareness and obsessiveness about order. It was also, as

he made clear, an anti-revolutionary text that corralled the threat of the new by justifying it as continuity. Its considerable influence was therefore, he noted wryly, 'greatest where the French *Beaux-Arts* tradition is strongest'.[79] Le Corbusier in this aspect at least was a counter-revolutionary. Here Banham reiterated a common enough view in English architectural circles at the time: that Corbusier was an inconsistent figure whose radicalism did not easily survive contact with reality. An elegant expression of that was Lionel Brett's assessment of recent work by Le Corbusier published in the *Architectural Review* in 1947. Brett, like Banham, was partially sceptical – less about the work on its own terms than the claims made for it.[80]

Banham had better things to say about Le Corbusier's urban theory book, *Urbanisme*, published in 1925, which contains the plan for the Ville Contemporaine.[81] Banham generally approved because it seemed to elaborate on the Città Nuova, complete with the lunatic airport between high-rises.[82] Banham also approved of the slightly later Plan Voisin (1925), noting that it would have demolished 'most of historical Paris north of the Seine', occupying all points between the Gare St Lazare, the Gare de l'Est and the Place de la République.[83] Inside this vast area a few monuments would survive, not always in their original locations, although an exception would be made for 'the Place Vendôme, which Le Corbusier greatly admired' – this was to 'be left intact and in place'.[84] The architect's intentions were partly to shock, as Banham described, 'even in progressive circles'. Banham's treatment of *Urbanisme* was largely positive: here Le Corbusier's revolutionary reputation was justified, and more to the point it was the most like Futurism. For the same reasons, Banham approved of the Villa Savoye, the celebrated house Le Corbusier built at Poissy in 1928–30. There was nothing much rational about it; the point of the pilotis at ground level was to create the impression of the first floor floating in space,

Le Corbusier, Villa Savoye, Poissy, 1928–30.

a dramatic image. The open ground floor – the stairwell up to
the first floor is the main element – was furthermore designed
around the minimum turning circle of a car, which could, he
wrote, 'having set down its passengers at the main entrance on
the apex of this curve . . . pass down the other side of this
building still under the cover of the floor above, and return
to the main road along a drive parallel to that on which it had
approached the house'. He described it, perhaps more in hope
than anything else, as a quotation of the rooftop test-track on
the roof of the Fiat factory in Turin, 'tucked under the building
instead of laid on top of it, creating a suitably emotive approach
to the home of a fully motorised post-Futurist family'.[85] Banham
had seen this house and remarked on its then dreadful condition,
the result of its occupation during the war; much later in his
career he might have celebrated its ruinous qualities, though
this was not the place or the time for it.[86] The point was well

made, however. In its sublimation of technology to produce
an aesthetic, this was not a functionalist building, but an
authentically Futurist one. Futurism was a lens to understand
the Modern Movement.[87]

## A Futurist Conclusion

The conclusion used Futurism to flag the contradictions in the
whole project of modern design. If it was, as it purported to be,
an architectural rationalization of new technology, then why,
Banham wondered, had it so conspicuously failed to take
account of technological advances in the 1920s, particularly
in vehicle design, an area architects invariably found attractive?
He wrote: 'The Burney "streamliners" in Britain, and the racing
cars designed in Germany in 1933 for the 1934 Grand Prix
Formula, the Heinkel He70 research aircraft and the Boeing
247D transport aircraft in the U.S. all belonged to a radically
altered world to that of their equivalents a decade earlier.'
(The Burney Streamliner was a terrible, but much discussed,
rear-engined car built in a very limited series from 1927.
The Prince of Wales allegedly bought one in 1930.) Banham
continued, 'one might have expected an art that appeared
so emotionally entangled with technology to show some signs
of the upheaval.'[88] It is a fair point, supported by Banham's
knowledge of aircraft design. The Boeing is a remarkably
different object to the stately Farman aeroplane illustrated by
Le Corbusier, or the tiny biplanes that punctuate the Città Nuova:
all steel, streamlined and enclosed, the 247D was built for speed
and altitude, represented by a radically new outward envelope.
So marked a design shift was this that the Boeing still reads as a
broadly contemporary object today, whereas the Farman does not.

In the conclusion Banham also celebrated Mies van der
Rohe's 1929 German Pavilion for the Exposición Internacional

in Barcelona, which in no sense was (or is, in its 1986
reconstruction) functionalist: here was a profligate building
that above everything celebrated the luxuriousness of the
materials, particularly where the modern chrome and smoked
glass bang up against the polished marble. Banham remarked
on the iconic leather chairs, designed especially for the Pavilion
and since popularized: 'rhetorically over-size, immensely heavy,
and do not use the material in such a way as to extract maximum
performance from it . . . they flout, consciously one suspects,
the canons of economy.'[89] In short, there is something rather
irrational about these chairs: big and throne-like, they are
emotive, sensual and generous.

Banham's conclusion was characteristically tough: if modern
design was to make claims to being of the Machine Age, it
needed to keep abreast of what the Machine Age actually was.
And in this, Banham argued, it failed: its version of the Machine
Age was no more than a style, the look of technology rather than
technology itself. It may have been an accident, 'but it is the kind
of accident that architecture may not survive a second time'.[90]
History has an activist cast about it here. Banham's Futurism

Ludwig Mies van de Rohe, German Pavilion, Barcelona, 1929,
reconstructed 1983–6.

was a method as much as a topic. It was also, for Banham
as much as the original Futurists, one based in experience,
which specifically included the war. Banham's experience of
technology in the 1950s was inevitably coloured by the war
because that is when by far the greatest technological advances
had been made in recent years. 'This vision', wrote Anthony
Vidler of the Futurists, 'was not of a merely symbolic order,
like that of Le Corbusier, but rather of an order of technological
understanding by those who knew the interiors of the racing
cars they drove.'[91] Banham implicitly was one of those people.
If he didn't know Marinetti's racing car, he certainly knew the
cockpit of the Bristol Beaufighter, strewn with shrapnel and
broken glass and who knows what else after it came in from
a sortie over the English Channel. His engagement with
technology was of a lived kind (the repeated 24-hour shifts,
the grease and the air raids), and the breakdown it produced
by the end of the war meant an engagement with technology
of a possibly greater intensity than anything the privileged
Marinetti had experienced. That, arguably, is where *Theory
and Design* comes from: its perversity is that of someone who
has not only lived with technology, but has been obsessed by
it, as well as been nearly killed by it. It was the view of someone
who has genuinely lived the changes in sensibility brought
about by technology, and has embraced the contingent, and
often violent world it has brought about. Futurism was the
means of accounting for that world.

# 3 THE NEW BRUTALIST

*Theory and Design in the First Machine Age* was one obvious product of Banham's flirtation with Futurism. Another was arguably the New Brutalism, the revolutionary architectural tendency for which he would arguably have liked to have been the Marinetti. He was its chief theorist, and ultimately its critic. As a movement it had a clear revolutionary 'moment' between 1953 and 1955 when something genuinely new seemed possible (the dates are Banham's).[1] It defined Banham's public identity as much as anything in the early 1950s. Banham wasn't the only person who could claim to be its theorist, for Peter and Alison Smithson had already published at least one short note about it, and continued to write about it after Banham had lost interest.[2] It is also important not to collapse Banham's New Brutalism into the work of the Independent Group (IG). There was overlap, for the Smithsons, Nigel Henderson and Eduardo Paolozzi were certainly identifiable as both, but Banham projected the New Brutalism far more widely, making an argument that ranged beyond the IG, and architecture, and London. It was certainly ambitious, global and multi-dimensional, and as a result Banham is inseparable from it.

The mythical origins of the term 'New Brutalism' were described in a much-quoted letter by the Swedish architect Hans Asplund, son of Gunnar. Asplund had used it in 1950 'in a mildly sarcastic way' to describe a tough-looking new house in Uppsala. The term caught on in London: Asplund wrote that 'it had spread like wildfire', and that it had, somewhat astoundingly, been adopted by a certain faction of English architects.[3]

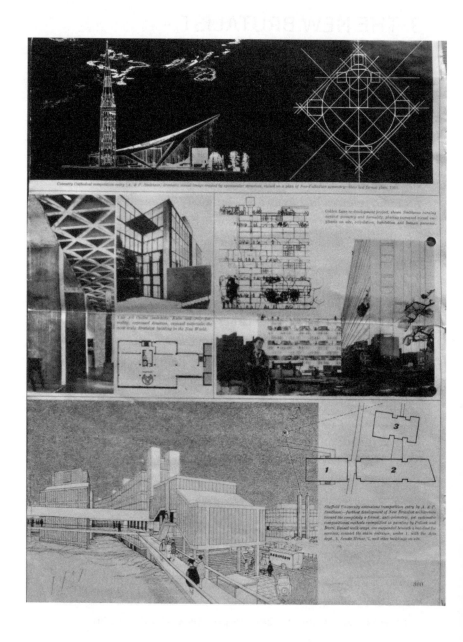

Illustrations from Reyner Banham, 'The New Brutalism', 1955.

It was, in other words, one of those aesthetic terms, like Impressionism, meant as abuse, but transformed into its opposite. (The name itself, as is well known, connoted many things including *béton brut* (raw concrete), as well as, Banham said, Peter Smithson's nickname, 'Brutus'.[4]) What it meant here for the Swedes Bengt Edman and Lennart Holm was a severe form of modern architecture making no concession to contemporary Swedish tastes favouring gently pitched roofs and natural materials. What the account left out, Banham remarked later, was the 'ethics': New Brutalism, as he formulated it in 1955, wasn't just a style, as it appears in Asplund's letter, but an attitude to the world that encompassed much more than architecture alone. (It is important here to keep a distinction between the New Brutalism, the tendency that is the focus here, and Brutalism, the more durable and lately revived architectural style.) New Brutalism was also an 'ethic' from the beginning, an attitude to culture as much as a way of doing architecture. Banham wrote later of Brutalism that it expressed what its architects 'urgently felt they must express even if they had, as yet, no architecture to express it'.[5] Arguably therefore there were New Brutalists before there was (New) Brutalism, an architectural style that really only flourished much later.[6]

To be one, you arguably needed to satisfy three conditions, the first concerning social class: a New Brutalist was, if not working class, then aligned with or empathetic to working-class culture. That was certainly true of Banham, whose class allegiance motivated much of his early work.[7] The same could be said of Peter and Alison Smithson, who were born in Sheffield and Stockton respectively, to ordinary backgrounds. Their birthplaces were quintessentially northern-industrial, they both studied in the Northeast, and while they never played up their origins, they retained a fascination for working-class vernacular forms. The working-class residential terrace was re-read through their invention of the street deck, the architectural form with which they are most associated. The Scottish-Italian artist Eduardo Paolozzi was the child of shopkeepers. The last member of the Independent Group to be associated with New Brutalism, Nigel Henderson, was, by the standards of the others, an aristocrat – but he had chosen to live and work in London's East End, and as his photography showed, he fetishized its street life.[8] If not working class themselves, they were working-class aligned.

To be a New Brutalist also involved demonstrable fascination with the emergent, particularly American, consumer culture; mass culture was to be consumed and appreciated, regardless of the political tensions it inevitably created. The Smithsons wrote directly of this in 1955, of their attempt to 'face up to a mass production society and drag a rough poetry out of the confused and powerful forces which are at work'.[9] The architectural historian Kenneth Frampton later wrote, somewhat critically, that the Smithsons were caught between their class allegiance and pop culture, 'ensnared in the intrinsic ambivalence of an assumed populism'.[10] Neither they nor Banham would have seen that as ambivalence, but rather an existential condition. The tension Frampton described can be seen in the best work of the Smithsons, whose collages of their unsuccessful but much-discussed entry for the Golden Lane housing estate in London depicted pop celebrities Marilyn Monroe and Joe DiMaggio surreally cavorting on the street decks. The New Brutalists could accept such tensions as natural; as they happily consumed these icons, they were simply illustrating everyday life.

The New Brutalist also had to accept the world as, in some important respect, a ruin. New Brutalism appeared in the immediate post-war period and was a product of austerity, bombsites and future promise – but as yet not much building,

and certainly hardly anything that could be described as
Brutalist. Its schemes were sometimes startlingly accepting
of their surroundings: Golden Lane, for example, was simply
a layer over a bombscape that the architects had made little
attempt to hide. That attitude long persisted: in a BBC TV
film made in 1970, Alison Smithson described a remarkable
acceptance of the East End landscape as they found it: 'right
from the start we begin to identify with a site to put down
mental roots hooking onto rosebay willowherb, the children
overturning wrecked cars, the smell of curry on the stairs of
rejected tenements, oddments of past character or obvious
large identifying fixes.' It was, she went on, 'the poetry of the
ordinary'.[11] As a New Brutalist, you were supposed to take
the world as it came.

If there is a defining image of New Brutalists as a group,
it is the photograph taken for the 1956 exhibition *This Is
Tomorrow*, which depicts four of them: the Smithsons, along
with Paolozzi and the photographer Nigel Henderson, sitting
on chairs in the middle of Limerston Street, Chelsea, where
the Smithsons then lived. They represented a subset of the
Independent Group who had discovered a set of shared interests
and met independently of the IG; they were, in effect, the New
Brutalists.[12] Their identification with the street was a working-
class alignment, as was the informality of the subjects' dress,
Paolozzi's work clothes in particular; the emergent consumer
culture was there in the cars, one of which is a contemporary
Morris Oxford, whose toothy grille is just visible in the background between Peter Smithson and Eduardo Paolozzi. And
if the street was not a ruin, it was certainly shabby and the city
was there 'as found', in the phrase that crops up with frequency
around Brutalism. The image, Mark Crinson has written, is both
'absurd' and 'serious': 'absurd' because the group is sitting in the
middle of the street, and in spite of the claim of the exhibition's

Left to right: Peter Smithson, Eduardo Paolozzi, Alison Smithson and Nigel Henderson on Limerston Street, Chelsea, 1956.

title, the scene looks nothing remotely like the future. But also serious because it made a claim for the street as the 'literal embodiment of urban thinking'.[13] That combination of absurdity and high seriousness was also characteristic, representative of the tension between the intellectual and mass culture.

Banham was certainly both of these things too. The New Brutalism, in his formulation of it for the *Architectural Review*,

emerged from the peculiar texture of London in 1955, in
a way that paralleled the Futurists coming to terms with the
industrialization of northern Italy.[14] The term had been first
used in print by the Smithsons nearly three years earlier,
albeit in passing, in a short piece for *Architectural Design* on
a proposed house in Soho; they stressed the house's deliberate
lack of finish and exposition of structure, both themes that
Banham would develop at far greater length and turn into
theoretical principles.[15] Banham's article occupies six – or
possibly seven – pages, half of which are illustrations. (The
ambiguity is because the left-hand page of the opening spread
is a collage of photographs of the recently completed Notre-
Dame du Haut at Ronchamp, Le Corbusier's startling exercise
in free composition and his greatest departure to date from the
rationalism of the 1920s. Banham didn't refer to it, but he could
well have done.) The text was printed on the textured art paper
the magazine used for opinion pieces, and that, combined
with the declamatory Clarendon font, with its heavy serifs,
boldly announced the essay. It looked like, and arguably was,
a manifesto, although it was representative only of Banham's
perspective rather than the view of a group. There was in fact
some disagreement between Banham and the Smithsons about
Brutalism, the latter feeling he had co-opted the term for his
own purposes.[16] The distribution of text and image made the
multimedia character of Banham's version of the New Brutalism
immediately apparent: whatever it was, in Banham's eyes, it
wasn't only architecture. It was a state of mind, he implied, as
Futurism had been. Only two of the buildings illustrated could
be visited in real life (Hunstanton School by the Smithsons,
and Louis Kahn's Yale University Art Gallery). The other three,
schemes by the Smithsons for Coventry Cathedral, Sheffield
University and a private house in Soho, were drawings for
unbuilt projects. The remaining images were diverse: sculptures

by Independent Group colleagues Eduardo Paolozzi and Magda Cordell, paintings by Jackson Pollock (who had totemic status among IG members) and Alberto Burri, plus photographs of graffitied windows in London's East End by Nigel Henderson. As in *Theory and Design*, Banham ranged promiscuously across the arts, and his confidence in doing this spoke to a cultural microclimate favourable to what the art historian Alex Potts described later as 'particularly active interchange' between art and architecture.[17] To call the New Brutalism into existence as a multimedia tendency was to call to mind 1920s avant-gardes, and certainly Futurism, with which Banham was already associated via the discussions at the IG.

That recollection of the avant-garde was also there in the text. One subtext was Marinetti's 1909 manifesto of Futurism (as already noted, Banham's 'muse' at the time was said to have been Marinetti).[18] 'The New Brutalism' consciously lacked Marinetti's technological optimism, but it had the same hostility to tradition, named here with a curious and anachronistic term, the 'New Art-history'. (This is confusing for art historians now, for whom it signifies Marxist-inspired critique of the discipline.[19]) What Banham meant in 1955 was the recuperation of the Modern Movement by History, a process involving style labels and categories, and a narrative trajectory – and its consequent emasculation. His PhD supervisor Nikolaus Pevsner was certainly implicated, although he was not named.[20] Banham complained: 'the New Art-history has bitten into progressive English architectural thought, into teaching methods, into the common language of communication between architects and between architectural critics.' There was a pithy quote from the architectural historian Robert Furneaux Jordan, lately principal of the Architectural Association School and architectural correspondent of *The Observer*, on Brutalism:

'Lubetkin talks across time to the great masters . . . the Smithsons talk only to each other.'[21] In one sense, of course, Banham was thoroughly disingenuous, complaining about history when down the road at the Courtauld he was simultaneously writing it, but it was consistent with his multiple identities: *there* he was an historian but *here* he was the leader of an avant-garde movement.

The essay was a Futurist-lite assault on the establishment, cultivating three impactful things: 'Memorability as an image', 'clear exhibition of structure' and 'valuation of materials as found'.[22] By 'image', he meant something precisely different from the historical understanding of architecture. In another time and place he might have used the word *gestalt*, as what he argued for was gestalt-like: simple, clear, immediately apprehensible form, not unlike the way Minimalist sculpture was described in the 1960s. Alex Potts wrote, 'he used the word "image" in a very particular sense, not as representation, but to describe a material configuration that is immediately striking for "raw" visual qualities that were not reducible to formal logic.'[23] 'Not reducible to formal logic' is important because, whatever the New Brutalism was, it wasn't logical, and therefore a challenge to the version of modernism inherent to the Art-historians. The value of the New Brutalism here wasn't history but affect.

The emphasis on 'image' also marked an oversimplification of the other New Brutalists, whose work was perhaps more about process than it was about image (that was certainly the case with the Smithsons' architecture, as it was with Pollock's painting, both included in the essay). But Banham's points about structure and materials could be clearly enough illustrated in the real building that Banham wrote most about, the Hunstanton School by the Smithsons, finished in 1954. Occupying a site in a small Norfolk seaside town, it is a simple, steel-framed building with a yellow brick infill, two storeys in height. It is rectangular and symmetrical in plan, punctuated with three square courtyards, one roofed to make an assembly hall. There are clear, free-standing elements: a gymnasium, clearly visible in the image in the essay 'The New Brutalism', and ancillary buildings with a distinctive, high water tower.[24] In the small image in the essay, the school appears a lot more refined than it actually is. The seemingly obvious comparison is Ludwig Mies van der Rohe's Illinois Institute of Technology (IIT) campus on the south side of Chicago, built from 1950, and a sensational object in the architectural magazines, which was the only place the Smithsons would have seen it at this point. Mies's exquisite work impressed through the quality of its materials and its attention to detail; the IIT looked like, and was, an expensive building, an advertisement for luxury through understatement. In the grubby picture in the *Architectural Review*, Hunstanton looks at first sight like an IIT knock-off. But in the text Banham made clear it was something else: 'Hunstanton appears to be made of glass, brick, steel and concrete, and is in fact made of glass, brick, steel and concrete. Water and electricity do not come out of unexplained holes in the wall, but are delivered to the point of use by visible pipes and manifest conduits.' He went on: 'One can see what Hunstanton is and how it works and there is not another thing to see except the play of spaces.'[25]

What he meant was illustrated by a well-known image of the school's toilets depicting a rank of washbasins, backlit by an opaque glass wall. There is absolutely no decoration in this space, no compromise. The basins are attached simply to a steel beam in a line, and strikingly not only is the mains piping exposed, but so too is the waste pipe, a simple tube that cascades water into a gully at the children's feet. The more you look at it this remains an austere space, the plumbing not much removed from what you might expect to find in a campsite. Nothing ameliorates the space, nothing hides the servicing. It simply

Alison and Peter Smithson, Hunstanton School, Hunstanton,
Norfolk: detail of the washbasins, 1954.

Ludwig Mies van der Rohe, S. R. Crown Hall, IIT campus, Chicago, Illinois, 1956.

is what it is. Mies's work, by contrast, is all about the illusion
of simplicity; in actual fact, at IIT as everywhere else in Mies,
simplicity requires a great deal to be concealed. Hunstanton
by contrast was all about the way it is built, what it is made of,
and its relative cheapness. Revealingly, the Smithsons were
happy to have their IG colleague Nigel Henderson photograph
the place under construction. 'The Smithsons' work', Banham
wrote, 'is characterised by an abstemious under-designing of
the details, and much of the impact of the building comes from
the ineloquence but absolute consistency of such components
as the stairs and handrails.'[26]

That is a strange idea: deliberately 'under-designing'
runs counter to what you might think architecture actually
is. 'Abstemious' also indicates the valuation placed on the
condition of austerity, something, then as now, from which
most wish for release. 'Ineloquence' too might invite pause
for thought: what is a critic doing here encouraging architects

to design ugly objects? These characteristics expressed in words make clear that this is, whatever the photography appears to say, a very different kind of architecture to that of Mies: tough, uncompromising and rough.

That affinity for material roughness manifested itself in the essay in a hostility to the picturesque, which had a Cold War politics to it all of its own. On the surface, the anti-picturesque stance was a generational revolt, for the picturesque meant old; it was the established power of the architect's department of the London County Council, which favoured an attenuated modernism with traditional elements ('people's detailing'), which Banham described as 'brickwork, segmental arches, pitched roofs, small windows . . . picturesque detailing without picturesque planning'.[27] (The New Brutalism was also, in one view, about the reassertion of private practice against the state.[28]) In any case, the picturesque, exemplified in Pevsner's work, meant compromise, continuity between past and present, and some order in the ruins.[29] The New Brutalists wanted none of those things, wishing to reassert the Modern Movement's revolutionary credentials: absorption by the picturesque was death, and the revolt against it was perhaps the most clearly Futurist-like part of the 1955 essay.

Among the best examples of what the New Brutalism might be in Banham's view was not a building at all, but an Independent Group installation called *Parallel of Life and Art*, produced collectively by the Smithsons, Nigel Henderson and Eduardo Paolozzi and shown at the Institute of Contemporary Arts (ICA) in 1954. For the design historian Anne Massey it was more than just an example of New Brutalism, like the Hunstanton school; it was the very basis of it.[30] It was a peculiar and probably unprecedented installation, a set of architectural scale photographs of scientific, engineering and art structures, the panels of which could be displayed in any way the curators saw fit, in an improvisation that gave them an unprecedented amount of control. In the original installation the panels were suspended at a variety of angles from the walls and ceiling; it didn't look stable and it wasn't. It was genuinely multimedia and interdisciplinary; it didn't offer solutions. For Charles Jencks, Banham's sometime PhD student and one of the first historians and critics to take the installation seriously, the images 'all had a compulsive violence as if they had just been torn from a context for their immediate impact'.[31] (Frampton also noted the violence of the images, as well as 'distorted and anti-aesthetic views of the human figure': this was not easy viewing.[32]) The images themselves, Jencks noted, were dominated by the sciences and could be, in the popular sense, brutal, citing number 100, 'a benign tumour made up of proliferated cells', and number 119, a 'section of a thrombosed pulmonary'. The flirtation with death was not mediated by any attempt to explain: life and death were just there. Lacking 'humanization' or 'anthropomorphization', Brutalism was 'undomesticated', the 'visual equivalent of cosmological truth as it was then known'.[33] It was thoroughly uncompromising in spirit, the exact opposite of the welfare-statism of the Festival of Britain. It confronted the viewer with the brutality of the world, rather than trying to ameliorate it.[34]

That confrontational position came through again in the 1956 exhibition *This Is Tomorrow*, for which the Limerston Street image was made. Partly curated by Lawrence Alloway, who had taken over leadership of the IG from Banham, it included the Smithsons' *Patio and Pavilion*, a quasi-architectural installation comprising a shed in an area of open space; compared to the rest of the exhibition, with its copious references to American consumer culture, *Patio and Pavilion* seemed to look back. Banham wrote in the *Architectural Review*: 'one could not help feeling that this particular garden shed with its rusted bicycle wheels, a battered trumpet and other homely junk had been excavated after an atomic holocaust and discovered to be part of a European tradition of site planning that went back to archaic Greece and beyond.'[35] Banham was somewhat critical here, feeling that the tradition was the picturesque one, and that the piece therefore lacked the appropriate critical edge (the Smithsons themselves laughed it off, knowing Banham was perpetually disappointed in them).[36] But critical or not, ruins were integral to many of the images the New Brutalists had produced. The world's fabric was 'bombed out', Kenneth Frampton later wrote, but it had technology: 'mobile consumerism was already being envisaged as the life substance of a new industrial vernacular.'[37] Banham, whatever his reservations about this individual work, understood this extremely well, and the curiously downbeat acceptance of the world as found was something that would have echoes throughout his work. The New Brutalist didn't imagine the world was transformable, but it could be civilized with technology, albeit in a bodged and contingent way. It implied coming to terms with the world as it was; it was to a certain degree comfortable with violence and its consequences. The world may have gone to hell, it seems to be saying, but you can still have a TV set.

That streetwise attitude was strongly visible in all the images that Banham included as illustrations of the New Brutalism in the 1955 article, none more so perhaps than the perspective for the unbuilt Golden Lane competition. Like the Sheffield University project of the same time, it was in effect a modern structure laid upon the devastation of the post-war city. There is no new world, they seem to be saying, no transformation. We survive, technologically assisted, in the ruins of what's left. It was certainly a bracing message, and an exciting one for a writer who was keen to try out a (quasi-) revolutionary pose. New Brutalism's message may have been

Peter and Alison Smithson, Golden Lane competition entry, 1952.

rather different from that of Futurism, but it demanded a similar kind of subject position from its leaders; it was Banham's would-be Marinetti moment – although it needs to be said that he was writing as more of an outsider than might immediately be apparent, and he did not command the support of a group. His New Brutalism was in some ways an overlay on an existing situation, like the buildings he described.

## Ethics versus Aesthetics

A revolutionary position does not always survive contact with reality, especially for someone as mercurial as Banham. Early hints of trouble could be seen in Banham's review of *This Is Tomorrow*, which he felt had diluted the revolutionary line.[38] Banham's doubts were also evident in a review of Sheffield's monumental Park Hill housing complex, built between 1957 and 1961, whose design was overseen by city architect J. L. Womersley.[39] A colossus on a hilly site overlooking the Sheaf valley, it was like nothing else yet built in Britain, comprising four connected walls rising to fourteen storeys in places, all connected by continuous street decks and bridges. Aerial photographs showed a clear debt to the Smithsons' Golden Lane project of 1952, for this monster was laid over the existing landscape. The fragments of the Victorian industrial city lay all around, while the street decks clearly invoked the Smithsons' design. Nowhere, curiously, did Banham mention the New Brutalism, although on the face of it Park Hill was everything it stood for. The problem, if there was one, was of aesthetics. Banham was largely approving of Park Hill, but the impressions it left on him were of its looks and the reference points of those looks rather than the architectural programme per se. In other words, it was a building for architectural trainspotters who would be able to elucidate the quotations: Le Corbusier's Unité d'Habitation in Marseilles, Affonso Reidy's Pedregulho complex in Rio, lately illustrated in the *Architectural Review*, and possibly, Banham thought, the Cerro Piloto housing in Caracas.[40] In its reference points and stylistic tics, it represented just 'the kind of building a great many young architects in Britain in the early fifties wanted to put up'.[41] He noted the presence of an artist, John Forrester, on the design team, there apparently to ensure stylistic consistency, pleasant colouring and some Mondriaan-like decorations: another disappointment, for it focused on aesthetic niceties rather than the 'much more creative and exciting possibilities at hand'.[42] At the same time, the elements that might have informed a more radical architectural programme in New Brutalist terms, namely the inhabitants, were not really to be trusted. Banham wrote that he would let 'qualified social scientists' explore the use and inhabitation of the building, although it was precisely those questions later and elsewhere in Banham's career that would provoke some of his most radical work.[43] But not here: it was in the end all about the aesthetic, in which case the resemblance to the imagined revolutionary programme of the New Brutalists of 1955 was superficial. And that impression was backed up by the photography of Park Hill, which as much as it nodded towards the ordinary lives of the inhabitants (children playing on the

Sheffield Corporation City Architect's Department, Park Hill, Sheffield, under refurbishment in 2020.

Sheffield Corporation City Architect's Department, Park Hill, Sheffield, 1961.

decks, shoppers queuing at the butchers and so on) repeatedly emphasized the cliff-like immensity of the exterior and the starkness of the materials. The *Architectural Review*'s picture editor emphasized drama.

## 1966: Ethics and Aesthetics

By 1964 the New Brutalism in the Banham universe was arguably all about the aesthetics. His enthusiastic review of Leicester University's Engineering Building by James Stirling and James Gowan is a brilliant, but straightforward formal analysis of a composition of unexpected elements.[44] The one residual element of ethics in the review was in the reference to materials 'as found', and the architects' refusal to embellish or hide. That had a class politics about it, albeit of a residual and buried kind.

Otherwise the revolutionary New Brutalism of 1955 was seemingly in decline, the term itself no longer in active use. By 1966 he had openly become the figure the 1955 essay had affected to disparage, the historian – and moreover, as an historian, in the book *The New Brutalism: Ethic or Aesthetic?*, he was complicit in the New Brutalism's historicization.[45] It was an understandable transformation, as Banham's personal situation had changed a good deal. In 1955 he was a jobbing journalist, with a doctorate on the side: he had presence but little security, and the thesis wouldn't be finished for another three years. By 1966 the PhD was done, he had found a secure academic position at the Bartlett School of Architecture, and he had already completed two books, *Theory and Design in the First Machine Age* and, also for the Architectural Press, a straightforward, illustrated *Guide to Modern Architecture* in 1962.[46] He had a substantial media presence, making regular radio broadcasts, contributing cultural criticism for mainstream political journals, especially *New Society*. He was also learning to drive. He had, in other words, become an adult.

An Architectural Press commission, *The New Brutalism* is not long, at perhaps 30,000 words, but is luxuriously illustrated, which keeps prices of used editions surprisingly high.[47] It made clear that whatever Brutalism had been, its avant-garde moment was finished and it had become a style. The book's conclusion was titled 'Memoirs of a Survivor', and its view of history was unequivocal: 'It is very clear that the most important fact about the British contribution to Brutalism is that it is over.'[48] Banham complained that little of the architecture of the original Brutalists had manifested the promise of *une architecture autre*, an architecture of pure feeling.[49] The Smithsons' complex for *The Economist* newspaper on St James's in London, completed in 1964, was perhaps the crux of the problem. The architecture of pure feeling that

James Stirling and James Gowan, Engineering Building, Leicester University, 1959.

was the promise of the 1955 manifesto had been transformed into an exercise in 'studied restraint', a polite building for an establishment client, thoroughly respectful of its surroundings; it was the exact opposite of revolution.[50]

Alison and Peter Smithson, Economist Building, London, 1964.

Banham elaborated considerably on the New Brutalism's
politics, and in retrospect this aspect of the book says much
about his and the New Brutalist position. The New Brutalists
were in his view broadly of the left, but, conscious of social
class, they were suspicious of the tendency of the mainstream
left leadership to preach, especially when it came to culture;
they all appreciated and consumed American popular culture.[51]
That put them at odds with the communist faction of the giant
architects' department of the London County Council, whose
housing department was split between card-carrying members
of the Communist Party of Great Britain (CPGB) and younger,
liberal-left members. The CPGB-supporting group, whose
members included Kenneth Campbell and David Gregory-
Jones, favoured a Swedish-style attenuated modernism;
the others were broadly in favour of Le Corbusier, whose
influence was nowhere more clearly visible than at the Alton
West Estate, Roehampton, in southwest London.[52] Banham's
account of it all, perhaps informed by his friendship with
Colin St John Wilson, IG member and sometime LCC architect,
was mischievously anti-communist, insinuating that the
organization was dominated by Soviet placemen ('an exemplary
piece of Cold War demonology', as Owen Hatherley wrote much
later on).[53] The communists at the LCC, Banham argued, wanted
a national style, equivalent to the USSR's under Andrei Zhdanov,
Stalin's influential Minister of Culture. Zhdanov was no more,
having died mysteriously in 1948, but his influence among
the LCC architects seemingly remained, at least in Banham's
imagination. The aim was to produce an English version of
Soviet Socialist Realism, enforced with (he wrote) 'a grotesque
mixture of Stalinist conspiratorial techniques . . . and the
traditional methods of English snobbery'.[54]

The effect on architectural design was clear, Banham
thought. In late 1954, he continued, the communists had

succeeded in having the LCC issue a directive on building height, so that anything less than four storeys was to be considered 'domestic' and should therefore have a pitched roof. It was controversial for modernists, for it would have banned almost all of Le Corbusier's domestic architecture. Order was restored shortly thereafter by the unexpected intervention of the USSR (wrote Banham). At the All-Union Congress of Architects, Nikita Khrushchev, then the premier of the USSR, intervened to bring the Zhdanov line into doubt, relieving Soviet architects of the need to follow an officially approved stylistic template. It threw the LCC communists into confusion: 'advocates of Socialist-Realist architecture all over the world' suddenly found themselves 'without ideological support'.[55] The episode had origins in fact, but Banham used it characteristically for humour as well as his own propaganda to serve the New Brutalist position, for it needed enemies in order to meaningfully exist, and in a neo-Futurist way, what Banham had done was identify an older generation (here, the LCC communists) as an obstacle. Here were the USSR devotees, absurdly following the twists and turns of party directives, but also, and more damagingly, they were identified as cultural conservatives, committed to perpetuating the picturesque. Criticizing the LCC's much-praised Alton East Estate, which was incontrovertibly Swedish, Banham attacked its 'Zhdanov precepts' along with its attachment to 'a romantic and fashionably morbid form of landscape/townscape painting exemplified by the work of John Piper and Graham Sutherland'.[56] This work had been vital in inculcating 'a mood of elegant despair' that had a tendency to dominate English culture.[57]

Banham's attack on the LCC was therefore more than simple 'Cold War demonology', identifying a problem with the cultural conservatism of the left. In other words, the architectural

culture of the LCC communists combined sympathy for the
USSR with a nostalgic and reactionary England. The landscape
art to which Banham referred was familiar enough. Piper was
a regular contributor to the *Architectural Review*, where in
articles and images he had advanced what might be described
as a refined fatalism: his *Bombed Buildings of Britain*, published
while the Second World War was still in progress, was an attempt
to come to terms with the damage caused by the Luftwaffe's air
raids on Britain by promoting a cult of the ruin – an attitude,
as Banham was perfectly aware, that stretched back to the
eighteenth century.[58] It was seemingly an odd combination with
the LCC's communism, but what Banham showed was how they
could comfortably be combined at Alton East, legibly a picture
of natural order. Whatever the New Brutalists were about, it
wasn't that. The New Brutalists 'had the depressing sense that
the drive was going out of Modern Architecture, its pure dogma
being polluted by politicians and compromisers who had lost
their nerve'.[59] To be a New Brutalist was also, as this newly
historical take made clear, to be part of a generational revolt.
Marinetti's 1909 manifesto again cannot have been far from
Banham's mind.

The material fact of the book, however, was evidence that
the revolution was over. The key buildings were all luxuriously
photographed. Hunstanton School had a chapter to itself,
Banham refining the earlier argument about Mies, and stressing
the lack of drama about New Brutalist buildings in relation to
the building services (unlike High Tech later on). If this was
implicitly an unspectacular architecture, it was also, by accident,
architecture that photographed spectacularly well, and the
book's ongoing appeal has a great deal to do with that.[60] An
architecture of enviable textures and of bold, sculptural shapes,
it needed only early morning sunlight and some sensitive
printing to reveal its attractions. The book's sumptuous images

included Le Corbusier's Unité d'Habitation, a key reference point for Brutalists, which in one photograph becomes a superlative abstract sculpture. An emergency stair at the end of the building, cast in concrete, twisting upwards over five floors, becomes an abstraction in that the function is no longer really visible, but it is also highly anthropomorphic in some unspecified way. A picture remarkable for its texture and light, and the power of the image, it says nothing about the building of which it is a part beyond its capacity to provide startling images. It was in the photography of the New Brutalism that ethic definitively became aesthetic. 'I make no pretence that I was not seduced by the aesthetics of Brutalism,' Banham wrote, 'but the persistence of an idea that the relationship of the parts and the materials of a building are a working morality – this, for me, is the continuing validity of the New Brutalism.'[61]

That ethical validity was based on a short revolutionary moment before anything much had been built and when it was possible to imagine an architecture of uninhibited potential, one where the architectural programme would be entirely driven by functions and materials, and its products (Hatherley's 'strange, angry objects') would be untouched by any stylistic considerations.[62] That moment has continued to fascinate precisely because its architecture scarcely exists in reality and has to be imagined. The American art theory journal *October* was captivated by it for precisely those reasons in 2011, exploring its 'latent critical potential' by reproducing the 1955 manifesto and a series of critical commentaries that stuck to the revolution, and largely avoided the architectural products (architecture, in the *October* universe, was always a disappointment).[63] Reiterating Banham, the journal concluded with some 'lessons' from the New Brutalism: it was a tendency that didn't seek to ameliorate the present, but 'rather create something of value in a confrontation with it'. Its modus operandi was therefore a 'productive tension' with its surroundings, a difficult position to hold in that it meant antagonism rather than amelioration, but an implicitly moral one.[64]

What would Banham have made of this posthumous laureation? He would have concurred with the view that the New Brutalism was more about cultural politics, less about style. He had surprisingly little to say about *Brutalism*, which is to say the architectural style that emerged later, taking the look but little else from the earlier experiments. Banham didn't have much to say once the revolution made contact with reality, as it were, not even when the Smithsons belatedly realized something like their Golden Lane housing in the Robin Hood Gardens project scheme, completed in 1972. That project reiterated a good deal of Golden Lane, in its street decks in particular, as well as its general form, but its existence as a building in the world was circumscribed by debate about its performance; by 1972 it was, in any case, twenty years out of date by the revolutionary standards of the New Brutalism.[65] Banham, typically, liked the idea of the architectural programme driven by the inhabitants of a building, but the reality of that was always for others to deal with (his remark in his 1961 Park Hill review about leaving those considerations to 'qualified social scientists' is instructive). The New Brutalism's afterlife saw its transformation into Brutalism, latterly a transgressive, sexy (and ultimately amoral) style. In one of the more popular recent book-length accounts of Brutalism, the architectural historian Barnabas Calder recounts a night spent in a remote Brutalist bunker, his whole body literally in contact with the concrete, an image in which concrete becomes a fetish.[66] The film *High-rise* (2015), directed by Ben Wheatley and written by Amy Jump, based on J. G. Ballard's novel of the same name, is an orgiastic riot in which a Brutalist apartment building (in real life the condemned 1973 Leisure Centre in Bangor, Northern Ireland) is a character as much as anything else. Most of all, Brutalism in its most recent phase was impossible to dissociate from the less palatable workings of the housing markets in the world's most costly cities: the Trellick Tower in London, one of the icons of the Brutalist style, designed by Ernő Goldfinger and completed in 1972 as social housing, became a fashionable address, with its original social purpose abandoned. The class transformation of public housing in London in particular is an inescapable part of the story of Brutalism. By the 2010s its transformation from ethic to aesthetic was complete. Banham's own engagement with it, his history as a New Brutalist, terminated in 1966.

# 4 THE AUTOPHILE

It is a monster of steel and glass and rubber and chromium plating, nearly six metres (20 ft) in length, and weighing two tons, powered by an eight-cylinder engine, six litres in displacement. In this particular example it is a rather sickly yellow. How you even begin to describe its form stretches an ordinary vocabulary. The basic alignment is easy enough to explain, with the various parts in the expected places: there are the usual four wheels, a standard three-box bodyshell which even an uncommitted observer would recognize as housing the engine at the front and a boot for luggage at the rear. A clearly visible passenger compartment lies in the middle, accessed by four doors, two on each side. There is relatively conventional glazing, with a curved windscreen, two opening ventilation windows in the front, and the normal horizontal ribbon all the way to the rear window. There is a steel roof, headlights, bumpers, indicator lights. It is, at the most basic level, a recognizable car.

But imagine you have not seen this thing before, and you have no context to understand it other than the tiny, feeble and rare cars of a bombed-out and austere post-war London – it is literally twice the size or more, and has a lurid colour scheme in a market where colour is rarely an option. The scale shocks, partly in contrast to the other cars on the road and the surroundings. It shocks too because, at a time of austerity, it is patently scale for effect alone, and if you poke under the surface you see immediately how much space the car occupies simply for the sake of taking up space. The engine, big though it is, needs little over a metre (3 ft) in length (it was actually a modern and compact design). The bonnet is so long because

Cadillac Sixty Special, 1951 (The 'Brian Tait Russell Cadillac').

there is a gap of nearly a metre again for empty space before the bumper/grille assembly, which occupies a similar amount of space again.[1] To put it another way, the space provided for the mechanical parts of the car is double what they in reality require. There is a similar profligacy at the rear end. The packaging, to use a modern design term, is remarkably poor. There is less interior room than in a modern Volkswagen Golf, yet the car occupies more than twice as much road.

However, it is not only the scale that is so arresting: the iconography for the outward form of this object has little to do with how it is supposed to work. This is an object that is all about style, and every inch of the outer surface has been worked over and considered, and designed to look a particular way. Every part draws attention to itself. Some of this extrudes forms recognizably present in European motor design, so there is some faux heraldry on the front hood meant to signify a noble heritage (the name of the brand supports this idea, a reference to the French explorer Antoine de la Mothe Cadillac, widely understood to be the founder of Detroit). The emblem that bisects the hood, a sort of extruded angel lying prone, head into the wind, is not so far removed from what might have previously been found on a European car. But the rest of it is something else. The bumper/grille assembly is vast, to begin with, all chromium-plated and wildly anthropomorphic. Unlike those of European cars of the period, it is aggressively horizontal, and therefore reads as a mouth. From this point on, car radiator grilles tend to read this way, but this is one of the first examples to make so much of it. It is a mouth alright – grinning, confident, toothy (those vertical bars!), aggressive. The bodywork bulges out below the glasshouse, and there is a legible nose at the leading edge of the hood. It is certainly stereotypically masculine, all big shoulders and swagger.

The headlamps introduce a note of doubt, at least as far as the car's gender is concerned: they naturally read as eyes, but they are delicate compared to the treatment of the grille, and moreover they are subtly hooded, which makes unmistakable reference to the trope of the Hollywood starlet, eyes half-closed in ecstasy (the reference was apparently Jane Russell in the publicity shots for *The Outlaw*). Then there is the question of those extraordinary extrusions of the bumper, two of them, breast-like in size and shape and referred to commonly as Dagmars, in reference to the famously pert actress and television personality of the same name.[2] The ambiguity continues inside. If this is a rocket ship, it is also at the same time apparently an ice-cream parlour. The seating comprises two wide, ribbed vinyl benches that really belong in that sort of establishment, while the controls are, by modern standards, basic and cluster around the steering wheel, with a smaller, more ornamental Dagmar as the central boss. The interior is definitely organized around the comfort of the passengers rather than the pleasure of the driver. Although part of the dialogue around car design in this period concerns the extent to which it refers to aviation design, the interior in this case is nothing at all like the cockpits of aircraft of the time, their interiors seemingly all instrumentation. The car interior is actually the reverse, a space of relaxation, consumption even. What an odd thing it is: huge and aggressive in parts, demure and female in others, a weapon and a space of comfort, anthropomorphic and sexually ambiguous.

The car in question is the Cadillac Sixty Special, 1951 vintage, designed by Bill Mitchell, and part of a fourth-generation design produced between 1950 and 1953. By the time the production run ended in 1953, the Sixty Special had sold nearly 14,000 examples, and was Cadillac's best-selling model by far. It was quite powerful for the time, its motor in the first instance capable of 160 brake horsepower (power outputs would routinely double over the next decade). It was reasonably quick and could comfortably reach 100 mph, but its soft suspension, along with the interior design, indicate a machine built for comfort not speed: that emphasis was deliberate and meant to be clearly legible to the average consumer, which it was, and still is. This particular Sixty Special appears in two places in Banham's work, first in two photographs by Mary Banham for a lecture by Reyner on car design at a Newcastle Polytechnic conference in 1975. The lecture, which reviewed a quarter-century of Banham's thinking on the topic, was later published

in a volume of papers.[3] The car was identified as the 'Brian
Tait-Russell Cadillac', on account of its owner, and subsequently
appeared in the BBC TV film *Fathers of Pop*, which Banham
made in conjunction with Julian Cooper in 1979 and which
dealt with the origins and development of the Independent
Group.[4] The car, in its lurid yellow glory, is a faintly comic
presence throughout the film. If you need an illustration of
the anthropomorphic qualities of this kind of vehicle, this
is as good as any. It serves the film's narrative purpose too,
transporting Banham from one historical location to another,
while there is an important sequence in the middle in which
he points out, with a combination of love and authority, the
car's outstanding design features. Ben Banham remembered
well the TV production and his last sight of the car: 'The filming
proved to be a close-run thing, as the car drove away down
Abercorn Place behind the closing credits the fuel pump failed
and it coasted to a halt as it arrived at Maida Vale.'[5]

The Brian Tait-Russell Cadillac is a stand-in here for a
much wider set of interests: it could have been a Buick, or
a Chevrolet, or a car from outside the General Motors stable
of brands. American cars, and cars in general, were of central
importance in Banham's thought and arguably one of his most
divisive concerns. Cars were (and are) often associated with the
political right with their connotations of individual freedom,
ideas that sat uncomfortably with Banham's mainstream leftism,
a contradiction of which he was well aware.[6] More recently cars
might be seen as connotative of rather normative gender roles.
As the design historian Penny Sparke put it, cars were 'public'
and 'masculine', and he was as a result indelibly marked with
those things.[7] Their importance was nowhere clearer than in
Sparke's own 1981 anthology of Banham's writings, from the
frontispiece with its fantasy vehicles designed by François
Dallegret to articles analysing assorted Volkswagens (he was

not a fan), Minis, Buicks, Pontiacs, Cadillacs, Jaguars, Toyotas and Fords, as well as the iconic Citroën DS and the Willys Jeep.[8] Banham, in that volume, could almost have been an automotive critic.

Cars as an intellectual project first emerged in the work Banham did with the Independent Group (IG) between 1952 and 1955. The IG was an informal organization that met intermittently at the Institute for Contemporary Arts (ICA) in London between 1951 and 1955; it had a semi-official status at the ICA, and had representation on that organization's management committee, but if it had a position, it was one, if not hostile to, certainly critical of the ICA's values under the directorship of Herbert Read. Its informality meant plenty of discussion happened away from the ICA, including at the Banhams' house. Some meetings attracted no more than a few participants, even some of the more celebrated ones such as Eduardo Paolozzi's legendary epidiascope lecture showing off his collection of American ephemera. It was hard to get into, a close-knit group of friends and their families that wasn't really open to outsiders, as the artist Richard Smith noted.[9] Banham however managed, and became central to it: he gatecrashed the Paolozzi lecture, and not long afterwards became the group's official secretary, as well as a regular contributor to discussions. He 'defined' the character of the IG through his interests in technology and popular culture, and his willingness to engage with all the contradictions involved in popular culture from the perspective of the political left.[10] The IG's topics ranged widely. All aspects of popular culture were of interest, especially American popular culture, art and the future of art, philosophy, the politics of class. Cars were inescapable. Richard Hamilton painted them, Paolozzi showed collages with them prominently featured, Peter and Alison Smithson collected advertisements illustrating them, and Colin St John Wilson drove one for the IG.

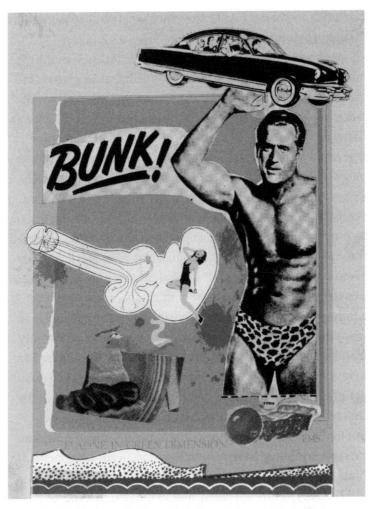

Eduardo Paolozzi, *Evadne in Green Dimension*, 1948, screen-print and lithograph on paper.

One of few members of the IG to own a car, he acted as the Banhams' unofficial driver using his Lancia: he took the Banham family on excursions to Silverstone for the motor racing.[11] The IG – specifically Hamilton and Banham – curated an auto-oriented exhibition in July 1955, *Man, Machine and Motion*, a straightforward photographic show of people and machines, its subject matter stretching what was conventionally thought appropriate for an art show.[12]

Above all, Banham talked about cars in lectures, in the most focused way on 4 March 1955 in a talk entitled 'Borax, or the Thousand-horsepower Mink'. ('Borax', a U.S. term that has fallen into disuse, meant manufactured goods whose design was flashy or hybrid, with overtones of shoddiness. It is recorded that eighteen people attended the talk.[13]) Banham was still a long way from being a driver himself. He had apparently seen a Chevrolet car at this point, a very rare sight in 1950s London. Precisely which model of Chevrolet was unclear, but it had made an impression.[14] He had also allegedly seen a Cadillac, glimpsed through the window of the Courtauld library in 1951 (again the precise model is unclear).[15] He had almost certainly never been a passenger in an American car at this stage, and it would be nearly a decade before he would visit America and see these monsters in their natural habitat, let alone drive one. The only member of the IG to have had that experience, or anything like it, was James Stirling, whose involvement with the group was peripheral. Stirling had spent some months as a student in the United States, mostly in New York, but with visits elsewhere.[16] But for Banham and the others, the apprehension of American cars was an almost entirely mediated one, in advertisements, films and rumour.[17]

The 1955 lecture appeared later in the year in a short-lived journal, *Art*, under the title 'Vehicles of Desire'. A short, polemical piece, it opens with an image of a car Banham had at best seen only fleetingly, the Cadillac Eldorado convertible, a two-door drophead development of the Series Sixty. He didn't identify it, apart from referring to it as an 'open Caddy', but this is the only model it could realistic have been. The next time, he wrote – with some imaginative licence, as if there had ever been a first time – one

wambles past you, its front chrome-hung like a pearl-roped
dowager, its long top level with the ground at a steady thirty
inches save where the two tail-fins cock up to carry the rear
lights, reflect what a change has been wrought since the last
time any architect expressed himself forcibly on the subject
of the automobile.[18]

What followed was a series of complaints, rehearsals for
the argument he would make at greater length in the book
*Theory and Design in the First Machine Age*. Le Corbusier didn't
understand cars, Banham argued. He cited them in his writings,
but he projected architectural fantasies onto them; he wanted
them to be enduring, timeless objects in the spirit of the
architecture they aspired to build. Banham's argument was in
some respects a self-serving one, and he required Le Corbusier
to be a dilettante aesthete whose interest in cars extended only

Cadillac Eldorado, 1955 model.

to the Bignan-Sport, a hand-built roadster that was thoroughly unrepresentative of modern car design – a somewhat unfair view, if a useful one for Banham and the IG, who needed foils for their arguments.[19] It was also inaccurate about Le Corbusier, who in fact had designed a car, the Voiture Minimum, in 1936.[20] The IG nevertheless persisted with their argument: cars weren't buildings. They were small by comparison, mass produced and, most important of all, impermanent, with a life cycle of perhaps three years at the time of writing, and going down. The classic automobiles beloved of architects (the Citroën Traction Avant and the Volkswagen that came to be known as the Beetle) were products of 'freakish' markets: Banham disliked the Beetle, which he thought unbalanced and poorly engineered.[21]

Where the car market was working as it should, its evolution would be shockingly swift: 'there can be no norms of formal composition', he wrote, 'while the automobile remains an object in evolution.'[22] Under these conditions, and concretely with drastically attenuated product lifecycles, the car could and would look like anything its designers wanted it to. Its difference from architecture did not however mean that there wasn't anything to say. The car was a richly endowed source of imagery waiting for interpretation, especially by someone with an art-historical training like Banham. In a famous passage, the Eldorado was 'a thick ripe stream of loaded symbols', 'symbolic iconographies' connotative of the important stuff of modern life, namely 'speed, power, brutalism, luxury, snob appeal and plain common-or-garden sex'.[23] An art-historical tease, it argued that a mass-produced design might be as symbolically loaded as high art. All it required was the appropriate tools to decode the messages. One of the rare persons with the tools to do the job was quoted by Banham, although not named – this was Deborah Allen, one of the editors of the New York-based journal *Industrial Design*, read keenly by the members of the IG.[24] She was one of only a handful of intellectuals anywhere at that time to discuss car design in any depth. This was almost certainly part of her appeal to Banham and the other autophiles in the group, given their misgivings about Le Corbusier's understanding.[25] Allen was an insider. She was not a natural auto critic, and had previously regarded cars as vulgar and profligate, certainly out of sync with her Manhattan-based professional life. She had written earlier that cars were 'senseless', a view that chimed with that of the New York cultural elite, for whom cars were mostly useless on a day-to-day basis. But in an episode described much later by the design historian Alice Twemlow, she had a form of epiphany when being driven by a friend in a new Buick Century from Connecticut into Manhattan: 'Inspired by her exhilarating experience of the car speeding along the coastal road, and her appreciation of the way her friend the driver inhabited its interior space, she wrote an uncharacteristically enthusiastic review.'[26] That review has passed into legend: it was, Banham wrote in 1955, criticism of 'almost Berensonian sensibility' –

Buick Century, 1955.

quite a claim, referring to the American art historian Bernard Berenson, then the pre-eminent Anglophone scholar of Renaissance art.[27] The passage Banham reproduced read, in full:

> The Buick . . . is perpetually floating on currents that are built into the design. The designers put the greatest weight over the front wheels, where the engine is, which is natural enough. The heavy bumper helps to pull the weight forward; the dip in the body and the chrome spear express how the thrust is dissipated in turbulence towards the rear. Just behind the strong shoulder of the car, a sturdy post lifts up the roof, which trails off like a banner in the air. The driver sits in dead calm at the centre of all this motion – hers is a lush situation.[28]

This remarkable passage imagined the car as having agency of its own, perhaps even life (this, and the incorporation of the viewer's emotional response, were probably what prompted the Berenson comparison).[29] The imagination of weight, speed and structure was finely done, and communicated something of what discussion must have been like among Harley Earl's partly female design team in Dearborn: Earl and his so-called 'damsels of design' presciently imagined the car as a fantasy-laden consumer object, rather than engineering.[30] Allen took this on board, considering the car as a consumer experience as much as anything. This was not the imagination of the showroom, but of the road. The architectural understanding of cars at this point generally had little to say about the experience of driving, which is one of the reasons why Banham in *Theory and Design* felt so impelled to invoke Marinetti, who at least knew how to drive, even if not always how to keep a car on the road. Allen wrote of the driver as a woman ('hers is a lush situation'). She did so naturally, yet this ought not to be overlooked given the everyday, somewhat chauvinistic, reality of the IG.[31] Banham concluded with a bracing address to the reader, the *'hypocrite lecteur'*: were they now so sure of their position vis-à-vis the automobile? Was there not something to value? The top body stylists, he wrote, had access to an exceptional range of 'symbolic iconographies', manifest in 'actual symbols' that might come from anywhere: 'Science Fiction, movies, earth-moving equipment, supersonic aircraft, racing cars, heraldry, and certain deep-seated mental dispositions about the great outdoors and the kinship between technology and sex.' Car design was not 'a farrago of meaningless ornament, as fine art critics insist, but a means of saying something of breathless, but unverbalisable consequence to the live culture of the Twentieth Century.'[32]

That is a remarkable set of claims, looking back on it: that largely anonymous car designers working invisibly and collectively might have access to an understanding of the modern world that art had largely missed. Hiding in plain sight and consumed by millions (if only in image, as Roland Barthes was to say at the same time) was the real art of the modern world.[33] 'Vehicles of Desire' was not only a challenge to the reader's value system, but, full of rhetorical sweeps and ornamental flourishes, it paralleled the stylistic baroque of the automobiles themselves.

Even at just a thousand words, 'Vehicles of Desire' is an important piece in Banham's oeuvre. What did it want? What did Banham want from cars? What did the IG want from cars? These questions are worth asking because they are sometimes occluded by the nature of the material itself and popular assumptions about it, cars being a stereotypically male province, for example. Banham's enthusiasms for things with wheels were at some level stereotypically boyish, but as they developed, in dialogue with both Mary and the IG, they became more complex, cognisant of their existence as consumer objects, defined in image and use increasingly by women.[34] Whatever the complexities of their gendering, however, cars were (and arguably, remain) distasteful for both the cultured elite and the intellectual left. That was undoubtedly an attraction for both Banham and the IG, for cars were vulgar, profligate, wasteful, anti-modernist and, most problematically for the left, American.[35] (There was a mischievous implication about class in all this – that cars, in spite of their costliness and rarity at the time, were a definitive working-class interest – a misleading idea at best.)

Something of those feelings comes through in accounts of Eduardo Paolozzi's April 1952 epidiascope lecture at the ICA, which showcased the artist's collections of advertising material, most of it American, and a great deal of it featuring car design.[36] The lecture is legendary, but accounts of it point up not only Paolozzi's jangling nerves but the ever-present danger of the epidiascope melting the material it was projecting, and how little it impressed the audience at the time – apart from Banham, who was captivated. Few of the IG owned cars at the time, a fact that was partly simple austerity, but one that could be rationalized into a badge of honour. Disgust at cars was real; to make something of them, especially the highly decorative American cars of the time, was a calculated provocation.

Part of the problem with cars, and especially American cars, was to do with their flagrant eroticism and the problem was right there in the title of 'Vehicles of Desire', which overtly connected cars and sex. Banham then described the designers' invocation of sex, without (as ever, when he wrote about it) being terribly specific. But then there was the invocation of Deborah Allen's piece for Industrial Design, which explicitly connected bodily and sensual form. Most commentaries on the essay ignore the car itself, a pity, as it is one of the most outrageously sexual cars ever designed, if anything more so than the Cadillac that Banham actually named. Starting from the front, there are some of the same design cues as the Cadillac, such as the toothy chrome grille, the Dagmars and the same hooded Jane Russell-quoting headlamps. But moving rearwards, the design has a more stereotypically masculine aspect; the headlamps cap a long front wing on each side, whose essentially phallic form is punctuated by four decorative portholes. These were non-functional, but to a 1950s male viewer were likely to recall contemporary military technology, such as the ventilation holes on contemporary machine guns, or the attenuated exhaust pipes bristling either side of the nose of a contemporary American fighter plane, or, for the nautically inclined, the distinctive limber holes in the hulls of u.s. Navy submarines to enable swifter diving.[37] Whatever they were, the allusions were certainly bellicose. The wings adjoin a wrap-around raked windscreen that is significantly shallower than the Cadillac's, introducing a lower roofline, and suggestive of a car built for speed more than comfort. That impression is continued inside with a bank of instruments implying much more technical prowess than the somewhat domesticated Cadillac. The Buick's dash is, and looks like, a machine; its instruments are round, aircraft-style, and there are a lot more of them, regardless of what is going on with the seating, which remains organized around well-upholstered bench seats that to later eyes look as if they belong in a diner.

The technophilia, at least as far as goes, stops rear of the dashboard and Deborah Allen's phrase 'lush situation' alluded partly to that; this is in reality still a car organized for comfort. The comfort is nevertheless of a serious and enveloping kind, accentuated by the softness of the car's suspension, designed to obliterate imperfections in the road surface (the bed-like

qualities of the front bench are in one possible reading
suggestive of and enabling of sex). Moving further rearwards,
there is some somewhat androgynous exterior decoration –
a chrome 'spear' (in Allen's phrase) that swoops dramatically
down and then up again, forming a 'V' in advance of the rear
wheel arch, and accentuating that form as well as the notch
marked by the junction of the frameless door. It suggests, Allen
wrote, the gathering wind behind the car, adding to the sense of
forward movement; it's also suggestive of the female body, and
precisely the place in the car's design where Allen's imagined
female driver might sit. The rest of the car reverts back to the
techno-militaristic imagery of the front of the car, with fins.
So there is sexual anthropomorphism here, and not a little
ambiguity that in the accounts of this and other cars never gets
entirely resolved. But the car certainly allows for sexual fantasy,
and in Banham's account of car design delivered at the ICA
and subsequently in print it is not hard to imagine the sexual
frisson generated by the image. When Allen wrote 'hers is a lush
situation', the eroticism was clear enough. A confident, affluent,
sexually empowered woman of a kind rare in austere Europe sits
in charge of a powerful machine. She is in control and knows it;
all that phallic imagery at the front of the car serves her ends, at
least for the duration of the drive.

Richard Hamilton's attitude to automotive imagery was very
much aligned with Banham's, and from 1958 he made a series
of multimedia artworks on the theme, including *Hommage
à Chrysler Corp* (1958), $he (1958) and the orgasmically titled
*AAH!* (1961). One further 1958 work referred directly to Allen
in its title, *Hers Is a Lush Situation*.[38] All connected sexual and
automotive imagery, reiterating tropes that had appeared
frequently in Eduardo Paolozzi's collages as early as 1948,
not always happily in some eyes – the works were criticized
in some quarters as sexist.[39] Formally, *Hers Is a Lush Situation*

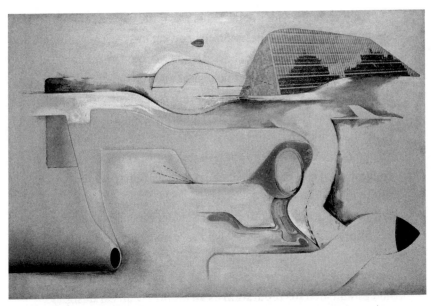

Richard Hamilton, *Hers Is a Lush Situation*, 1957, collotype, screen print and foil on paper.

included metal and other collaged elements from the just-completed United Nations building in New York to details of the Buick Century, all presided over by Sophia Loren's lips. The imagery was clearly both fascinating and ludicrous. Here was bathos, with images of high seriousness (the UN) bang up against popular culture, with automotive imagery as a structuring thread. The sexual nature of the image figured not only in Loren's lips, but the abstracted car imagery too, decontextualized to play up the eroticism. The Dagmar of the Buick's bumper was extruded into a pointed phallus, while on the left-hand side of the image, the rear fin arrangement of the contemporary Eldorado exposed the exhaust pipe built into the rear bumper, here anthropomorphized as a sort of automotive anus. Then in the middle of the image there was something strained and sexual going on around the front headlight of the Buick, although precisely what was unclear.

As ever, nobody in the IG nexus was quite explicit enough about the connections between sex and car design; they alluded, and hinted, and suggested, and juxtaposed, but the reader was left to draw their own conclusions about what exactly is depicted or represented. There was much ambiguity. Sometimes the driver was imagined as male, sometimes female, sometimes containing both male and female elements. Meanwhile the design of the car interiors showed that it needs both to be suggestive of sex, and (realistically) the location in which it might take place.

These questions about sex were evident in a little-reported but interesting exchange in the literary magazine *Encounter* on car design between the painter and critic Andrew Forge and Banham in 1956, the year after the still non-driving Banham had established his reputation as an authority on car design.[40] Forge wrote, disturbed, about the new Cadillac Espada (Forge's misspelling was the meaningless 'Esparda'), 'the double bed, it seemed, had suddenly turned into a machine', and he went on to instantiate the ways in which the new Cadillac had taken sex out of the bedroom and inserted it into a world of symbolic war machines. The remainder of the article wondered about, and ultimately came down against, the tendency of American designers to separate form and function. Even relatively restrained designs such as the Lincoln Continental, he wrote, 'are as much a carnival float as La Esparda only its subject happens to be a car'. He concluded, from a European perspective, 'we demand a design that enhances the car's movement not the reverse. For no Borax machine can keep up with the imaginary wind that moulds it.'[41] Banham was the only source Forge cited, and he described him as the 'spokesman' for the design profession, which, if flattering to him, was also an indication of how far he had come, and how quickly. Banham responded two months later in a somewhat

pompous letter that complained about Forge's inability to get
either the Cadillac's name right or, embarrassingly, Banham's.
(If Forge had really known his stuff, Banham wrote, he would
have realized that 'espada', the Spanish for 'sword', was right in
line with General Motors' policy of naming cars after swords.)[42]
But one of the key problems, Banham complained, was Forge's
Eurocentrism (the word of course had yet to be invented).
European cars were meant to look like cars, their forms, in
theory at least, allied to function. American cars had detached
themselves almost entirely from that functionalist position (this
was a gross generalization, of course, and only really applied to
some mass-market cars; certainly not the Rolls-Royce, which, as
Erwin Panofsky would point out a few years later, was designed
to look like the frontage of a Greek temple).[43] Sex was the big
differentiator between European and American design; the
Europeans were only indirectly interested in sex, while the
Americans, Banham thought, were concerned with little else.
If Forge hadn't been so coy about sex, he wrote, he would have
recognized that the correct female body to reference in relation
to the Cadillac was not the complex, frightening Joan Crawford
but the straightforward sex-symbol Jane Russell, for which
there was plenty of 'iconographical evidence'. Forge was simply
determined to keep sex 'out of the discussion'. The American
experience showed, Banham wrote, that 'the relationship
between automobile styling and sex is probably the biggest
industrial design problem awaiting a solution.'[44] There was
a response from Forge immediately following Banham's
comments, which argued, perhaps fairly in retrospect, that
Banham was overstating the case.[45] In some ways he was, in
some ways not, because his purpose was less analytical than
polemical, using the example of American car design to insert
sex into the discourse about popular culture, based partly on
the evidence, partly on the fact that sex was what the IG found

so fascinating about it (see Hamilton's pictures). But typically, if Banham could say it was about sex – and criticize others for failing to see that – he didn't have the vocabulary to say exactly what 'sex' meant in terms of car design. As we have seen, it could be all kinds of things, from representations in chrome of penises, vaginas and anuses, to the spaces (those bench seats) where sex might reasonably take place, to what Freud would have described as a sublimated erotic experience, in which driving stood in for sex. That, surely, was one of the lessons of Deborah Allen's car criticism.[46] Could sex really have been explained at this moment? Could Banham have himself been less coy, at least in print? These things are doubtful, but it does mean that what sex means in this context never really got explained. Banham's autophilia remained generalized.

## Banham on the Mustang

After the IG Banham's autophilia was transformed into speculation about Marinetti's cars in *Theory and Design*, and after that it was generalized into a theory of driving, leading beyond that into speculation about the urban morphology of Los Angeles.[47] There were scattered writings on car design per se, but not many. 'Night, Mrs Jagbag', an account of Jaguar car design, appeared in 1961, and then in 1967 a piece on the then-new Ford Mustang.[48] The Mustang article ('A Horse of a Different Colour') appeared in 1967 in *New Society*, to which Banham was already a regular contributor.[49] The article discussed the Ford company's unexpected hit, the Mark 1 Mustang, a cheap and cheerful coupé designed to appeal to the youth market, although in practice appealing much more widely. The Mustang was 'voluptuous' first and foremost, the Coke-bottle kink in its lines much emulated and widely understood – this was a line that referred, not very obliquely, to the female body. The imagined

customer was a 'man who reads *Playboy*', which is to say at that
stage a wide cross-section of affluent and/or aspiring-to-be-
affluent men whose interests centred primarily on sex and cars,
and, every so often, literature.[50] The car was fun, Banham noted,
but its fun wasn't only driver-oriented as there was plenty of
room inside for 'traditional back seat pursuits'. In the drop-head
version, 'you might have to tuck your legs in a bit during such
pursuits as the storage for the hood when folded reduces the
seat space', but the fact of its being a convertible was in some
way erotic compensation enough. That said, Banham continued,
the opportunity to fill the back of the car with 'swinging bird life'
was a 'fringe benefit', not much in evidenced by the car in use, at
least in Europe. This was a car for solitary drivers, 'a one-man
car, a driver's car, an expert's car'.[51] (The viewpoint here, in
retrospect, borders on a caricature of normative masculinity.)

He produced the surprising story that his friend, the
academic planner Peter Hall, was about to buy one to commute
between London and Reading. The point of the *New Society*
story was less sex, present in the usual ways in the car's design,
but the way it appealed to a new public who only a few years
previously would have regarded cars with disdain. The Mustang
was helped in Europe by its appearance in 'no less than five'
French films: one was certainly Jean-Luc Godard's 1965 *Alphaville*,
a cool interstellar detective story in which the car was as much
the star as its lead, Eddie Constantine. The Mustang's popularity,
which Banham illustrated with quotes from importers, official
and otherwise, paralleled the emerging understanding of Los
Angeles as a city of global importance that needed to be understood on its own terms. Banham *would* say that, as he had just
started visiting the city and had developed in prototype form
his argument about freeway driving in articles for *The Listener*
and elsewhere.[52] The *New Society* piece on the Mustang looked
forward to that adventure, as it did back to the earlier fascination

with Detroit metal. Sex was certainly present in the Mustang, but in an athletic, modern and masculine way: Steve McQueen, in other words, not Jayne Mansfield.

## Detroit in the Rear-view Mirror

Banham revisited the topic of car design in detail once more among several other interventions on the topic at a conference on design history in September 1975 at Newcastle Polytechnic. The papers, published in 1977, included Banham's contribution, 'Detroit Tin Revisited', which as the title indicated was a review and revision of his position on car design since the 1950s.[53] It was also the first mention in print of the Brian Tait-Russell Cadillac, the vehicle that would star in the 1978 film *Fathers of Pop*. In the paper Banham stressed the polemical value of the Cadillac at the time, it being so much the opposite of the European understanding of what a car was: it was indeed a 'monster', a 'visitor from another planet'.[54] It was an insult not only in terms of the exterior envelope, Banham wrote, but in multiple ways in engineering terms too. It had air conditioning, for example, at a time when 'there were possibly five air-conditioned buildings in the whole of the British Isles'. The tail fin was a source of particular offence in the design establishment for its frank rejection of functionalism. What followed was a long take-down of the establishment position on American design, its prejudices and inconsistencies (Banham mentioned here for the first time Roland Barthes's seminal essay on car design, 'The New Citroën', originally published in 1955.[55] Barthes (also a non-driver) made a strikingly similar point to Banham on the Cadillac: the car was primarily an 'object' whose purpose was symbolic; the engineering, the functional parts, were really just a pretext for the symbolism. The Council for Industrial Design, the official wing of the British design establishment at the time, might, Banham thought, have taken his argument about car design more seriously had they known about Barthes, who would have given a suitably intellectual gloss to what was essentially the same thing. But they didn't, because Barthes was not widely known until the translation of *Mythologies* in 1972.[56]

Banham's argument, yet again, linked sex and cars: 'It is extraordinary that practically every commentator on Pop art has commented on underwear advertising in general and the Exquisite Form ad in particular.' The Exquisite Form ads held particular fascination, partly for the qualities of the models photographed, partly for the technophile nature of the text, which presented bra design as an engineering problem to be solved. As he showed in accompanying images, the connections between underwear design and car design were strong at the time (the Dagmars have already been mentioned). But sex was also Detroit's undoing: Edsel, a short-lived sub-brand of the Ford Motor Company, introduced a model in 1958 with a radiator grille so unmistakably vaginal that the brand failed to sell. Banham commented that it was 'the most frankly sexual bid to every male chauvinist on the road . . . and it bombed in the showroom'.[57] Banham was coy about what the grille represented or appeared to represent, and, if it did represent what it appeared to represent, what that actually meant for the life of consumers. Did the Edsel sexualize the drivers of the car, who, given its size and market segment, were likely as not to be women? Was it meant to create a spectacle for (heterosexual male) drivers on the freeway, an orgy of pseudo-genitalia? As ever, Banham left the questions hanging – sex was *there* but at heart unexplained in itself. Banham, like the rest of the IG, was more interested in the idea of sex than sex itself. Sex was a provocation for the design establishment and its functionalist norms. In Banham's case, alertness to sexual symbolism was another way to do art history, so this 1975 talk was in the end a way of tracing aesthetic development in Wölfflinian terms, with High Renaissance, Baroque and possibly Mannerist phases. That led to his tentative conclusion, which was more about art-historical methodology than it is about sex:

> If you insist on the art historian's view of the rise and fall of styles, then the Brian Tait-Russell Cadillac is at the Masaccio point of bright beginnings and within ten years there would be post-Michelangelo or Mannerist Cadillacs. But the El Camino (a 1957 prototype design) is just about the middle – that is a Cadillac as Bramante would have designed it.[58]

In the end, Banham's autophilia was an ordinary kind. It was up to the writer J. G. Ballard to take it further, through his work for the science fiction magazine *New Worlds* and on to the 1973 novel *Crash*.[59] There is some overlap between Ballard and Banham, for both of whom Futurism was a reference point. Ballard's work moves well beyond anything in Banham towards a violent pornography that has no remote equivalent in Banham's work. If there is any violence at all in Banham, it is of a Buster Keaton-ish, slapstick kind, and the near total absence of Ballard from his work suggests incomprehension.[60] As the architectural theorist Mark Dorrian wrote later, Ballard's work drew on Richard Hamilton's 1958 car imagery to illustrate the residual violence inherent in the sexualized imagery of consumer culture; its logical conclusion was the orgasmic conjunction of twisted metal and body fluids, the ghastly leitmotif of *Crash*.[61]

## Banham's Cars

Part of Banham's mythology of himself was the engineering training, and the riposte to Andrew Forge in *Encounter* is an example of his playing that card. I was there, Banham says; I knew how to fix a carburettor. Ironically or not, he wasn't especially good with cars, and he took a long time to learn to drive them: Mary was the family's chauffeur.[62] A list of the cars the Banham family owned reveals a thoroughly pragmatic approach to them, at odds with the enthusiasms in the writing of the 1950s. Most of Banham's driving was, Ben Banham has said, done in rental cars of 'utter anonymity'. In terms of the cars the family owned, the London cars were, in order, a Heinkel KR200 *Kabinenroller* bubble car (1958–61), an Austin Mini Se7en 'Super' (1961–4), an Austin 1100 (1968–72), an Austin 1300 (1972–6); between 1970 and 1972 there was also a Ford Escort GT estate, allegedly one of a kind. In the United States the cars were a Ford Pinto estate (1976–7), a VW Rabbit (1977–88) and a Plymouth Voyager minivan (1986–8), 'in beige with every optional extra'.[63] In other words, the choices of car were determined by price and other extraneous factors, which certainly included the availability of automatic transmission in the early days, since the Banham family's main driver was Mary, who, disabled by the loss of a leg, could not drive a car with a manual gearbox. The choices of car in the United States were similarly pragmatic: Ben Banham noted the difficulty of buying anything in the first instance due to strict currency exchange controls. The Banhams' most extravagant car, the Voyager minivan, was a machine built entirely for comfort and ease of use. Precisely none of these choices represented the erotic themes that so preoccupied the IG in their discussions about car design. The cars they discussed really were Vehicles of Desire. The real-world choices the Banhams made were the opposite. Banham was an autophile more in the theory than practice.

# 5  THE ENVIRONMENTALIST

By the middle of the 1960s Banham had become an
environmentalist, albeit one of his own invention. His
environmentalism had three main principles: the world
was an interconnected system, or set of systems; those systems
were really more important than any individual elements, such
as buildings; there were however no limits to growth because
humans and their technologies were ingenious. By 1965 there is
no question that Banham's interest in the environment, broadly
conceived, was taking over from his interest in buildings. But
it was a singular, anti-Malthusian one that on the face of it
had little to do with the emerging environmental mainstream
defined by Rachel Carson's hugely popular *Silent Spring*.[1]

Carson worked as a marine biologist for the u.s. Fish
and Wildlife Service until 1952 before devoting herself to
writing. Her understanding of the environment also meant
an understanding of the interconnectedness of human and
natural systems, of the consequences of unforeseen actions
and circumstances. But she saw limits, real and moral, to
human agency. *Silent Spring* posited a benign nature to which
humans were alien, so the chapter headings of the book depict
a natural order threatened by human activity in and of itself
('Elixirs of Death', 'And No Birds Sing', 'Nature Fights Back').[2]
Banham would complain about the extent to which this
attitude, without naming Carson, had informed architectural
attitudes by the end of the 1960s.[3] To be a responsible architect
at that point, he indicated, had come to mean to wish to limit
human activity: 'rather than calling for more efficient air
conditioning, the call was for the abandonment of air
conditioning altogether, no matter who might suffer.'[4]

Banham's environmentalism was certainly real – but unlike the mainstream, it was positivistic. There were always technological fixes in Banham's universe, the 'boffins' always had a solution, the humans would always come out on top.[5] His version of environmentalism might have put him in conflict with the emerging environmentalist mainstream, but he also contributed to the curriculum design at the Open University, where his *Architecture of the Well-tempered Environment* strongly informed its course on the history of design.[6]

There is a well-known picture of Banham in his new guise, published in 1965. It depicts him and a Montreal-based architect friend, François Dallegret, in a transparent inflatable bubble, both disconcertingly naked, the effect ameliorated a little by the posterization of the original photograph. Banham had the same luxuriant beard with which he graced London, but he had swapped his usual heavy plastic spectacles for fashionable

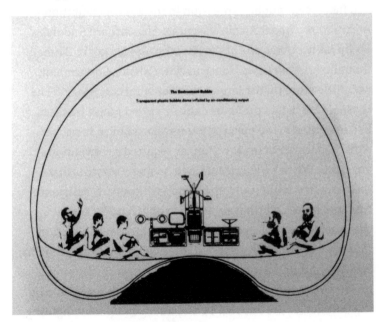

Reyner Banham and François Dallegret, 'A Home Is Not a House', 1965.

teardrop-shaped RayBans. The effect was transformative: with the posterization and the shades, he suddenly seemed modern and American, and vaguely Beat, as if he had just stepped off Ken Kesey's bus (Kesey and his Merry Pranksters had made their first transcontinental road trip the previous year, 1964, and images of it had been widely disseminated).

The image comes from 'A Home Is Not a House', written by Banham, with Dallegret supplying the illustrations, and published in *Art in America*, an unusual venue for both of them.[7] In its imagery the piece vaguely alluded to the Beats and their back-to-nature sentiments. But the argument was for a more subtle form of architectural environmentalism: in short, they wrote, building services had so evolved beyond the capacity of architects to understand them that the future of architecture itself was in doubt. There was something of the desire for the primitive hut in all of this too, an idea that had had recent public expression in the MOMA exhibition *Architecture without Architects*, curated by Bernard Rudofsky.[8] Philip Johnson was one of the few who already got it, Banham thought; his 1949 Glass House in New Canaan, Connecticut, was 'little more than a service core set in infinite space'.[9] The Glass House in fact prefigured the dissolved house Banham had imagined in the opening paragraph: a house so packed with modern servicing it no longer required a conventional envelope. When a house contained 'so many services that the hardware could stand up by itself without any assistance from the house, why have a house to hold it up?'[10] Hence the inflatable bubble, perched on a rock and seen in section inhabited by two Dallegrets and three cigar-smoking Banhams, squatting around a multifunctional service core containing the air con (necessary not only for temperature regulation but the inflation of the bubble), TV and audio equipment, lighting, and what might or might not be a microwave. It needed plenty of power. No problem, they wrote: Americans had always been prepared to pump more power into their buildings than Europeans, and in the modern world few of them were ever far from 'a source with between 100 and 400 horsepower – the automobile'.[11] It was not, all things considered, a universally attractive scenario: an inflatable plastic tent full of naked, cigar-smoking Banhams, attached to a rumbling V-8 engine. But it was certainly an arresting one.

'A House Is Not a Home' and its environmental bubble were a dry run for his book on building servicing, *The Architecture of the Well-tempered Environment*, first published in 1969.[12] (His friend, the film-maker Julian Cooper, referred to it less grandly as 'your plumbing book'.[13]) In a book of striking descriptions, one of the most striking of all occurs eighty pages in, introducing the reader to the mechanical ventilation system of the 1903 Royal Victoria Hospital (RVH) in Belfast. Banham wrote from inside the system, which he had visited on a winter's day with his family in 1967. A Plenum system of mechanical ventilation, powered by a giant fan in a separate engine house, it produced an unprecedented interior. 'The duct', he wrote, 'is one of the most monumental in the history of environmental engineering; a brick tunnel with a concrete floor over five hundred feet long and nine feet wide, twenty feet deep at the input end, tapering upwards to only six feet deep at the downstream end.'[14] Banham went on to elaborate the functioning of this vast system with its slow-moving currents distributed through a series of channels and then into the wards themselves. The air itself was literally conditioned on its journey through the duct system. It was

> pulled through hanging curtains of coconut fibre robes kept moist by sprinklers in the roof of the filter-chamber ... Cleaned of soot, smuts, and other impurities for which the Belfast atmosphere was notorious, the air then passed

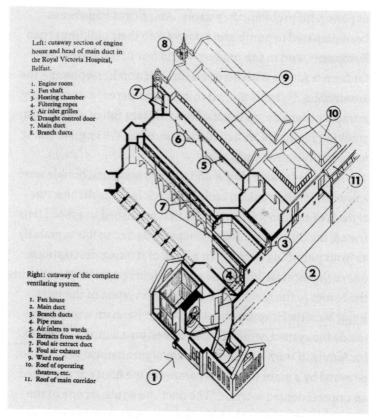

Left: cutaway section of engine
house and head of main duct in
the Royal Victoria Hospital,
Belfast.

1. Engine room
2. Fan shaft
3. Heating chamber
4. Filtering ropes
5. Air inlet grilles
6. Draught control door
7. Main duct
8. Branch ducts

Right: cutaway of the complete
ventilating system.

1. Fan house
2. Main duct
3. Branch ducts
4. Pipe runs
5. Air inlets to wards
6. Extracts from wards
7. Foul air extract duct
8. Foul air exhaust
9. Ward roof
10. Roof of operating
    theatres, etc.
11. Roof of main corridor

Sketch of the ventilation system of the Royal Victoria Hospital, Belfast,
by Mary Banham.

through batteries of heating coils before entering the fans
and being propelled up the duct.[15]

Because the air passed through the sprinkler system, it
wasn't just a ventilation process that was being described,
but something more sophisticated. The process affected the
relative humidity of the atmosphere, which was not 'left to
happy accident' but monitored using a thermometer, and
the rate of flow of water through the coconut fibre robes
regulated accordingly: the drier the exterior atmosphere,

the heavier the compensating flow of water through the
system.[16] The RVH had, in effect, invented air conditioning.
The term wasn't yet in use, but the principle of passing air
through a humid curtain to regulate the moisture content was
the same. There were even some contrasting arrangements
in the same building to illustrate the point; if the sick had
this primitive air conditioning to the wards, the well were
served by conventional methods, 'gas fires and . . . opening
windows, since it was known that the fit would insist on
controlling their own environment even if the sick could not'.
It was a most forward-looking building, the RVH, at least in
these terms. It was an unlikely starting point for the history
of air conditioning, although it pleased those specialized
architects who had known about its significance all along.[17]
It made sense once it was clear that down the road at Harland
& Wolff, the shipyard dominating the city's economy and
skyline, was a ready source of expertise, and the firm Samuel
Cleland Davidson was producing some of the world's most
sophisticated ventilation systems for marine use. While they
were not cited as part of the hospital's design team, Banham
noted that shipbuilding interests were well represented on
the hospital's board, as well as 'the suspicion that some of
them may have talked the architects into the final bulk form
of the building'. Whatever was the truth of the matter, the
RVH had a primitive air conditioning system and in the local
environs there was plenty of expertise to keep it going.[18]
That was not quite the end of the matter, however: if Banham
established an unlikely primacy for the RVH, he also pulled
back from attributing it canonical status, because, for a
modernist such as himself, the exterior was stylistically
retrograde. An attenuated Neo-Gothic in red brick favoured
by the project's Birmingham architects, Henman & Cooper,
it was hopelessly outdated by 1903, belonging, he wrote 'to

a concept of "Welfare" architecture initiated by the London School Board some forty years before, and out of fashion among consciously progressive architects of 1900'.[19]

There is a great deal going on in this story, not least the stylistic assessment, leaving even its status as architecture in doubt. (It is also a good example of Banham's inconsistencies, for as a New Brutalist he was still ostensibly an advocate of an architecture defined by programme, not style – he was certainly still pushing that line in *The New Brutalism: Ethic or Aesthetic* in 1966, when this environmental work was already under way.[20]) But in every other respect this account places the RVH centre stage, not only for being first in the air conditioning game, but for the aesthetic qualities of the engineering. Banham's account of the ducting was made during a family visit, which the surviving members easily remembered for its spookiness and freezing temperatures.[21] What Banham seemed to be doing at first sight was making a case for a new kind of aesthetic object, perhaps not intentionally meant to be seen or experienced as art, but one that nevertheless had artistic qualities. Banham's status as an art historian, and his desire to extend that academic tradition, was clear to some early reviewers.[22] Whatever *The Architecture of the Well-tempered Environment* was, it was a work of architectural history first, and its judgements were aesthetic ones. In the case of the RVH, there was an appeal to the Sublime.

The passage also confirms the more general trends in the book: the attraction to non-canonical architecture and architectural figures, the elevation of unforeseen elements in the design process, and the elevation of technology over the building shell.[23] It is a remarkable passage if you can picture the Banham family grubbing around in the hospital ducts, finding in the most hidden parts of the building a revelation about architecture. Ben Banham recalled the trip well, in an account that elaborates the visceral experience described in the book:

they stayed at the Europa Hotel, not long afterwards notorious for being the most bombed hotel in Europe. Banham had just learned to drive, and they rented a big Vauxhall Victor, perhaps the most American-looking of all British family cars at the time. 'PRB & the engineer in charge ventured into the main duct with torches to examine the construction,' he recalled

> all properly in accordance with laws of aerodynamics; the main duct acted as a diffuser to exchange air velocity for air pressure. I didn't join them, remaining in the doorway of the engine room near the fans; it was dark, noisy & windy in there! Later we all went & examined the 'filter gallery', walking between the louvres & the rope curtain while the engineer in charge explained how the humidity in the wards could be controlled by applying more or less water to the ropes (originally the ropes had been wetted purely to increase their effectiveness as filters). The building was, of course, slightly pressurised to keep the coal-fired filth of industrial Belfast out.[24]

The truth of the Belfast RVH, and of architecture in general, was therefore to be found in its guts; the authentic experience of that building was in other words to be found in the dark and windy ducts, examining the entrail-like ropes of coconut-fibre filters. It was a visceral place and an exciting one, and in its authenticity morally charged in a way that readers of Banham would reasonably connect with the New Brutalism: Hunstanton School or the Leicester Engineering Building were uncompromising places to visit and their appeal lay in structural vigour rather than comfort. The story was about depth over surface, structure over decoration, the health of the body over frivolous aesthetic delights, and in all this there was an incipient, albeit singular, environmentalism.

Two factors enabled the book. One was Banham's receipt of funding from the Graham Foundation for the Advanced Study in the Fine Arts, in Chicago, which allowed him to visit the United States purposely to study the relationship between building services and the outward design of buildings.[25] The Graham Foundation was a good fit: it was chaired at that point by the architect and journalist John Entenza, who, while editing the journal *Arts and Architecture*, set up the remarkable Case Study Houses programme, which had already produced a series of iconic houses integrating new technology and design (Pierre Koenig's bungalows, for example, made use of aerospace technology to both reduce weight and increase the speed of construction). Graham Foundation money allowed the work to be done. The other factor was Banham's work situation, which had radically improved. Not only had he become a full-time academic, with a lectureship in 1964 at the Bartlett School of Architecture, he had entered a situation that strongly favoured an environmental approach to design: under Richard Llewelyn-Davies, the Bartlett became University College London's School of Environmental Studies after a 'bloodless student revolution', the intention being to reorientate it towards the social sciences and away from art.[26] Banham was in the right place at the right time and *The Architecture of the Well-tempered Environment* was on message.

Belfast was perhaps the most suggestive part of the book, and the one most indicative of its programme – although, frustratingly for some readers, Banham pulled back from a total re-evaluation of architectural history in terms of building services. The RVH was less of a building than it should have been because of that facade, but it indicated a way towards a new, environmentally oriented architectural history. The politics of that history was the subject of Banham's opening chapter, which blasted the architectural profession for its historic failure to engage with building services. 'It fell to another body of men to assume responsibility for the maintenance of decent environmental conditions,' he wrote,

> 'another culture', so alien most architects held it beneath contempt and still do. The works and opinions of this other culture have been allowed to impinge as little as possible on the teaching of architecture schools, where the preoccupation still continues to be with the production of elegant graphic compositions rendering the merely structural aspects of plan, elevation and sometimes section. 'Never mind all that environmental rubbish, get on with your architecture!'[27]

This passage is both revealing and ambiguous: revealing because of the frustration it shows with architecture as is, and its implicit sense of entitlement. Here Banham's social background comes into play, setting off engineers against architects as a way of, again, needling the establishment. But it is also ambiguous in its messaging: was Banham arguing here for the dissolution of architecture, for its replacement by engineering, by technologists who implicitly know what they are doing? Or was it, perhaps more likely, a call to architects to acknowledge a threat to their existence and to neutralize it before it neutralizes them? That position is also possible and is perhaps the more likely one given the overall stance of the book. There is a flirtation here with the end of architecture, but as several reviewers pointed out, Banham failed to carry it through to its logical conclusion.[28] It was still, in the end, a book about architecture, not engineering, and it both reinforced the canon and took it apart.

The object choices of the rest of the book were similarly mixed, a combination of canonical and non-canonical

architectures. The non-canonical, engineering-led cases
included the Octagon, a Liverpool house built by two doctors
with concern for health, the Sturtevant ventilation system, a
mid-Victorian furnace technology system used for heating
commercial buildings, and Catherine Beecher's American
Woman's Home of the 1860s, a prototype suburban house
designed by a non-architect. Later on Banham discussed
off-the-shelf air-conditioning units in a way that linked to his
discussions of consumer culture for *New Society*, and looked
forward to *Los Angeles*, which was all about such things. The
book's canonical objects included the Larkin administration
building in Buffalo, New York, by Frank Lloyd Wright, which
was an office building with an early air-conditioning system
that, to Banham's approval, significantly defined the exterior
envelope; turn-of-the-century houses by Charles and Henry
Greene (the Gamble House, Pasadena) and Wright again, this
time in the Baker, Gale and Robie Houses; Bruno Taut's Glass
Industry Pavilion; the Bauhaus; Le Corbusier's Cité de la Refuge,
and assorted private houses; Ludwig Mies van der Rohe's
Lafayette Park apartments in Detroit, contrasted in their
deployment of air-conditioning units with I. M. Pei's Kips
Bay apartments in New York; the Johnson Wax Company
headquarters by Wright, and the Arizona Biltmore hotel;
Erich Mendelsohn's Universum Cinema, Berlin; Rudolf
Schindler's Lovell Beach House; the UN building and the
General Motors Technical Center, Warren, Michigan, the
latter by Saarinen & Associates; Philip Johnson's Glass House
in New Canaan, Connecticut; Olivetti's 1964 factory in Merlo,
Argentina; and the Queen Elizabeth Hall in London, ostensibly
designed by the London County Council architects' department,
but really by Archigram, the radical group of Banham-friendly
fellow-travellers, who were arguably beginning to provide
propaganda for his theories.[29] Later editions of the book

naturally included the Centre Georges Pompidou.[30] If there was ever a building to make a fetish of its servicing, it was this one, for never was a building designed to look so much like a node in an environmental system. (Banham was developing this argument at the time of his death in the proposed *Making Architecture: The Paradoxes of High Tech*; his critical purchase on the topic had to do with the unresolved tension between the architect's attraction to technology for the look, and the engineer's for what it could do. Banham's sympathies were for

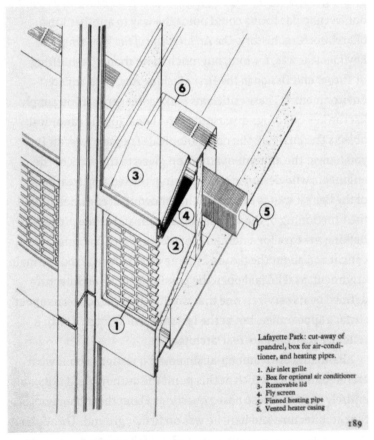

Lafayette Park: cut-away of spandrel, box for air-conditioner, and heating pipes.

1. Air inlet grille
2. Box for optional air conditioner
3. Removable lid
4. Fly screen
5. Finned heating pipe
6. Vented heater casing

189

Ludwig Mies van de Rohe, Lafayette Park Apartments, Detroit, and air-conditioning package. Sketch by Mary Banham.

the engineer, but the parts of the project that survive suggest, as ever, ambivalence.[31])

For the design historian Nigel Whiteley, writing in 2002, this list was evidence of the book's timidity: if the point was to reinvent the canon of Western architectural history, then why was so much of the old canon still there?[32] Or if the point was the exploration of energy use in buildings, then its success was also circumscribed by the lack of the data such a study would need. Banham also purposely neglected vernacular architecture on the grounds that he didn't like it – yet as Whiteley also pointed out, vernacular forms could point the way to another kind of architectural history. *The Architecture of the Well-tempered Environment* was, for him, not much more than a 'reshuffling' of *Theory and Design in the First Machine Age*, with added Environment.[33] These criticisms make some sense if you simply list the key buildings discussed in the book, for the canonical objects far outweigh the non-canonical. They are less fair if you look at the amount of attention given to the work of the engineers who designed the servicing: the lengthy treatment of the Belfast RVH is a case in point, showing in enormous detail the functioning of the ventilation system and in the process making the case for a new kind of technological sublime. His conclusion about the facade in some ways contradicted the main argument, as if he laid open the possibility of an architecture defined by its services, one that would be free of concerns about surface appearance, but at the last moment refuted it with a reflexive turn back to 'real' architecture.

Banham's environmentalism posed questions about what architecture was, which at this point the author could not entirely resolve. It also posed questions about the inhabitants of that architecture and here he was on firmer ground. Throughout the book there was an understanding of the odiferous bodies of building users, and early on it was 'stuffiness' and 'draughts' that were understood as the driver for the development of air conditioning. Victorian and earlier interiors were invariably rich with the smell of human beings, but opening a window in northern latitudes, even if it corrected the smell, brought the temperature uncomfortably low.[34] The smell of other humans was important in class terms, returning to a key theme of Banham's environmentalism, because poor humans historically smelled worse. To notice smell in an account of building was to notice a key differentiator of social class, and to celebrate building services, as the *Well-tempered Environment* did, was to celebrate class-mitigating technologies. A well-serviced building did not smell because it disposed of the air fouled by its inhabitants. By enabling humans of all social classes to live together more comfortably, well-serviced architecture could be socially progressive. That idea, running all the way through the book, elevated the concern for ameliorating differences of social class above that of reducing energy consumption, a key point of difference with mainstream environmentalism.

Banham's environmentalism was also decidedly American in flavour. He had more or less convinced himself of the superiority of American environmental engineering before he had even visited the place, and nothing about his first real encounter with the u.s. in 1963 seems to have changed his opinion.[35] In terms of approaches to the environment, air conditioning was one of the key markers of American superiority: Americans got it, and Europeans did not.[36] It was a European, Le Corbusier, who came in for particular criticism in *Well-tempered Environment*, for repeatedly opting for the wrong technology by failing to understand his buildings' environmental performance. It was a critique that reiterated something of the argument of *Theory and Design in the First Machine Age*. The 1933 Cité de la Refuge, a Salvation Army hostel for six hundred, featured a multi-storey, double-skinned glass facade supposed to maintain an even temperature in the building by circulating treated air between the glass skins (a *mur neutralisant*, or neutralizing wall). But in reality, wrote Banham, budget cuts meant the absence of cooling equipment, meaning that if it performed well in the winter, six months later it was 'an intolerable glasshouse', and the architect was driven to make some revisions, including, at the behest of Paris's conservative planners, 'openable *fenêtres d'illusion*' (Le Corbusier's usage). These (literally translated) 'illusionary windows' were meant to provide a modicum of stylistic continuity with the surrounding architecture, rather than address the environmental perform-ance of the building. The difference between the before- and after-facades was notable, as illustrated: the early one was an entirely smooth reflective surface, in image at least, self-consciously reading as modern, the replacement a concrete 'egg-crate' (Banham's phrase) that anticipated Le Corbusier's post-war work at La Tourette and elsewhere. Banham praised the solution as architecturally appropriate, while lamenting that it appeared only as a correction to an existing building.

Le Corbusier, Cité de la Refuge, Paris, 1933.

And he was critical of Le Corbusier's understanding of what he was attempting to do with the *mur neutralisant* even if he had had access to the plant that would provide the cooling air. Not only was the plant needlessly duplicated (Le Corbusier: 'two fans: one blowing, one sucking'), but the architect insisted 18°c to be the standard interior temperature regardless of location in the world. It was, Banham retorted, a rhetorical, authoritarian approach, 'all over the world, pegged to a standard temperature of eighteen degrees centigrade whether you like it or not'.[37]

All this was a continuation, by other means, of an established position on Le Corbusier and technology and it ought to be taken with a certain scepticism. Le Corbusier was consistently set up to fail, largely, one suspects, because of his status in the British architectural establishment. The judgement about the Cité de la Refuge was made on limited evidence in any case, namely Le Corbusier's own account, from two pages of 1937's *Quand les cathédrales étaient blanches* (published in English in 1947 as *When the Cathedrals Were White*), with some interpretation by Banham.[38] The 'intolerable glasshouse' he described was Banham's poetic interpretation, Le Corbusier merely suggesting that ambiguous 'difficulties' emerged after two years of 'perfect operation'.[39] Similarly invented was the suggestion a little further down the page that the environmental performance of the building after the fitting of openable windows was better than the architect imagined, which elaborates anything in Le Corbusier's account. There were no other sources, beyond the architect's own words.

Banham liked to puncture the myth of Le Corbusier for a variety of reasons. He was capable of an entirely opposite argument when it suited him: just months before the publication of *The Architecture of Well-tempered Environment*, for example, Banham had robustly defended another modernist glasshouse with well-documented problems of heat control, specifically his friend James Stirling's Cambridge History Faculty library, which he reviewed at the end of 1968. Here Banham reported turning up unannounced on a hot mid-August day to experience the design. With notable precision he declared that

> at 2.15pm and with outside shade temperatures of 74 deg – 77 deg F and no mechanical ventilators working . . . I found the interior warm, but not so much that it was necessary to remove my jacket. If it had been any hotter I would not be writing this article.[40]

At the same time, if Banham was critical of Le Corbusier, in giving over quite so much space to him he also affirmed the architect's status. He could have left out the masters, but he didn't. Attention is also respect, and Le Corbusier survived the interrogation because Banham approved of the belated invention of the *brise-soleil*, that crude but effective means of mitigating solar gain. But Le Corbusier emerged from the critical encounter caricatured as a dogmatist, happy to boil the poor inhabitants of a Salvation Army hostel in order to achieve the right look.

Banham continued in the same vein on lighting, Le Corbusier sharing the modern movement's predilection for exposed electric bulbs mounted on batons. In the case he illustrated here, the Villa Cook of 1926, the illumination from the bulb was too intense for the photography: it 'burned a hole in the emulsion of the negative so . . . the block maker has had to redraw the bulb by hand'.[41] That is certainly the case, looking at the final image; it is slightly disingenuous of Banham given the limitations of all photography in dealing with high-contrast situations. In this case the focused intensity of the bulb would have done little for the scene's general illumination, which would have required a long exposure to get any result at all;

it was a typical photographic problem. But Banham's point made sense in contrast with the description of American works of the same period, such as, for example, the Lovell Health House in Los Angeles designed by Richard Neutra, which incorporated recessed ceiling lighting. By the early 1960s, Banham argued, the direct lighting strategies of the early moderns had authoritarian overtones: 'pure white light was to survive only as the weapon of the Secret Police interrogator, the brain washer and the terrorist.' The impression they left behind, he continued, 'was of a luminous environment close to the threshold of pain, probably made tolerable only by the notorious willingness of intellectuals to suffer in the name of art'.[42] This was mischievous, to say the least: Banham was prepared to overlook or downplay issues of comfort in buildings he liked (the work of the New Brutalists, the Cambridge library, tangentially the ventilation ducts of the RVH). But when it suited him, especially when it allowed the use of Le Corbusier as fall guy, it mattered.

It was nevertheless a compelling, often funny narrative with some clear preferences: the engineer over the architect, America over Europe, pleasure over pain. And while the book remained canonical in many respects, canonical architecture very often appeared as a foil, an image of bad practice.[43] The book's heroes were the engineers and their designs: the anonymous designer of the American Woman's House, Thomas Edison, Willis Haviland Carrier's primitive air conditioning units, the Rivet Grip company's commercialized suspended ceiling, the designers of life support systems for space suits.[44] What Banham wanted, however, was not to displace the architects with a new canon of engineers, but to use the engineer as a means of making a critique. So in the chapter on air conditioning, the virtues of the self-installed, DIY air conditioner did not ultimately displace architecture – but they called into question the limits of architectural practice when (as in I. M. Pei's Kips Bay complex in New York) no provision for the technology had been made. It really should have been, Banham argued, but that said the random pattern made by the self-installed units was, in the end, 'not unattractive'.[45] Banham's position here was halfway to the environmental position that characterized the later part of his career. What mattered here was still, in the end, buildings, but their status had been considerably eroded. It would be *Los Angeles*, however, before the concern for the environment really displaced architecture.

*The Architecture of the Well-tempered Environment* was published in 1969. The following year, however, at the International Design Conference Aspen, which was on the theme of 'Environment by Design', Banham's confidence in its thesis was battered in an enduring and profound way.[46] It was, he reported to John McKean for a *Building Design* interview in 1976, 'the most bruising experience of my life . . . I could suddenly feel all those changes that ran together in a spasm of bad vibrations that shook the conference. We got ourselves together again but an epoch had ended.'[47]

Banham, who had been chair of the 1968 iteration of IDCA, was heavily implicated in the 1970 event, giving one major presentation on themes related to *The Architecture of the Well-tempered Environment*, as well as a closing talk bringing together the conference themes. Set up as a philanthropic exercise by the Chicago businessman Walter Paepcke, IDCA was the living embodiment of professional positivism: three days of boisterous high-altitude eating and boozing, its partying leavened by well-intentioned debate that wrestled with the place of design in society. In 1970 Banham was one of a relatively diverse (for IDCA) platform of twelve key speakers, who also included the African American lawyer Cora T. Walker, the ecological activist Cliff Humphrey, and Banham's friend and sometime collaborator, the planner Peter Hall, who along with Banham

was one of the authors of the polemical *New Society* article
'Non-plan'. The relative diversity of the panel was recognition
of the fractious macropolitical situation in the U.S. and beyond.
It was an awkward event on every level. The trouble came not
from the main platform, however, but from sections of the
audience, whose noisy activism forced a vote covering, Banham
recalled later, 'every current "problem" from abortion to Vietnam
and the abandonment of design for profit'.[48] He added to
this in a first draft of the introduction, describing 1970 as a
moment of 'radicalization and polarization' that put an end
to a 'previously cosy conference of professionals getting their
knees together under the seminar table to investigate mutual
advantage'.[49] Those friendly arrangements were over. 'Instead',
he remembered, 'a body of up to a thousand designers, architects, artists and students were sitting down in the tent to have
their ears burned off by crusading biologists, fault-finding
philosophers, subversive sociologists and peddlers of every
variety of apocalypse from pollution to Black Power.'[50] (That
casual equation of 'pollution' with 'Black Power' has dated
particularly badly.) In the same memoir, Banham lamented
the decline of deference among student participants and the
growing tensions with the business community in Aspen, with
their 'well-nourished paranoia about long hair, bare feet and
all the rest of it'.[51] The meeting was tempestuous: half the
conference attendees left during the session, and a series of
bad-tempered interventions attacked the ethical legitimacy
of the entire conference. Banham wrote later to Mary, 'I was
sorely tempted to pull the plug on the whole operation and
leave the board with the shambles I felt they deserved.'[52]

A revealing account, it shows Banham's own identification
with what must no doubt have been regarded as the forces of
reaction by the activist parts of the IDCA audience. That bubble
image of him by François Dallegret was, one might say, both

misleading and uncannily accurate: misleading because Banham
on this stage was far from the hippyish radical his appearance
in that image suggested, but accurate because it depicted him
in a literal bubble, protected from the real world by technology,
which is presumably how his opponents saw him. It was
certainly a highly individualistic, anti-collectivist image.
The difficulty of Banham's position was already quite legible
in *Well-tempered Environment*, although perhaps not so much
to its author: there was an exposition in the last chapter on the
1959 United States Atomic Energy Pavilion, designed by Victor
Lundy and Walter Bird and exhibited worldwide, including, as
the illustrations clearly showed, at the Aterro do Flamengo in
Rio do Janeiro, Brazil, a major piece of reclaimed land in the city
between the financial centre and the southern beaches.[53] That
location in itself was controversial given the United States's
history of interference in the region and its role shortly afterwards (1962) in installing a military government: it was in that
image a literal projection of U.S. power. Like many things in
Banham, that history, about which something was certainly
known in 1969, went unexplored and suggests some political
naivety. Then there was the pavilion itself, a massive inflatable
comprising two overlapping half-shells, a distant cousin of the
Sydney Opera House, and a power-hungry one requiring constant
energy inputs to stay up. On neither count was it really the kind
of structure that was easily defensible in the face of environmental activism. Banham may have meant its inclusion to be
provocative, of course, but by 1970 it was liable to make his
position look vulnerable.

Back at IDCA, Banham had earlier been forced to endure an
intervention from the French delegation, led by the sociologist
Jean Baudrillard. 'We have chosen not to make a positive
statement,' Baudrillard began, ominously, before proceeding
to demolish the intellectual basis of the conference.[54] To

focus on the environment, Baudrillard stated, might appear a progressive move on the part of IDCA's organization, but it was a way of sidestepping politics:

> Professor Banham has clearly shown the moral and technical limits of the illusions of Design and Environment practice. It is not by accident that all the Western governments have now launched this new crusade and try to mobilize people's conscience by shouting apocalypse . . . in the United States it is no coincidence that this new mystique, this new frontier has been developed during and parallel to the Vietnam War.

Environmentalism, in other words, was a means of ensuring the survival of the political class by distracting attention from its operations elsewhere, and from the possibility of political change. To address the environment was to address symptom and not cause, because capital had made the environment the way it was, so to effect change one needed to address politics. Architects and designers were nothing more than 'medicine men', complicit in a 'hoax' designed to direct attention away from politics.

Banham was no mainstream environmentalist, as we have seen, but he did, as his 1970 interventions made clear, believe in the ability of humans to solve environmental problems through technology. It was as good as an ad hominem attack. As Alice Twemlow writes, Banham had been recently sympathetic to striking students in London, and had not long before that supported students at the Architectural Association in developing their own teaching programme in parallel with the official one.[55] But he was often uneasy with radical politics and his interventions at IDCA were all about pragmatism and reasonableness, and the need to trust experts.[56] He generously included the French contribution in an edited selection of essays from IDCA from its earliest iteration in 1953.[57] But it was framed by a regretful introduction about the split that had emerged at the conference, and the erosion of trust in progress. Banham was not alone in his position: support came from Peter Hall, whose talk at the same conference praised the unglamorous achievements of planners regarding land use in post-war Britain, meant to remind the audience that progress was possible within the context of the political establishment. But the conclusion to the conference left Banham disillusioned and baffled, after which his involvement with IDCA, except as its sometime historian, largely ceased.[58] Banham found himself in an uncomfortable place here. Having been accustomed for nearly twenty years to being the provocateur, here he was cast as the voice of the establishment, or worse, of the military-industrial complex. To be critical of environmentalism as it was being constructed was a difficult position to hold if one also wanted to retain one's critical position in the world. As the architectural historian Felicity Scott put it subsequently, Banham's stance could easily be interpreted as collusion with authority, 'something close to "liberal-capitalist oppression" according to the ideals of a new generation of radical thought'. And at the same time his fascination with technology could easily seem 'naïve techno-optimism'.[59] Perhaps this was Futurism coming back to bite him. What was a relatively harmless provocation in the 1950s, a means of pricking the British architectural establishment, at this point might seem more dubious, with its glorification of technological violence. Futurism in 1950s London was at best a way of coming to terms with war-ravaged surroundings and an avalanche of technological change, much of it driven by the military (certainly Banham's speciality, aviation). But Futurism had no ethical position on those things, apart from acquiescence to them, a position that in the highly polarized USA of 1970 was unacceptably apolitical. Banham's environmentalism, without a political gloss, could render him vulnerable, as IDCA 1970 palpably showed.

## Long Life/Loose Fit/Low Energy

He was not quite done, however. He revived and refined his environmentalist position in an aggressive, but lucid piece for *New Society* in 1972, arguing against the emerging trend towards the reuse of existing buildings, particularly (in the English context) Georgian ones. 'Long Life/Loose Fit/Low Energy vs Foster' was about two things: first the argument made by the then President of the Royal Institute of British Architects, Alexander Gordon, in early 1972 for a '3L' strategy of 'Long Life, Loose Fit, Low Energy'.[60] What Gordon meant was clearly communicated by the title: a perspective on construction that favoured adaptation and reuse over new development, and the encouragement of architectural practice that favoured keeping buildings in use as long as possible. It chimed with a public mood increasingly sceptical of development, and modernist development in particular. This emerging architectural orthodoxy, Banham pointed out, was produced in a context that itself largely took place in buildings of this description – Georgian terraced houses: 'At Liverpool, Cambridge, Edinburgh, Bristol . . . and above all at the Architectural Association, generations of students have been conditioned by up to seven years of daily exposure to accept Georgian as a kind of universal environmental failsafe.'[61] It was, in other words, a post hoc rationalization of taste. He did not mention social class directly but it is certainly there in the invocation of Georgian, the default architectural style of the English establishment. To spend seven years in such a setting was arguably a process of affirming its values. But it was, according to Banham in his own rationalization after the fact, not evidently true that Georgian houses

were much good for the environment in any case. They had
energy requirements like any building or they would cease to
function – just in this case the energy input was not obviously
named. It was provided by a 'serving wench and the fact that
she doesn't appear on the architect's plan doesn't mean she
wasn't there'.[62] At the Architectural Association, he continued,
the spending on energy far exceeded rent: £2,000 on the former,
more than double the £900 of the latter. That tells you about the
condition of rental and energy markets at the time, rather than
consumption per se, but Banham was an engineer, not an
economist.[63]

The second part of the argument concerned Foster &
Partners' sensational new IBM building in Portsmouth, a big
single-storey all-glass office campus, 10,000 square metres in
all. It had come in for criticism due to the allegedly high cost
of energy, stemming partly from the requirement that warm
air was blown over the glass to prevent condensation. Banham
countered that all buildings required energy inputs and that
to pretend otherwise was naive, implying (but not elaborating)
that it was important to take into account whole-life energy
systems: condensation is an energy cost, he wrote, invoking the
dripping walls of a Glasgow tenement after cooking, a situation
relieved only by opening a window and thereby losing all the
heat. It was not the place for quantitative analysis – but
nevertheless, as Whiteley argued later on in relation to *The
Architecture of the Well-tempered Environment*, to make that
argument really required a more systematic approach,
comparing the energy consumption of buildings in use.[64]
Banham appeared to have little interest in such analysis. But
her nevertheless made an important point about early 1970s
architectural environmentalism: once one understands the
importance of the image of the Georgian terraced house, one
understands environmentalism as, in part, reactionary

anti-modernism, and the post hoc rationalization of aristocratic taste. He noted later that Alexander Gordon said that he preferred 'proper brickwork' to 'drains'. In other words, Banham wrote spikily, the RIBA president preferred 'the niceties of bricklaying to the necessity of hygiene'.[65] Not all architectural environmentalism was like this, of course, but a lot of it was, as the Prince of Wales would show in his interventions in architecture in the 1980s. Here Banham again connected social class with environmentalism as he had done in *The Architecture of the Well-tempered Environment*.

That book was originally published in 1969, to largely reasonable and uncontroversial reviews. If there was a controversy about it, it came later. It gained significant support in a review by Walter Segal, the advocate of self-build housing, whose work became popular in the 1970s in the mainstream environmental movement. Banham's pragmatic attitude and his challenge to architectural convention chimed with Segal's approach; perhaps Banham's environmentalism was not so eccentric as it might have first seemed.[66] The last (1984) edition added some commentary on High Tech architecture, a tendency Banham increasingly supported, as well as on the book's origins and history. For the first time there was some acknowledgement of the difficulty he faced regarding his position on environmentalism: the book, he acknowledged, had encountered increasingly hostile reviews as the 1973 oil crisis and the resultant spike in oil prices made energy-intensive building unfashionable where it was not actually unsustainable. That memorable remark in the introduction about the book being seen as 'a tract in favour of wasting energy' was there because he, unlike his critics, did not make energy use an 'anathema'.[67] He had not in fact continued much beyond 1972 in the environmentalist mode, although he continued to believe in the position he had worked out. What happened next, as the following chapters make clear, was the move prefigured by *The Architecture of the Well-tempered Environment* – from a focus on architecture, to, literally, the environment in which it sat. The first example of that approach was Banham's only large-scale study of a city, *Los Angeles: The Architecture of Four Ecologies.*

# 6 THE ANGELENO

Reyner Banham first visited Los Angeles in 1965, and although
the city was never home, it defines his work more than any
other. 'I love the place beyond reason,' he stated in the smoggy
opening to the 1972 BBC film on the city he made with the
director and producer Julian Cooper, and there was a high
degree of the irrational in Banham's approach to the city,
which allowed him more than anywhere else to indulge his
taste for paradox.[1] Los Angeles was a vehicle for two broad
intellectual projects of Banham's: first the ongoing historical
revision of American architecture to reveal its technological
superiority over Europe's, a key theme of *The Architecture of
the Well-tempered Environment*; second, a move to the study
of the environment, much developed here. By the conclusion
of the film, Banham was arguably not much concerned with
architecture at all, as normally conceived, but 'ecologies', the
term that defined the book on which the film was based.[2]
His impatience with architecture, and architects, was plain
enough in the conclusion: 'the common reflexes of hostility
(to Los Angeles) are not a defence of architectural values
but a negation of them, at least in so far as architecture
has any part in the thoughts and aspirations of the human
race beyond the little private world of the profession.'[3] (For
Anthony Vidler, the project was essentially a methodological
one, about 'blowing up' traditional architectural history.
LA was literally and metaphorically vehicular, and it offered
a historical counter-model, 'a freeway model of history'.[4])

Los Angeles was also the vehicle for another identity
to add to all the others, the Angeleno. As ever, it was no off-
the-peg identity but an invention. It was there most clearly in

the introduction to the BBC film, as Banham stepped out of the terminal of Los Angeles International Airport and into his rental car, still colossally bearded, wearing a brown leather jacket and shades and a flat cap. While he sounded as Norfolkian as ever, his dress and confidence in the new environment spoke of a profound identification with it. He no longer looked especially English, or seemingly wanted to; he had become, temporarily or not, something else. That identity was associated with mobility to begin with, expressed above all by driving the city's freeways with pleasure and confidence; it was contemporary, little concerned with the past; it was enthusiastically, unapologetically consumerist; and it was hedonistic, with both the book and the film of the city structured around pleasure-giving elements. The cover of the first edition of *Los Angeles* was a simple reproduction of the iconic painting *A Bigger Splash* by David Hockney, like Banham another provincial Englishman captivated by the sensual pleasures of LA.

Banham's Angeleno identity was also self-consciously a touristic one and he evoked tropes of the eighteenth-century Grand Tour sometimes ironically, sometimes not, to make clear the continuing distance. All of these things had been present already in Banham's work, at least since he started reporting on America in the middle of the 1960s. But by 1971 and the publication of *Los Angeles*, they had cohered into an enduring and memorable public image. *Los Angeles* was probably Banham's most popular book and for many, perhaps most readers, the Angeleno Banham *was* Banham.

When Banham first wrote about Los Angeles in 1968, it was a city of roughly 2.8 million in a metropolitan county of about 7 million.[5] It had become an object of considerable theoretical interest for urbanists, having organized itself in an unusually polycentric and horizontal way. It had not been the first U.S. city to embrace the freeway system, but it had done it with greater enthusiasm and commitment than anywhere else. Among Banham's peers, it was an object of particular interest for the planner Peter Hall, whose visionary book *London 2000* had reimagined the capital region as essentially an English LA – a vast tapestry of freeways connecting the Kent coast and the city, whose restless inhabitants would be constantly mobile.[6] The actually existing LA underpinned the work of another visionary urbanist, Melvin Webber, who advocated for the separation of community (an idea, he thought, rather than a location) from place, hence the 'non-place urban realm'.[7] But contemporary LA in 1968 was not especially well known by Europeans; it was 'as remote as Mars' from the perspective of Norwich, Banham said, memorably, in the 1972 film.[8] It was a place you could report on for *The Listener* confident that very few of your readers would have actually visited.

Banham's LA work had multiple origins. In the 1972 film there was an artful sequence that found him back in childhood Norwich in picturesque scenes including the cathedral ('in whose shadow I played manly sports') and the respectable but modest terraced housing in which he grew up.[9] Banham, like most of his generation, was already familiar with the city through the local cinema – he had already been there countless times in his imagination and knew it, or at least a version of it, intimately.[10] That fascination was fed shortly after the Second World War by his first encounter with actually existing Americans, service personnel stationed in Norfolk, regular visitors to the Maddermarket Theatre where for a time he worked.[11] Banham's first real view of the city was in 1965, funded by the Graham Foundation grant that allowed him to do the research for *The Architecture of the Well-tempered Environment*.[12] It revealed a place organized in a radically different way from any European city, and one that in particular would require a driving licence to understand. That, mainly, was the impetus for Banham's taking up driving lessons the following year, 1966, and his gaining a licence at the end of the year (reported in an article for the *Architects' Journal*).[13] If he was going to be there at all, he was going to need to be able to drive for himself, and Banham characteristically made this otherwise mundane rite of passage into an existential moment. Banham's interest in cars up until that point had been to some extent like Roland Barthes' in the pages of *Paris Match*: cars were symbolic objects, and he wrote about them as if they were in effect sculptures. Cars, once Banham could drive, were experiences, and his attention towards them shifted, as it had done with architecture, from the object to the environment and its perception. Banham would return to the topic of the cultured non-driver in 'Unlovable at Any Speed' (1966), which commemorated his belated accession to the world of driving, a short but lucid exposé of the passions evoked by the subject.[14] The title referred to the consumer rights campaigner Ralph Nader's devastating 1965 book *Unsafe at Any Speed*, which criticized the American auto industry's lax approach to car safety.[15] The article itself narrated the precise experience of passing the driving examination, and the consequences, professional and personal, for acquiring the skill ('But you've spoiled everything by learning to drive. People who rave on about technology are supposed to know nothing about it.')[16]

From that point on, in any case, Banham was a driver, and the skill enabled him to deal with the uniquely car-oriented city of Los Angeles. LA appeared substantively for the first time in 1968 in 'Encounter with Sunset Boulevard', one of a series of four radio talks whose texts were published in the BBC's literary magazine *The Listener* in August and September.[17] The four were the basis of *Los Angeles*, although in concept rather than form: they were very substantively reworked and expanded for the book. That first article, 'Sunset Boulevard', was notably autobiographical even for Banham, beginning with his panic on being lost late in an unfamiliar city where ordinary journeys might be a hundred or so miles. The only picture, a photograph by Dick Miller of Sunset Boulevard with a blonde woman gratuitously surveying the scene, was titled 'the bus stop Reyner Banham missed'; the inference was clear – the article was really about *him*, his expectations, his unfamiliarity, his attempt to relate it to other versions of other cities, his sense of the city's destabilizing what *he* understood a city to be, his inner experience intimately connected with the outer one of the city. This self-reflection was not exactly new in itself, but it was new in its exaggerated quality, as if LA in some way permitted and encouraged it.[18] That essentially existential work would be developed further in *Scenes in America Deserta*.

The second and perhaps best-known piece of *The Listener* quartet is 'Roadscape with Rusting Nails', which reflected on the outline of the city made by its overlapping layers of transport history.[19] Banham again appeared as an actor in the piece: he arrives after a visit back to London, impossibly tanned – impossible, according to his interlocutors, none of whom had been to the city, because of its reputation as a smogbound hole. Not so, wrote Banham, delighting in putting them right, it was no worse than London. The freeways, he wrote, were productive of the city's form and the unhappy situation of Watts, the poor neighbourhood that was the epicentre of the city's riots in 1966. Watts's problems, Banham argued (on the basis of what evidence it was unclear), derived from its relative isolation from the freeway system. These arguments were developed in relation with a historical account of the city's transport networks that would be worked up later as a chapter of the book ('The Transportation Palimpsest'), the argument being that the Pacific Electric (PE) tram system provided the form of the metropolis, and in many cases the paths for the later freeways;

the freeways, in other words, weren't the obliterating force
they had been in London. The PE had also, counterintuitively,
survived much longer than LA's European critics might have
supposed, through to 1961, later than many of the mourned
tram systems in the UK. More counterintuitive and possibly
counter-factual argument followed: the smog was overstated,
part of the city's discursive performance in the same way as
the weather in London; it might in any case be caused by
gardening ('pouring prodigious quantities of mist-producing
water on the soil of the Los Angeles basin . . . this must have
done something to the local climate. But the automobile is
man-made and therefore a suitable scapegoat.')[20] The heart
of the article, though, was the account of driving in Los
Angeles, written as if by an experienced driver of the city's
streets, as if he had always known them. In fact he had passed his
UK driving test only eighteen months previously.[21]

He was not an especially confident driver, let alone an
experienced one, but here he was describing arranging his day
by making sure that he 'finished it by driving down Wilshire
Boulevard in the late afternoon towards the Pacific sunset'.[22]
He described Wilshire as that rare thing in the urban world, a
street that one might drive for pleasure alone. That pleasure
was not, and is not, especially architectural, but rather derives
from its spaciousness, and the experience of the sunset as one
drives west. Dead straight, easy to navigate and slow, it was an
ideal starting point for the novice motorist, here, by the miracle
of post hoc rationalization, reported as one of the world's great
urban experiences.

But Wilshire was the street-level accompaniment to another,
more durable Banham experience, lying some fifteen miles
due west of downtown, and not far from a sprawling junction
with Wilshire: this was the intersection of the San Diego and
Santa Monica freeways. It was and is architecturally spectacular,

Intersection of
San Diego and Santa
Monica freeways.

with high, narrow vector-like ramps carrying traffic between the broad freeways. Their seemingly weightless qualities made them a place of interest to photographers including Julius Shulman, chronicler of the Case Study houses. The intersection seen from a single viewpoint was, Banham wrote, 'convincingly monumental', with 'the unmistakeable stamp of great engineering' (it remained anonymous, here and elsewhere like most engineering projects, although the designers could no doubt have been identified had Banham cared to). 'But to drive over those ramps', he continued, 'in a high sweeping 60-mile-an-hour trajectory and plunge down to ground level again is a spatial experience of a sort one does not normally associate with monuments of engineering – the nearest thing to flight on four wheels I know.'[23]

These are some of the most characteristic lines in Banham's writing, partly because they set out so much of the territory for what would become *Los Angeles*, but also because they push so hard at traditional architectural history; here in these lines is the shifting of focus from the static object of a building to an embodied, kinetic experience involving a total environment; in that environment, the observer becomes an actor/participant, one whose actions both constitute and define the work. Here there is also a very modern aesthetic sensibility: in a widely cited piece, the American sculptor Tony Smith, interviewed in 1967 for the house magazine of the New York art scene, *Artforum*, recalled his experience driving in the middle of the night, at some unspecified time in the 1950s, on the then-unfinished New Jersey turnpike and emerging enraptured by the kinetic experience, accompanied by the blazing lights of the surrounding New York megalopolis. Art from that point on was an art of 'postage stamps', Smith said. How could it possibly compete against the all-encompassing immensity of this thing, whatever it was – enormous not only in its physical scale, but in the enveloping quality of the human experience. It wasn't art, he said in a remark that really got the attention of the younger generation of minimalists, but it was art-like, and yet it also did things that art had never before done for him.[24] It is not hard to imagine Banham writing these things: the frustration with the old world, the sense that the world of art has been taken over by the world of technology, the overwhelming excitement at the new technology: this is Banham's sensibility and LA above all was the place to explore it.

What was perhaps most important in this early encounter with LA, besides the experience of it, was the suggestion of a new kind of person created in relation to the city, in much the same way that Haussmann's Paris was supposed to have created the figure of the *flâneur*. The comparison is perhaps too easy to make: for Charles Baudelaire, the *flâneur* was simultaneously an observer of the urban scene, and a participant in it – but always in motion, he was never entirely committed; he was always moving on.[25] Banham himself didn't make the connection, here or later, perhaps because he had already invoked the trope of the Grand Tourist in relation to the city and there was no need for another human type who was simultaneously expert and enthusiast, simultaneously of and not of the thing he observes. That dual position lay at the heart of his invented Angeleno identity. (He came close to resolving that duality in favour of a permanent move to the city in 1968. There had been a job offer from UCLA, and the family spent the 1967–8 Christmas vacation in the city ostensibly, it seems, to scope out the viability of a move. They decided to stay put, for practical reasons, but the duality vis-à-vis the city was a function of circumstance, as well as an intellectual position.[26])

To be an Angeleno in Banham's sense could be transferrable to other situations beyond LA, for example 'Non-plan', the *New Society* piece from 1969, which wondered, heretically, if Southern

California might have produced a better built environment than highly regulated England. Banham was one of the four authors, the others being Paul Barker, the editor of *New Society*, the academic and planner Peter Hall and the architect Cedric Price.[27] The polemical introduction sounds remarkably like Banham but was a joint product; Barker had written it in response to a series of meetings over a year or so in pubs at which all four were present, and had all of them sign it off as an accurate reflection of the discussion.[28] It began with a seemingly inconsequential detail, a guide to planning produced by Dorset County Council about which a controversy had arisen: its recommendations for an appropriate design resulted in the blandest of speculative buildings, which would, they argued, have happened anyway. Architects had complained. The story, they wrote,

> illustrates the tangle we have got ourselves into. Somehow, everything must be watched; nothing must be allowed simply to 'happen'. No house can be allowed to be common-place in the way that things just *are* commonplace: each project must be weighed, and planned and approved and only then built, and only after that discovered to be commonplace after all.

It was an argument against planning; more accurately, an argument against the paternalist policing of taste in planning that the authors thought productive of a stifling, anti-architectural conformity. Doctrinaire and dreary, it suppressed what might be, were it allowed to emerge, the 'hidden style of mid-20th century Britain'.[29] The authors were deliberately vague about what they meant by planning, implying in the first instance an international culture that was anything from Haussmann in nineteenth-century Paris to Robert Moses in 1950s New York: planning as the literal embodiment of authority. More specifically, and locally, they meant the 1947 Town and Country Planning Act, the legislation that for the first time in the UK required official permission to be sought for development.[30] They referred to an amendment to that in 1968, and an increasing, albeit vague, sense of planning being under threat, mentioning Milton Keynes, a planned city that, with the assistance of Melvin Webber, was trying not to be planned at all.[31] What the Non-plan authors seemed to want was a version of Southern California, and a landscape celebratory of the car. Hints of it, they argued, could already be found in car design and advertising ('the popular arts of our time') and these things came together in the automotive landscape around petrol stations, although they lamented that British motorway services, then novel, had been 'damply overplanned' and whatever exuberance they might have had, had long been lost.[32] To illustrate the point, the authors had Christopher Ridley, a photographer, drive around central London at night taking photographs of neon signs. They didn't reproduce very well on *New Society*'s newsprint-grade paper, but they gave an indication at least of the modernity and movement they were after, each punching a single word into the darkness: 'Shell', 'Jaguar', 'Tesco', 'BEA', 'Fish Bar'. It is hard not to see them now in relation to the photographs of neon signs of Las Vegas published three years later by Robert Venturi and Denise Scott Brown; that use of images was part of a vastly bigger and more systematic research project, but the impetus and the intellectual provocation were similar.[33] It was a world of bright lights, movement and simple messages: food, petrol, travel. The second part of the article showcased three deliberately provocative interventions in the English countryside, each of them delineating an area that for a limited time would be free of planning controls, the conceit being that freedom might

Christopher Ridley, photographs for 'Non-plan'.

build better than paternalism. The proposals had a distinctly libertarian, hedonistic feel, and Barker found a children's book illustrator, the New Zealander Graham Percy, to draw them. The result was a pseudo-Angeleno roadside fantasy, all neon hotel signs, advertising billboards, solid traffic and airliners piercing the sky.[34]

Was it serious? The border of that image with its wizard-hat decoration, all stars and lightning, suggested a high degree of whimsy in the whole enterprise, as did the light-hearted tone of the text. There was also something in Percy's illustrations that was weirdly reminiscent of Gordon Cullen's sketches illustrating Iain Nairn's 'Outrage' column in the *Architectural Review*.[35] Weird, because Cullen's images were specifically designed to attack the unplanned suburban sprawl the Non-planners actually advocated. It may have been unintentional, but more likely it was deliberate in the spirit of the IG, a rejection of potential criticism by simply embracing the object of that criticism. Whatever it was, all of the authors of 'Non-plan', and especially Banham and Hall, had found something by that stage in California that had got their attention; the previous year Banham had written that he knew of 'no greater enthusiast' for the city than Hall.[36] LA had forced them to reconsider many of their existing assumptions, from the presumed superiority of European design to its supposed liberalism, to something as fundamental as their assumptions about the suburbs. For Banham, as late as 1964, suburbia was a bad place: his film for the BBC, *A City Crowned with Green*, was an account of London that depicted Metroland (the transit-oriented suburbs of the 1930s) as a terrible void, free of culture and human life during working hours, the opposite of the city.[37] But by 1968 Los Angeles had made nonsense of that traditional dichotomy between city and suburb. That openness to urban design, that sense of old hierarchies being turned on their heads, strongly informed 'Non-plan' and, beyond, Banham's sense of Angeleno-ness.

First published in 1971, *Los Angeles: The Architecture of Four Ecologies* was a hybrid book bridging both academic work and

Graham Percy, illustrations for 'Non-plan'.

journalism. Banham often made a distinction between the two forms of output, but in reality the traffic between the two was substantial.[38] It had the length and structural complexity of an academic work, but in tone, and the breadth of its reference points, it drew clearly on the four BBC radio talks, as well as the quirkiness of the work he had been doing for *New Society*, which under Barker's editorship had left him more or less unsupervised to report from the front lines of consumer society.[39] *Los Angeles* had, like Banham's articles for *New Society*, discussion of cars and car culture, buildings that were not really architecture, and junk food.

 *Los Angeles* also maintained the autobiographical quality of the radio talks and in this it was quite unlike the previous book, *The Architecture of the Well-tempered Environment*, which was a straightforward historical narrative. *Los Angeles* blended geography with travelogue and autobiography, so the Banham of the book was even more a construction than usual, adding something of the Grand Tourist to the character. He was not alone in this at the time, for it had become an occasional habit of those describing the modern American landscape to do it picturesquely; at the same time Robert Venturi and Denise Scott Brown were writing of Las Vegas in terms of the monuments of ancient Rome in their *Learning from Las Vegas*, often written about in the same terms as Banham's book.[40] *Los Angeles*, however, made something of the author's own position, which Venturi and Scott Brown did not. Banham-the-tourist was also a keen photographer: many of the images in the book were his, and where they were not, he had tried versions himself with his new Pentax SLR that were then worked up by professional photographers including Julius Shulman. His own pictures, such as the image of Johnnies, a bar on Wilshire Boulevard, had a simple, snapshot-like quality, an unvarying 50mm lens providing the closest to the eye's natural perspective.

He was an enthusiastic photographer, especially here, and taking pictures was in effect a way of thinking.[41]

Los Angeles's peculiarities – horizontal extension, mobility, wild variety of landscapes from alpine to ocean – meant that for an imaginative reporter like Banham new terminology was needed: hence 'ecologies'. He was already thinking in environmental terms, and here, as with *The Architecture of the Well-tempered Environment*, the terminology was twisted to mean something slightly new. 'Ecology' here wasn't discussed, or explained, but by inference the reader understood it to mean a loose structure that could accommodate the built environment, landscape and anthropology, as well as what Banham would later call 'the eye of the beholder'.[42] As Anthony Vidler put it later, Banham's ecology was 'self-fabricated'; it 'provided an open framework for heterogeneity in subject matter and observation'.[43] Specifically it allowed him to discuss areas of the city that were not so much places as states of being: the beach, the plains, the hills, the freeway. These 'ecologies' structured the book, interspersed with more conventional explorations of architecture and urbanism.

The first chapter, 'In the Rear-view Mirror', set up two allusions to the picturesque: the rear-view mirror itself, although Banham didn't comment on it in depth, was a device that could be of similar size, shape and purpose to the Claude glass. The former has an ostensibly practical role, the primary means of observing traffic behind a car, and is of obsessional interest to driving instructors. The Claude glass was a piece of polished metal, of sometimes similar size and shape, used by the Grand Tourist to observe a scene by reflecting it. Tinted, it produced a view that resembled a heavily varnished landscape painting. Both devices were means of literally re-presenting a landscape; both (curiously) required the viewer to sit or stand with their back to the view itself; most importantly, both were means of resolving a boundless landscape into a comprehensible image.[44] That comparison was implicit rather than explicit, however. Banham was clearer about the picturesque in what is probably the most famous line in the book: 'So, like earlier generations of English intellectuals who taught themselves Italian in order to read Dante in the original, I learned to drive in order to read Los Angeles in the original.'[45] (No matter that this contradicted the line in 1966's 'Unlovable at Any Speed' in which learning to drive had been for the 'love of a woman', like growing a beard.[46]) Here was the city as picturesque site, the visitor as Grand Tourist, with all of the implications that entailed – the visitor as privileged subject, rendering the city as a unique aesthetic object for pleasurable consumption. Banham insisted repeatedly on the city's unique qualities: 'I make no apology for it', he wrote,

> The splendours and miseries of Los Angeles, the graces and grotesqueries, appear to me as unrepeatable as they are unprecedented . . . Once the history of the city is brought under review, it is immediately apparent that no city has ever been produced by such an extraordinary mixture of geography, climate, economics, demography, mechanics and culture; nor is it likely that an even remotely similar mixture will ever occur again.[47]

He put the reader inevitably in mind of ancient Rome, a uniquely powerful city state with a dynamic and civilization all of its own. Los Angeles was no prototype city, no 'harbinger of universal urban doom', but its own civilization *sui generis*, almost entirely self-referential. Against this theatrical backdrop Banham, both in the book and even more so in the film, was a performer: his history of the city in both cases was a narrative of his personal encounter with it and his acquisition of local habits and behaviours: here he eats a hamburger, there he notices someone's driving behaviour on the freeway, then he visits the beach, ruminates on downtown, or tells you about where he is living. What he experienced as an individual was revelatory of the uniqueness of the city's culture, and it is his position as a privileged but knowledgeable outsider that permitted him the insight. His Angeleno personage was above all an expert consumer of the city, constantly seeking out its pleasures.

That sensibility found itself naturally enough on the beach on the first instance, for this more than any other aspect was the defining aspect of this particular metropolis, 'the greatest City-on-the-shore in the world'.[48] That claim might have been contestable, but its main rival (at least the only rival beach city he mentioned), Rio de Janeiro, was not somewhere Banham had visited. The appeal of the beach was, broadly speaking, erotic. The landscape itself was the result of the visible geological process that had lifted it out of the ocean, and in this primeval landscape, humans themselves were attractively returned to the primitive. Banham clearly enjoyed the primitivism of the scene, which was, he thought, 'a symbolic rejection of the consumer society where a man needs only to own what he stands up in – usually a pair of frayed shorts and sun-glasses'.[49] On surfing, which Banham observed, fascinated but distanced, the participant was a well-muscled 'noble savage', pitting himself against the 'mighty hulking Pacific Ocean'.[50] The rest of the description of the beach city, all eighty or so miles from Malibu in the north to Huntingdon Beach in the south, stressed the lightness of the overlay of civilization: things had come and gone leaving traces, and ruins sometimes predominated, and in the middle of it all humans wander, semi-naked, in search of pleasure. It could scarcely be more picturesque, put like that. To start with the beach was the right place to start with Los Angeles, given its symbolic and cultural value, but it was also a measure of how far he had travelled imaginatively – from a world of war and violence described in *Theory and Design in the first Machine Age*, to one that seemed almost exclusively about pleasure.

To visit this landscape now is to visit a place that has been considerably developed since Banham's time, particularly around Venice, where the houses lining the boardwalk are today among the city's more expensive properties; Venice's ruins have largely gone. At the same time, the contingency of the scene is still striking. This is still not, as at the Rio suburb of Copacabana, a monumental civilization imposed on a tropical beach, but rather something more like a state of nature that happens to lie adjacent to a metropolis. The tsunami warning signs remind the visitor of the scene's fragility; it could all disappear under a wave. That sense of contingency, so important to Banham's understanding of the city, was perhaps most strongly present in the chapters on mobility, 'The Transportation Palimpsest' and 'Autopia'. Both contributed to an exaggerated sense of a city defined by its movement, and that to be a citizen of it was to be naturally and continually mobile. Here he revisited the intersection of the San Diego and Santa Monica freeways, a work that persuaded him that the city's freeway system was 'one of the greater works of Man' (it is hard not to think this remark was calculated to upset as many RIBA members as possible).[51] The images Banham chose of the intersection of the two freeways, the 405 and the 10, underlined a somewhat idealized and otherworldly quality; the aerial picture supplied by the California Division of Highways showed the complete structure in all its swirling complexity, from the west, looking towards Downtown. The distance from the scene means that you can scarcely make out the traffic, or the grid of suburban streets with which it collides at ground level; from up here it is a delicate, almost floral pattern, gently laid over the city.

There was certainly none of the sense of disruption you get as a pedestrian in this landscape, nor the crudeness of the road surfaces themselves with their noisy and uneven joints. The same is true of Julius Shulman's image on the following page, which has some of the unearthly quality of Catherine Opie's more recent photography of LA freeways. Banham sketched an ever more contingent future that saw conventional architecture dissolve further into landscape, as the highways were themselves overlaid with an invisible network of commuter flights using de Havilland Twin Otter aircraft originally designed for rural use. Although the airlines running these routes (Cable and Aero Commuter) were never more than marginal operations, Banham's alighting on them at the end of the chapter referred to his own long-standing obsession with flight, and the prefiguration of a city of pure mobility, whose physical infrastructure might very well disappear.[52]

If LA was a uniquely contingent city, its citizens, wrote Banham, might have evolved new forms of social life, as he reported in perhaps the book's most suggestive chapter, 'Autopia'. This anthropological reflection on freeway driving extended the frame of reference beyond Banham's driving experience to the freeway as culture. In arguably the book's second most famous passage, he reflected, somewhat voyeuristically, on the sight of a young woman passenger in a convertible being driven at speed on the freeway. As the car left the ramp to exit the freeway, he reported, she pulled down the sun visor to access the personal mirror, fixing her hair and makeup as she did so.[53] Who knows whether it was real or imagined? But the story identified LA's freeways as challenges to the European traditions of public space; the freeway *was* in effect public space, the off-ramp a transition zone, and everything else effectively indoors. That fantasy extrapolated from the life of the beach, explored in Chapter Two, titled

'Surfurbia', and it developed the idea that the city's life, public or private, was fundamentally lived out of doors. Banham cited the enduring urban myth that there were families who in fact lived their lives on the freeway, the car literally as home (it was sadly no more than a myth, but a popular and suggestive one).[54] And that idea was developed at greater length and more seriously in the concluding chapter, where Banham hinted that the freeway might be considered genuine public space, of an equivalent kind to the conventional spaces of the city. The freeway might be such a space because acceptance of its rules also conferred special freedoms, a contradiction of a kind familiar to urbanists – in recent American history it had been expressed most clearly perhaps by Jane Jacobs in her book *The Death and Life of Great American Cities*, which described the street life of lower Manhattan as a self-regulating system, with rights and responsibilities producing a uniquely urban experience.[55] Banham did not mention Jacobs, but there is something of that classic sense of urbanity in his account of the freeway. It represented one of modern society's most 'spectacular paradoxes', he wrote, a materialization of the tension 'between private freedom and public discipline that pervades every affluent, mechanized, urban society'. Banham wrote, 'the private car and the public freeway together provide an ideal . . . version of democratic urban transportation'. Yet, he continued 'the price . . . is the almost total surrender of personal freedom for most of the journey.'[56] Banham's Angeleno was therefore a secret disciplinarian. It was also someone who did not have to live with the freeways on a daily basis. As the architectural historian Thomas Hines wrote in an otherwise careful and positive review of the book, Banham's view that the two hours Angelenos spent on the freeway each day were among its most rewarding was 'a sad commentary on the other twenty-two hours of the Los Angeles day'. It was in the ecstatic, fantasy-laden account of the freeways that the reader was 'most aware of the author as a voyeur'.[57]

There was architecture in the book too, with short chapters focused on the Gamble House in Pasadena, the innovative work of the Viennese immigrants Rudolf Schindler and Richard Neutra, and the remarkable Case Study programme started by John Entenza of the magazine *Arts and Architecture*. Much as these were important, however, the weight of Banham's polemic was directed towards those forms of architecture that most challenged the definition of what architecture might be. 'Architecture: Fantastic' started not with an account of a building as such, but a 'fantastic hamburger' whose arrayed delights had entirely displaced nutrition for visual effect (for more on that, refer back to Chapter One). The fantastic architecture itself continued the theme in Banham, its purpose spectacle rather than function, with roofs or fire pits designed merely to attract attention from the road. Banham wrote of the profligacy of this architecture:

> From the Brown Derby onwards, through the Velvet Turtle at Redondo Beach, and onwards into a plushly under-lit future of 'Total Meal Experience', restaurants have been the most intensely and completely designed buildings in the area – few, even the most expensive houses can have had so much detailed attention devoted to them inside and out.[58]

This is the point: LA's real architecture, its most alive form, was its most ephemeral, along with dingbats (the name Banham gave to the speculative apartment buildings along major roads), Disneyland, the Watts Towers and all the rest. To be an Angeleno in Banham's sense was to be comfortable with ephemera, to expect no meaning below a play of surfaces, all in ways that anticipated postmodern thought in the subsequent decade. That argument was staged as film in 1972 in *Reyner Banham Loves Los Angeles*, made with Julian Cooper, and which faithfully explored the themes of the book. It was first broadcast on 11 March 1972 and again in June the following year.[59] The difference with the book was the visual presence of Banham himself; here, in flat cap, shades, seemingly even more prodigiously bearded than ever, he ranged over the city in a rented Ford to the accompaniment of Baede-Kar, a fictional guide that anticipated satnav, although with added commentary for the tourist (the name was a play on the Baedeker tourist guides that had, in what was no doubt a Banham joke, given their name to the Luftwaffe raids that had disproportionately hit cathedral cities). Banham was shown in the mostly African American suburb of Watts reflecting on the 1966 riots, but rather uncomfortably observing the local population from the safety of the car, as he did a great deal of the city. And there he was later observing the life of the freeway from the driving seat,

Banham poses as tourist in LA's Downtown.
From *Reyner Banham Loves Los Angeles*, dir. Julian Cooper (1972).

a process that distanced the viewer from the city as much as approached it. Observations could only be made, distracted at 60 mph though the windscreen, and anything that grabbed the attention needed to be big and obvious. He revisited the San Diego/Santa Monica freeway intersection he had written about for *The Listener*, and here he and Baede-Kar navigated the tricky junction in traffic, Banham's nerves slightly the better of him in front of the camera as a result of the traffic conditions. But it was still the affecting, aesthetic experience Banham had described a few years earlier in print, and at some level pleasurable ('Now wasn't that fun?', says Baede-Kar in her soothing tones).

The touristic dimension and Banham's own peculiar presence (the bonhomie, the clothes, the weird vocabulary) can make aspects of the film uncomfortable viewing now, especially when it encounters the questions of whom Banham's city excludes. Those aspects of the project were the subject of probably the most critical review Banham's work received in his lifetime, by an LA-raised artist then based in New York, Peter Plagens.[60] Writing for *Artforum*, Plagens savaged the book for its touristic approach.[61] The city of his imagination was a fantasy; the authentic city was one of exclusion, violence and ecological degradation, which as a resident one would know. Plagens's real beef with Banham was more reactionary, however: Banham just wasn't a Los Angeles native. His prose, Plagens wrote, was 'an embarrassing cocktail of officialese and hip; he uses or makes up ridiculous, un-euphonious slang I've never heard anyone here use: "San Mo" for the freeway or town of Santa Monica, "surfurbs" for the beach communities, and "autopia" for our car shtick.'[62] That may be correct, in the film as well as the book, as there Banham (consciously or otherwise) affected a peculiar mid-Atlantic accent as he negotiated the freeways at the start of the film, neither Norwich nor Southern California, with a vocabulary and intonation all his own. It was nothing new, of course: Banham had been making things up all his life (see, for example, the Louis Hellman cartoon the *Architects' Journal* published on 6 November 1968, in which a lightly fictionalized Banham, wearing swimming shorts and riding a penny farthing bicycle, intones 'it's a sock-it-to-me candy-coloured plug-in clip-on pop culture folks!').

Plagens's more substantial charge was the breezy reiteration of a set of Los Angeles clichés: the city as the beach and the Hollywood hills, and the admittedly new freeways, in other words, Plagens thought, 'conventioneer bullshit about "freedom" (mobility, sun, sex, affluence) for everybody which bloats LA with eager seekers and a quick-buck economy.'[63] This was fair enough: Banham deliberately skewed his analysis to these

Louis Hellman, cartoon featuring Reyner Banham from *Architect's Journal* (6 November 1968).

Louis Hellman, detail
of cartoon featuring
Reyner Banham,
*Architect's Journal*
(31 December 1969).

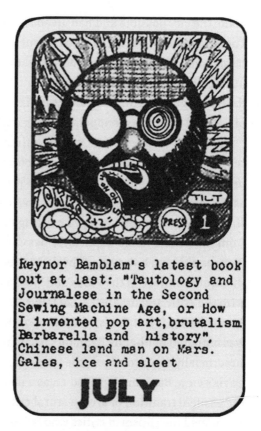

aspects of LA, rather than downtown, and he devoted only a
chapter to the endless-seeming flat grid of the main city, 'the
Plains of Id', where nearly everyone actually lived. That plain,
with its iron grid stretching unbroken twenty miles in any
direction, and its thousands of undistinguished bungalows
was, according to Plagens, the real city. Banham didn't ignore it,
but he suppressed its banality in favour of its more picturesque
elements. He said it himself: the book was principally about
the city's 'splendours and miseries', not the boring bits.[64]
For Banham and his publishers, LA was interesting for its
exceptionalism. The most serious criticism of all perhaps was
Banham's lack of interest in capital, the sources of finance that

made the city possible and had given it its peculiar form. There was nothing, Plagens noted, about the actions of capitalist monopolies: 'banks, savings-and-loans, oil, insurance, public utilities, and the division of highways . . . Banham is hardly the one to give us a Marxian analysis of the class structure of L.A. and what the monopolies wrung out of it.'[65]

Plagens's review was out of step with the largely positive reception elsewhere.[66] Indeed, for a book pitched as a provocation, seemingly not many were provoked; Banham, as if in anticipation, had to stage his own controversy at the start of the book, with outraged existing reports on the city from the writers Adam Raphael, James Cameron and others.[67] Plagens did hint, however, at the darker version of LA criticism that would surface in the 1980s and '90s, particularly associated with the critic and urbanist Mike Davis, especially in *City of Quartz* (1990).[68] But Davis, himself a Southern Californian, was bothered neither by Banham's peculiar language nor his superficially sunny outlook; the prose was 'brilliant' and, in Davis's view, Banham deployed LA as a means of attacking the ossified tradition of architectural criticism. Banham 'excoriated the elitism of critics who failed to consult the actual desires of the masses', and the book was 'a turning point in the valuation of the city by the international intelligentsia'.[69] Another Southern Californian native, the geographer Ed Soja, was similarly unconcerned by Banham's interloper status: like Davis beforehand, he regarded the project as one that had opened up the city for analysis, and had done so treating it with relative dignity – 'If there was irony or sarcasm in Banham's portrayal of LA it was joyfully hidden.'[70] There certainly was irony in Banham's account of LA, in his own performative approach to the place, in his treatment of it as a play of surfaces, and his focus on its perverse and eccentric aspects. It was a postmodern exercise before its time and Banham the Angeleno

a prototypical postmodern *flâneur*. He would have disliked
that description because of the terminology, but with half a
century of distance, Banham's Angeleno identity has all the
ironic distance, restlessness and preoccupation with surfaces
that characterized postmodern accounts of cities.[71] Thomas
Hines described Banham's approach to LA as that of a 'voyeur';
he meant it in a mildly critical way, to draw attention to the
limits of the book's project, as well as to refer to the nature of
his observation.[72] It does, however, perfectly describe Banham's
position on the city, with all the scopophilia and distance it
implies; it was a position with flaws, a little too interested in
the exceptional and the surreal to be generalizable, but also
identified something new in Banham's approach to the world,
and it anticipated postmodern approaches to the city elsewhere.

## Los Angeles, Revisited

The most suggestive part of Banham's Los Angeles for me
remains the intersection of the San Diego and Santa Monica
freeways, the I-405 and I-10. Whatever the traffic conditions
when you visit, it always creates some pause for reflection, for
it is still spectacular as a construction, still graceful from many
angles, and as you traverse it you still catch glimpses of the
Santa Monica mountains and the epic sprawl of Wilshire
Boulevard. It's a huge landscape in every way, with mountains
and ocean and skyscrapers all simultaneously in view, framed
by one of the city's great pieces of engineering. Knowing
Banham's account of this place you can appreciate the extraordinary qualities of this ordinary part of the city as you drive it.
He recovered it as a place.[73] Doing that was important because
it developed the possibility of a history of environments beyond
discrete architectural objects, and a history that was implicitly
about the extraordinary qualities of the everyday. That approach

had already been prefigured in *The Architecture of the Well-tempered Environment*.[74] *Los Angeles* went a long way towards developing it further, nowhere more than on the freeways. Admittedly to have the experience Banham had on the Santa Monica/San Diego intersection is now challenging. On the freeways themselves, while off-peak speeds can routinely reach 70mph or more, the condition of the high connecting ramps and their narrowness suggests Banham's account was an exaggeration (especially given the poor handling characteristics, not to mention tyres of 1968-vintage American cars). A speed of 60mph was probably fantasy then – it certainly is now most, if not all of the time as traffic routinely backs up for a mile or so, converting the ramps into de facto parking lots for cars shuffling slowly onto the main freeways. Speeds build rapidly after the junction, after some judicious shuffling, but the experience of the ramps is stasis rather than flight.

To walk this landscape inevitably poses questions of Banham's fantasy too. The slimness of the connecting ramps impresses from the ground as a pedestrian, as does their height

Intersection of San Diego and Santa Monica Freeways, 2019.

Intersection of San Diego and Santa Monica freeways in 2019.

and the paucity of support: these really are sculptural. The scale
of the whole intersection also impresses, for it takes a good ten
minutes to traverse the whole thing on foot from south to north.
And the movement of traffic (when it moves, as it eventually
does) has a slightly otherworldly quality from the ground;
shielded from direct traffic noise, the barriers alternately hiding
and revealing the trucks and cars, and it is a spectacle that
takes some time to grasp for it to make sense. But the ground
level of the intersection also has something Banham couldn't
or wouldn't have anticipated, specifically (as was common
throughout California from the mid-2010s) a substantial tent
city housing the homeless. In 2019 nearly all of the underpass
sidewalks had tents, packed tightly together, and vans line
the kerbside for the same purpose. It is orderly enough, and
has become a semi-permanent feature, further speaking of
stasis rather than movement. This has, traffic jams and all,
become for many a place to live in, rather than fly through.[75]
An updated *Los Angeles* would no doubt have had to find a way
to acknowledge this, and perhaps more of the city beyond the
fantasy; as realized, it remains the work of a privileged, albeit
brilliant, voyeur.

# 7 THE DESERT FREAK

Banham's book on deserts, *Scenes in America Deserta*, does not normally get much more than a footnote in accounts of his work.[1] This is a mistake: it is a quietly radical work, as well as the one that says most about Banham himself. In 1998, ten years after his death, when his children were looking for an appropriate place to bury his ashes, they chose one of the book's key locations, Zzyzx in the Mojave Desert. There was simply no competition, they said: the Mojave was the place he loved more than any other, and Zzyzx, a bizarre ruin of a health resort by a dried-up lake, was the place in the Mojave that meant the most to him.[2] If Banham was associated most with the modern movement in architecture, the place on earth that held the most personal significance in the end was neither typically architectural, nor typically modern – if anything, it picturesquely represented the folly of architecture in such harsh surroundings. It pushed further the idea of the environment and stretched the category of art history. Along with all his other identities, Banham was a self-confessed desert freak.[3]

*Scenes in America Deserta* was uncategorizable: not architectural history or art history or history, but a hybrid. My own copy is one I found dog-eared and abandoned on the floor of the architecture school where for some years I had an office. I picked it up, curious because it had Banham's name on the cover, but it didn't look like any of the other titles: it was a decorative, vaguely art-nouveau cover with the title in a box against a wallpaper background of schematic saguro cacti; the colours, a deep brownish-red, ochre and dark green, alluded to natural phenomena rather than architecture, which, on the evidence of the first leafing through, was scarcely present.

Ruins of Zzyzx in 1980.

There were attentive descriptions of Mojave scenery, some
references to the author's Norwich childhood, and a startling
account of an emotional breakdown on learning of the death
of a desert acquaintance, the 'Nipton Troll'.[4] It was a strange
book. My copy had been abandoned along with miscellaneous
debris from a PhD career by a student who had recently vacated
the postgraduate room: it was as if it didn't fit and wasn't worth
keeping, a puzzling, awkward object. I kept it on my shelf along
with the other Banham books until five or so years later when
I returned to it – or, rather, a first, handwritten draft – in the
special collections of the Getty Research Institute.[5] Like most of
Banham's drafts, it was written in pencil on yellow lined paper,
and also like all of them it was remarkable for the neatness of
the script, and the near absence of errors, as if the entire text
had emerged fully formed and merely needed to be transcribed.
(It may well have simply been a final draft, of course, the first
drafts having been binned along the way; the impression
of supernatural clarity was nevertheless hard to shake, and
somehow appropriate to the subject.) I settled down to read.
What a remarkable text it was, how lucid, and how far it had
stretched the boundaries of art history to describe an entire
landscape. And also how far it had gone to consider an inner
landscape as well as an outer one, how much further it placed
Banham himself centre stage, how his thoughts and feelings
were central to the narrative, even more so than in *Los Angeles*,
of which it was a development.[6] There was a consciously
performative quality to the work. In papers I found at the Getty
there was an undated proposal Banham had drafted which
showed, succinctly, how this thinking was present at the earliest
stages of the project:

> it is a landscape where I will always be an observer, a
> traveller – a *tourist* if you will because I am unlikely to live

long enough in that terrain to acquire the deeply ingrained knowledge of an old desert hand. It will be the deserts as seen – but not seen by innocent eyes; as a Briton I am heir to a powerful literary tradition, back through Doughty's *Arabia Deserta* to the rolling rhetoric of the King James Bible that colours all perceptions of deserts wherever they may be. Englishmen carry a private desert in their heads against which other deserts are measured [Banham's emphasis].[7]

The biblical character of desert work required Banham somehow to match it, and he invoked Charles M. Doughty's *Travels in Arabia Deserta*, a book he had likely known since childhood.[8] Doughty's work was biblical from the start; the 1936 edition with its introduction by T. E. Lawrence has a picture of Doughty on the frontispiece, an Old Testament prophet come to life.[9] Banham's language occasionally approached Doughty's ecclesiasticism. But just as important in some ways was Doughty's portrait: that prophet-like figure was also arguably Banham himself, albeit once he had been Westernized and given a bicycle in the well-known photograph of him at Silurian Lake.

Placing Banham in the desert, that picture identified him personally with it, describing a location (unlike the historically distant locations of *Theory and Design*) with which he was personally engaged, in the present. It also suggested an attitude to the desert celebratory of human activity, the more unlikely the better. That was a vital theme throughout the book: that the desert was not a void, despite its etymology, the Latin *desertus*, literally meaning 'left waste'. Instead the desert was full of life, particularly human life, and at a certain level it existed because of, rather than in spite of, human activity. *Scenes in America Deserta* therefore continued and developed the environmental approach of *Los Angeles*. It was geographically only a small step to the Mojave, which, if not a suburb of the megalopolis, is certainly one of its recreation grounds. The desert was not therefore the opposite of the city, but an adjunct to it, and for that reason Banham preferred the relatively unregulated Mojave to the de facto outdoor museum of Death Valley, with its curated viewpoints and exhibits. *Scenes in America Deserta*, for all its peculiarities, was most like a work of art history, but it activated a debate about the limits of that discipline and what should, or might, be its objects of attention. Architecture and art were relatively minor presences here, the book's concern being the all-enveloping landscape. The scale of that object and its complexity raise questions for the scope of art history, for what it could achieve as a discipline, even more so than *Los Angeles* (if this even was a work of art history). Banham at this stage of his career was conscious again of the discipline, having moved in 1980 from the department of architecture at SUNY Buffalo to the tiny department of art history at UC Santa Cruz, where he took on an eclectic range of teaching from the foundations of the discipline.[10] By a circuitous route the desert project brought him back to it.

Some of the rationale for that can be understood in the touristic aspects of *Los Angeles*. *Scenes in America Deserta* took that specialized tourism much further, a fact that is obvious from the first sight of the book, which resembles a travel memoir more than anything else, along with Banham's literal appearance in it, with its invocation of the Englishman abroad. His dressing up in Western garb (the bolo tie, hat and so on) was of course in that tradition: T. E. Lawrence affecting Bedouin dress to signify both imaginative engagement with the subject and a calculated flouting of convention.[11]

Doughty's *Arabia Deserta* was the model for Banham's book in both content and title. It is a sprawling, two-volume account of the author's travels throughout the Arabian desert in the

1880s, written in a high style based on the King James Bible. Lawrence was connected: although the book was long out of print, he arranged for it to be republished in 1921, as well as providing an introduction. Doughty was an important model for Banham, providing not only a title but a modus operandi. Doughty was a poet and explorer rather than an academic; his priorities were beauty and adventure. In Doughty's book, as well as Banham's later on, the desert was foremost a place of human activity, so the opening chapters dealt with the hajj, the long journey to Mecca. Those pages were about human life and human culture, and they teemed with people, the desert a full, rather than an empty, space.[12] Banham took much from that assumption, as well as the language, which he made more expansive and poetic than anything else he wrote.

There was also Doughty's own position in the story: as Lawrence wrote in his 1921 introduction, the book was about Doughty as much as it was about the desert. A sickly, pious man, he wrote a book about human suffering as much as anything else, and as much as Doughty might have wished to suppress his more narcissistic qualities, he was, Lawrence wrote, 'very really the hero of his journey and the Arabs knew how great he was'.[13] For Banham, Doughty was a model in his approach to the desert as a cultural phenomenon, in his poetic language, in his subjectivity and perhaps, even down to the huge beard, the theatricality of his authorship. It was a book about the Arabian desert, however, and the imperial circumstances that brought Englishmen of a certain type into contact with that place. Britain's imperial interests in the Arabian peninsula included the Aden Settlement at the time of Doughty's writing; in 1915, in the period described by Lawrence, Britain concluded the Treaty of Darin with Ibn Saud, giving the territory that became Saudi Arabia the status of a British protectorate. Looking upon deserts for an Englishman of the time was inevitably at some level about power, for you looked in order to know, and ultimately to control. It was an attitude Banham certainly absorbed at a certain level, and his looking at the American desert has an odd sense of entitlement about it, as well as humility. It was a very long way from home, but it was also an environment to which he felt he belonged in some peculiar way, and had a right to belong to. The English were meant to be in deserts, or at least that is what the experience of Empire told them; Banham, in this strange book, somehow continued the tradition.

For the American desert there was another model, equally poetic. This was *The Desert* by John C. Van Dyke, a fortuitous discovery of Banham among the possessions of the Gamble House in Pasadena, where he was staying courtesy of the University of Southern California. He read it, he said, more or less in one go, standing by the nook where he originally found it.[14] Van Dyke (1856–1932) was an American art historian of wide range who had written extensively on American art, nineteenth-century French art and Dutch and Flemish art of the medieval period, as well as methods and approaches to studying art.[15] His eclecticism was furthered by *The Desert* (1901), a book that expanded the category of art history to include the desert landscape itself and its perception. Van Dyke made brief mentions of art, for example in one of many accounts of colour, in which Van Dyke compares Impressionist renderings of French landscape with what might be seen in the deserts of the American West. But mostly it was a book about the experience of the desert, which in its optical, physical and bodily sensations quite literally equated to that of art. Van Dyke wrote frequently in the present tense, as if working out in real time in his own mind what it was that he was seeing, tactics Banham shared. A memorable passage explored the visual peculiarities of the desert, such as its tendency to collapse distance. One might ride all day towards a range of mountains that in the morning looked only a mile or so distant: 'this deception of distance is not infrequently accompanied by fatal circumstances,' he warned.[16] In its collapsing of visual and bodily experience, this was one of the parts that most prefigured Banham's later work.

The greatest innovation of Van Dyke's work was, Banham wrote, perhaps his 'color vocabulary', as he repurposed or invented words to describe transitory phenomena in the desert that were a combination of geology, climate, weather conditions and the eyes of the observer: his descriptions, which are quite lengthy, are in other words an attempt to describe the impossible. 'The desert air is practically colored air,' he wrote.[17] One of the parts Banham quoted at length read:

> The veil or sheet cloud might be called a sunset cloud giving out as it does its greatest splendour after the sun has disappeared below the verge. It then takes all colours and with singular vividness. At times it will overspread the whole west as a sheet of brilliant magenta, but more frequently it blares with scarlet, carmine, crimson, flushing up and then fading out, shifting from one colour to another; and finally dying out in a beautiful ashes of roses. When these clouds and all their variations have faded into lilac and deep purple, there are still bright spots of color in the upper sky where the cirri are receiving the last rays of the sun.[18]

He elaborated: there were at least six words for red in the passage, one of them implicit ('flushing'), and they were 'all true', as he had seen the same effects Van Dyke had described in the Mojave. What impressed Banham here was quality of attention, the attempt to describe subtle effects that had perhaps never been put into words. The phenomena themselves were ineffable, or actually impossible to see, as he remarked in a later passage when he elaborated Van Dyke's largely convincing attempt to imagine the end of the Saltoun Sea 'with its melodramatic visions of prehistoric marine creatures thrashing about in the shrinking shallows of the disappearing sea'.[19] What he found in Van Dyke was an account of an aesthetic experience that exceeded art, and he also found a model of how to write a book on deserts. That model meant the desert as aesthetics, the desert as a cultural phenomenon, a product of human as much as natural activity, and the desert as a space for the exploration of the self as much as the external world. *Scenes in America Deserta* took up all of these challenges, and, like Doughty, some of the language, which could be equally romantic and excessive. Banham absorbed enough of these poetic qualities for his text to be set to music by the composer John McCabe for *Scenes in America Deserta* (1986), which was commissioned by the King's Singers and first performed by them the following year in Houston, Texas.[20]

The book's origins lay partly in a film made for the BBC in 1979 and broadcast as 'The Roads to El Dorado', part of the pop-anthropology series *The World About Us*.[21] Produced and directed by Julian Cooper, who had made *Reyner Banham Loves Los Angeles*, it described a journey across the Mojave from Los Angeles to Las Vegas, portraying the desert as a site of human activity, often highly entrepreneurial, rather than a void. Every moment of this television version stressed this idea, from the aerial shots of Las Vegas that opened it, to the accounts of the bizarre history of Zzyzx, to the culture wars around the Sierra Club, the environmental organization that simultaneously *was* human activity and the desire to restrict it.[22] Banham already by this stage portrayed himself as a 'desert freak'; he used this description in an interview for *Radio Times* and the interviewer indulged him, spending some lines on his style of dress, noting the bolo tie and beard. Banham helpfully pointed out that

the Mojave was really 'moustache country'.[23] Explaining
the fascination with deserts, Banham connected them with
religious belief. They were puritanical, he said, referring to
his own mixed Protestant background; 'A lot of the people
I met in the deserts reminded me of Primitive Methodists.
You felt they had a hotline to God, and of course you need a
hotline to God in the desert.'[24] The appeal of the project from
the start was therefore different from architectural history:
this was bigger stuff, and it was connected, as he also said in
all his pronouncements on the topic at the time, with boyhood
experiences in Norwich, where he certainly had a copy of the
two-volume edition of Doughty.[25]

The book emerged at much the same time as Banham
developed literary connections with desert enthusiasts,
especially with fans of Van Dyke, whose *The Desert* had become
a cult item.[26] The project developed initially with a Utah-based
publisher, Peregrine Smith, whose list had a particular focus on
desert books. He cut a complex deal later with Nikos Stangos
at Thames & Hudson, but the initial contact in 1979 was with
Smith, prompted by the BBC TV programme.[27] This was a desert
book, not an architectural one, and Banham found a receptive
audience among literary groups with an interest in writing
associated with the desert. In 1987 he spoke at a National
Endowment for the Humanities-funded conference in Tucson
called 'Writers of the Purple Sage: Origins of a National Myth',
declaring it in a letter to the organizers, 'my favourite conference'
(at the same time, it is worth noting, he was speaking at the
Society of Architectural Historians and in Paris: if he had a
found a new home, he had by no means abandoned the old
academic one).[28]

The book announces itself differently to any of the
architectural histories; it looks like an early twentieth-century
travelogue, and from the start it reads like one. The first chapter,

'On First Setting Foot', recounted the author's first visit to the
Mojave, which in the book's high style appears to have taken
place in another century. It was in fact 1968, and an impromptu
deviation from the I-15 just south of Baker, a fuel stop midway
between Los Angeles and Las Vegas. Banham stopped the car
and, typically, noted a mechanical detail as the engine died, 'the
usual convulsive clatter and shudder of American v-8s of the
period'.[29] The overwhelming sensations reported were heat,
light and colour, and the general unfamiliarity of the scenario
that manifests itself in a range of bodily ways: the writing was
as much about Banham's physical response to the scene as
anything, and in its gradual working through perceptions
as if in real time, it recalls *The Desert*. The rest of the chapter
meditated on that initial contact with the Mojave, its snakes, its
peculiar human characters, its indelible links with nineteenth-
century Protestantism and, less predictably, its personal
connections with the childhood scene of Mousehold Heath
in Norwich, a most unlikely comparison. Being in East Anglia,
that Heath could scarcely be any further from a true desert,
but it was a dry landscape, 'the most nearly desert place I had
seen before the Mojave', he wrote.[30] It was also, perhaps more
importantly, a wild place on the edge of town, a place where
things were possible that, back in civilization, were implicitly
not. That might be as prosaic as catching lizards in summer,
or it might be (Banham noted, by now in full Doughty mode)
'as grand as recovering one's belief in God'.[31] The desert was
populated, a human and cultural product as much as anything
else, and that was as true of Mousehold Heath as it was of the
Mojave. And crucially the desert, wherever it was, was '*seen*.
It is a visual pleasure, visual response, and what else can it
be for the first-time tourist, the wheeled *voyeur*?' [Banham's
emphasis].[32] The intellectual project here was lucidly of
landscape displacing the object of art; in this process the

viewer's perception, both visual and bodily, would play an increasing role. It was a lively idea for art historians at least, for the desert, if it was to be considered an appropriate object of study, collapses the usual hierarchies of value. It also carried with it the implication of a radical subjectivity – something about Banham's book, and desert books in general, collapsed inner and outer worlds, making their authors central. The *Seven Pillars of Wisdom* was in large part about the creation of the Lawrence myth; *Scenes in America Deserta* was about Banham's creation as a 'desert freak'.[33] Here he used the label for the first time in the book, writing of a kind of creation myth: 'I knew . . . that not only had I become a desert freak but that this was a very improbable thing for me to become and I had uncovered an aspect of myself that I did not know.'[34]

What, or who, was it, this desert freak? It was certainly another exercise in hat-wearing, both literal and metaphorical (the literal hat and the accompanying Western accessories

Silurian Lake, Mojave, California, in 2019.

Zzyzx Road in 2019.

were fascinating to the *Radio Times*, for whom Banham was
reliably good copy).³⁵ However the metaphorical hat was
more important, for there was more to being a Desert Freak
than entertaining journalists. It signified a closer personal
engagement with the subject matter than any of the other
projects, *Los Angeles* included. The Desert Freak was an
enthusiast, a believer whose object lay fundamentally beyond
criticism. The job was one of eschatology rather than critique.
The Desert Freak was also introspective in a way that had never
been revealed before; Banham had certainly been a presence in
the earlier writing, but *Scenes in America Deserta* had passages of
autoethnography and autobiography that were more personally
revealing than anything in his previously published work.³⁶

Among the first (neo-) architectural sights in the book, and
the most conceptually and personally significant, was Zzyzx,
a resort complex built on the edge of the great Soda Lake, just
off I-15 and not far from the town of Baker. Built by a radio
preacher, Curtis Howe Springer, in the 1950s, it was seemingly
a failure from the start, consistent with Springer's own shaky

history: according to a local expert he had spent some time in prison for exaggerated claims about his health products. The name was chosen to be the last entry in the telephone book.[37] Zzyzx survived as a ruin, Banham wrote, with – bizarrely – 'a couple of electric massage machines . . . in the open portico overlooking the plunge and looked as if they only needed to be plugged in'.[38] Zzyzx was rebuilt from 1976 as the Desert Studies Center of California State University, Fullerton, and the ruins are now mostly gone. What Banham saw in 1968 was straight out of science fiction: an abandoned resort town on a dried-up beach, an epic, entropic scene redolent of the novels of Ray Bradbury, who had based his Martian fantasies on the Mojave. It was a smart call: as was clear from the Viking expedition onwards, the Mojave effectively was Mars, albeit with a breathable atmosphere.[39] Banham's account of Zzyzx is one of the book's more memorable passages: the resort's rooms, he wrote,

> stand among palms and laurels by a strip of green along the 'beach' – there's no other word for it – and command as spectacular a view as does any habitable room in the whole desert Southwest. It is a view of a lake gone solid – the image, for me, of Ray Bradbury's 'fossil sea' ever since I first saw it – a broad calm surface of differing greys, striped sometimes with silver when there is water on the further surfaces, sometimes mirroring perfect inverted duplicates of the Cowhole Mountains veiled with layers of mist that have been lifted off the lake's surface by the heat of the sun. The lake is some six miles across at this point, the Soda Springs promontory thrusts well out into it, and one has an almost reassuring sense of being comfortably surrounded by this sea of, as it were, eternal repose with its small brown and blue conical mountains on the further shores.

It was an arresting sight for Banham, and his account of it embodies a characteristic, and here acute, sense of being 'there', suggestive of repeated visits under different light conditions, as well as of physical presence in the landscape ('one has an almost reassuring sense of being comfortably surrounded by this sea'). It was also an image of human failure and epic natural destruction, described in an image by Tim Street-Porter depicting the remains of the treatment rooms with the dry lake in the midground, and the distant mountains in the distance. Banham was largely unconcerned with the architecture, mentioning in passing that it was the work of local builders, but the image here shows a single-storey modernist pavilion, roofless and stripped bare, a building of some sophistication in its proportions and fenestration, not too far from a house by Richard Neutra. It looked clearly modern, but was also clearly a ruin, and the landscape beyond was otherworldly. Banham did not have much time for the work of contemporary artists who had worked in the desert, dismissing as 'trifles' the works of Robert Smithson, Michael Heizer (misnamed here as 'John' Heizer) and Robert Morris: 'trifles' because they were, he wrote, the result of 'personal decorative fancy', rather than the epic purpose of the Kitt Peak Observatory in Arizona (a vast solar observatory, the subject of a later chapter).[40]

But the importance of Zzyzx also put Banham in the conceptual orbit of these artists, especially Smithson, who was obsessed with ruins and the picturesque, and images of modern failure. A copy of Smithson's 1968 essay 'A Sedimentation of the Mind' can be found in the Getty papers, along with a few notes on the artist. The essay was a melancholy but playful comparison of geological change with intellectual labour, in which both the earth's surface and the mind's ideas were subject to destruction and decay ('Slump, debris slides, avalanches all

take place within the cracking limits of the brain').[41] It was on
the face of it the opposite of the positivism with which Banham
was usually associated. But here in the desert they were much
more aligned, and Street-Porter's images of the ruins of Zzyzx
could quite easily have been Smithson's. Banham's later career
was one increasingly focused on ruins, and his objects were
increasingly the failures, the outcasts. Zzyzx, this obscure
place, hard to pronounce, let alone reach, was merely one
point in the broader history of entropy that *Scenes in America
Deserta* largely was.

That position cast much of the human production of desert
as ruin, as in the entertaining account of Frank Lloyd Wright's
Arizona work in the desert, 350 miles to the southwest of Zzyzx.
Wright, according to Banham, first visited the high desert
in the early 1920s, passing through it on the way to the West
Coast as he worked on the Imperial Hotel in Tokyo.[42] He was
then recorded as visiting Death Valley in 1928, and was in the
running, although ultimately unsuccessful, for building Death
Valley Ranch, better known as Scotty's Castle. He then built two
disastrous projects in the environs of Phoenix: the Rose Pauson
House, which burned down in 1942, and Ocotillo, a project
started and abandoned in 1929, comprising low pavilions with
monopitch roofs in canvas, built from lightweight materials.
The experimental design was a failure, because the lightness
of the construction and the canvas roof resulted in terrible
performance in the summer heat, and it became apparent
it would be uninhabitable after April each year. Banham's
introduction to the chapter on Wright began with the debris
remaining from Ocotillo's failure. It was a 'very queer site of
modern archaeology', he wrote,

> a mess of broken fragments scattered over an area the size
> of a middle sized room. Elsewhere amongst the chollas

and cacti there are areas of burned ash, holes containing broken porcelain insulators and what may be pieces of toilet fitting, broken china and other domestic detritus, and areas of compacted ground that may have been the sites of small buildings. These are the remains of what may have been the best building project ever to have come from the mind and hand of Frank Lloyd Wright.[43]

It was seemingly a mysterious project: it rose and fell in the same year, and it is unclear what exactly happened to it to bring about its end. Wright claimed, apparently, that 'local Indians' had stolen the building materials; it may have caught fire during the unusual heat of the summer of 1929. Banham's attraction to it was derived from the boldness of the design, a low encampment emerging from the peculiarity of the desert site; that site specificity, along with the highly contingent quality of the architecture ('little more than stiff tents of wood and canvas'), were obvious attractions, reiterating the preoccupations of *The Architecture of the Well-tempered Environment*.[44]

But new here in the treatment of Wright was a preoccupation with his failure, not only in the boneheaded misunderstanding of the desert climate, but in the perversity of the project's history, its fleeting quality, and its almost total annihilation, alongside which there was Wright's somewhat biblical character (his family included several Unitarian ministers, including an uncle, Jenkyn Lloyd Jones, prominent in the American branch of the church). Starting with the tiny remaining fragments and the blasted site, Banham seemingly celebrated rather than mourned destruction; there was something in that account of the ruins of the site that made a fetish of the fragments.

It is quite a contrast, too, with what Banham said in 1969 in *The Architecture of the Well-tempered Environment*, where

Wright is a hero: in that book Wright's 1908 Baker House in Wilmette, Illinois, stands for a natural, modern use of heating technology to produce a uniquely comfortable environment, in spite of the extreme temperature variations of the Midwest. It was a eulogy to the sensitive, intelligent use of contemporary technology; here, Banham wrote, technology 'was finally and naturally subsumed into the normal working methods of the architect, and contributed to his freedom of design'.[45] Wright's genius (that is the right word for the way he was treated in *Well-tempered Environment*) was his understanding of the environmental aspects of architecture and making it central to the design process. Here he was the opposite, imposing an environmentally illiterate structure on a landscape that rejected it. The evidence for either version of Wright was admittedly thin, beyond Banham's visits to the sites: these were ideological Wrights, inventions to serve different purposes. They had in common, however, technology and the environment – Banham's interest in Wright was consistently marked by those things, rather than the symbolic and formal aspects of his work that could dominate other accounts, as well as the figure of Wright himself.[46]

Banham's scepticism of Wright continued with Taliesin West, the sprawling desert campus Wright built from 1937, and which reiterated in a more durable form the expansive pavilions and shallow pitched roofs of Ocotillo ('pretty well a reworked repeat of Ocatillo camp on a larger scale').[47] It survives today as a combination of museum and private architecture school, which since its opening has required its students to build and live in a shelter in the surrounding desert as their first project. Banham's interest was partly that architectural form, and the way the master plan was designed for the possession of an epic view across the great landscape bowl in which Scottsdale and the wider city of Phoenix sits: on a clear day you can see for a

Frank Lloyd Wright, Taliesin West, 1937.

hundred miles. But here, as at the beginning of the chapter, there is a preoccupation with failure. Wright himself, whom Banham met several times in old age, was depicted as a cane-brandishing monster, railing at the Scottsdale development that he had helped bring about. He was a 'pompous, senescent old show-off with a lot of style about him still, but nothing to say except clichés and quotations from his own former utterances'.[48] And the place itself in its actually existing condition raises all kinds of questions about its authenticity. The original buildings were an unlikely combination of massive walls built partly of fieldstone recovered from the surrounding desert and canvas roofs – but the canvas, a conceit from Ocotillo meant presumably to put the visitor in mind of camping and Japanese architecture, was also a liability, lacking both thermal insulation and protection against rain. The canvas was retained, but plastic tiles were installed above, a material Wright abhorred. Banham poked fun at the tourists' experience, the guides with their silly deference to the master ('Mr Wright') and their nervousness at interrogation as visitors are 'shepherded around in controlled groups under the guidance of Taliesin fellows and apprentices who never seem to deviate from meticulously prepared scripts and if asked an unusual question, tend to clam up for minutes while they regain their composure and get their mental cassette players running again'.[49] Wright's failure is perhaps manifest most clearly in a story the Taliesin fellows do in fact, to their credit, tell, concerning the electrical power lines that appeared shortly after he arrived on the site. The problem was partly, as Banham described, their curvature: specifically they sag in the opposite way to the horizon. But it is something more fundamental than that. Wright's reported rage was 'pretty typical of the kind of paranoia that grips so many desert freaks: he had come here to avoid contamination by the works of other men, and other men – doing exactly the same thing as he – had invaded his *cordon sanitaire*'.[50]

This was, you could say, classic Banham: a delight in the perversity of process, in what happens when architecture gets out into the world, subject to forces beyond its control.

View from Taliesin West with power lines.

Taliesin West however also represented an ideal of living in the desert that had considerable appeal. It addressed (even if not entirely successfully) the specifics of the desert site, making use of technology to make the desert inhabitable. Partly this was electricity and fuel applied to the landscape, partly the use of thick walls, partly the allusions to camping with the canvas roof materials and the informal layout of the site. Taliesin West might have been a critical node in the Wright universe, but it had the informality of the campground, regardless of the actual activities on the site. The desert itself was and is a powerful presence, and the complex was a way of safely experiencing it, rather than insulating the visitor from it. It was, however imperfect as architecture, a perfect object for Banham's argument, identifying the desert as a human, cultural phenomenon as much as a natural one, and demonstrating that its mistakes (for example Wright's fury at the power lines impeding the view across to Phoenix) were as important a part of its visual culture as anything else; human interaction made the desert.

The other outstanding architectural case study in *Scenes in America Deserta* was Arcosanti, 70 miles north of Taliesin West on I-17, the visionary complex started by the transplanted Italian architect Paolo Soleri in 1970. Soleri, who had studied at Wright's architecture school, had set up a home/workshop complex called Cosanti in 1956, which trialled some of the techniques and structures that would later define Arcosanti, as well as providing an income stream for the project via its foundry, which makes the bronze wind bells found all over the complex. Arcosanti is now in its fiftieth year and continues its glacial progress towards a unitary settlement of 25,000, itself a prototype for the metropolitan-scale settlements Soleri imagined. You can stay there, arriving by a two-mile dirt track that in poor weather is close to impassable. The surrounding

Paolo Soleri, Arcosanti,
started 1970.

landscape is bleak and scrubby; the nearest town, Cordes Junction, is a scattering of gas stations and convenience stores at the junction of I-17 and Route 69. It is not a promising place. Arcosanti itself occupies one side of a steep gorge, at the bottom of which runs a river. It faces southwards, making the most of the light. You arrive at the top of the city, from which the main development drops away. The initial view is not promising, especially if you arrive at the end of a winter's day when much of the surrounding landscape can be impassable with snow. When it emerges, it is certainly strange, somewhere – it is not clear – that could be both the distant past and the future. It is a mess, first, a construction site with red earth and mud everywhere. Then some larger structures start to become clear: a five-storey multifunctional complex in *béton brut* and glass that you enter from the top, built around a three-storey atrium at the top of which runs a gallery. There is a public square covered by two concrete vaults, used intermittently for sports. Adjacent to that is the biggest and newest part of the complex, the East Crescent, built around an open-air amphitheatre and comprising flats for the sixty or so residents of the complex, including a 'sky suite', an airy roof terrace with views all over the complex to the mountainous landscape beyond. On a still day the background hum of the trucks on I-17 can be heard, but mostly the place is quiet, the silence broken by the croaking of the ravens nesting on the other side of the gorge, and the tinkling of the ubiquitous bells. In form and materials Arcosanti vaguely resembles the priory of La Tourette, Le Corbusier's last work, and also in its ecclesiastical atmosphere, an impression reinforced by the monastic demeanour of the mostly young residents who pay the Foundation for the privilege of working on the site. The image of Soleri, Arcosanti's founder, appears frequently: he smiles, saint-like, from a portrait mounted on the wall of the Vaults.

Banham wrote about Arcosanti on at least two occasions before *Scenes in America Deserta*. A very short account of it appeared in the 1976 book *Megastructure*, mainly about the pseudo-science of Arcology, which envisaged vast structures of unprecedented density leaving as much of the earth's surface as possible free of human influence. Banham didn't have much time for that, having already established himself as an apologist for human influence in *The Architecture of the Well-tempered Environment*, and of sprawl in *Los Angeles*. For these reasons it was no surprise to read his scepticism about Soleri, who, he wrote, 'emerges as a maniac for compactness; even his vastest projects are claimed to be "about miniaturisation".'[51] That was not good because it suggested a residual formalism, rather than allowing the programme to define the envelope; the best and most appealing examples of the tendency in *Megastructure* were those that had done precisely that, in other words, activating the largely unrealized potential of the New Brutalism. His scepticism about Soleri was in fact typical. Arcosanti was popular with students in architecture schools in the 1970s, but less so with architects themselves; a decade later, in one account, it was 'archaic and utterly anachronistic'.[52]

Soleri's designs were also rigid, wrote Banham, implying strict divisions of function built into the very concrete, with little possibility of change. On Arcosanti itself, his suspicion of Soleri was partly that of gurus in general, and post-Beatles gurus in particular (as seen at his IDCA confrontation in 1970, he was no hippy).[53] Banham complained that Soleri somehow had allowed the myth to develop that the project had required no energy to build, and that by extension Arcology was an architecture that had eliminated energy consumption. That was, he argued, nonsense. The myth was a result of the first parts of the complex having been constructed by hand 'using only the most primitive of technical aids. Such manual

performance which few other architectural educators have
been able to command is clearly a response to Soleri's status
as a natural guru-figure.'[54] Soleri's charisma was enough, in
other words, to persuade young people to pay for the privilege
of giving their labour, and in so doing helping to create the myth
of the zero-energy construction site.

Banham visited Arcosanti in 1976 for *New Society*, when he
could at last describe Soleri at close range: 'at once guru and
craftsman. Greying now in his cut-off shorts and workman's
vest he looks a cross between a quattrocento John the Baptist
and one of those wire-muscled Sicilians you see on building
sites in Milan and Rome.'[55] He went on to say something about
the prototypical nature of the project, and its relation to other
world buildings – at a planned 3,000 population it was not far
off J. L. Womersley's Park Hill complex in Sheffield that Banham
had reviewed so enthusiastically in 1961, but it had a baroque
quality that set it completely apart: 'a vast symphonic composition of superposed vaults and apses up to fifteen storeys high,
with another ten or so more of superstructure cragging up in
concrete above that'.[56] That was quite aside from the primitive
construction methods, with the labourers' camp down in the
valley amusing Banham with its similarity to the one that had
built Le Corbusier's designs at Chandigarh – as did the paradox
of this post-1968 generation of architects acquiring a taste
for archaic, cathedral-like forms and monumentality. Those
paradoxes drew Banham's attention, as well as, here, the same
observation that he made of Arcology in general, that it was a
mode of building that was nothing if not energy-intensive and
imposing on the landscape despite ambitions to be the opposite.
It might have been an alternative to sprawl, but it only reversed
the direction of travel from horizontal to vertical: 'Better to live
in huge superblocks and travel vertically. And get stuck in lifts,
pollute the air and overshadow the landscape? Whom art thou

kidding, Master?'[57] That scepticism was developed further in *Scenes in America Deserta*, which raised the problem that the scale of the proposed Arcologies could only be achieved with the assistance of corporate America, finance and all 'that most of Soleri's followers loudly despise'.[58] It was also a tyrannical vision: why put 25,000 people in a place that previously had none, and in a structure that by concentrating so many people in such unprecedented density might be a sociological disaster, perhaps 'as harmful to humankind as the atom bombs that were also tested in secret seclusion in these deserts'?[59]

*Scenes in America Deserta* was, however, less about architecture or even environments than it was about looking. Hence the phrase 'the eye of the beholder', which was the title of the last chapter. This chapter was both performative and theoretical, a working out of a problem seemingly in real time for the benefit of both writer and reader, the problem being how literally to see the desert.[60] It had something of a traditional art-historical approach in it: it assumed the primacy of the individual, and of the individual experience of looking, detached from any preconceived view. It supposed that an interpretation could reasonably be worked out in this way, and that the process of working out the interpretation might be the subject of the commentary. It was a rhetorical mode Banham deployed throughout his career, but perhaps most self-consciously here.[61]

In the 'The Eye of the Beholder', that mode was deployed first to attempt to account for the most fleeting conditions above the Soda Lake near Zzyzx in the Mojave. Unique atmospheric conditions caused him and his photographer to stop to capture something that would last a few minutes at most. It was a scene of 'exquisite and evanescent beauty – the time, the temperature, and the angle of the sun had together caused the early mist not to fray away in wisps and fragments, but to lift in uniform horizontal layers, which now banded the face of the mountain in pale veilings of faint luminescence'.[62] The language is partly meteorological, but here, as elsewhere, what Banham is trying to account for is a whole scene, occurring at a particular time, under particular circumstances, with multiple dimensions to it, only some of which can be captured by photography or words. It seemed to be an extension of the 'ecology' that defined *Los Angeles*, a desire to capture the completeness of a scene.[63] The language is always grasping towards something that ultimately resists description: 'pale veilings of faint luminescence'. That scene might be huge, as it is here in this Soda Lake episode, a whole landscape encapsulating geology, weather, climate and human activity. Or it could be, as it is a few pages later on, something tiny, such as, Banham wrote, 'the blown sand that wedges against the footings of the dry mountains throughout America Deserta', visually separating the mountain from the plain.[64] What followed, after a straightforwardly art-historical exploration of the eighteenth-century categories of the Sublime and the Picturesque, was the possibility, absent from Banham's writing up until this point, of a 'pure aesthetic response'.[65] What if, in other words, the desert simply *was* beautiful in a natural, unmediated way, nothing to do with any pre-existing beliefs or expectations? That question remained unanswered to the end: Banham wrote on the last page that he had 'lost' himself in the desert, 'in the sense that I now feel I understand myself less than I did before'.[66]

That acknowledgement points to a book that was more tentative than the others. There was humility about it in that Banham as Desert Freak knew the limits of what he was doing, and that he was necessarily a voyeur (to use a revealing word that cropped up repeatedly in and in relation to the book).[67] At the planning stages with Peregrine Smith, Banham was clear about both his enthusiasm for the desert and his understanding that he would be a perpetual outsider: would that, he implied, be enough? It was a position of sometimes surprising humility in relation to the desert – surprising because Banham's earlier material could sometimes be bombastic in its certainty.[68] That hedging, tentative position defines the material in the Getty archives on the project, which contain numerous fragmentary sense impressions in note form: a time recorded, the condition of a road surface, the clicking of Tim Street-Porter's camera, an epic silence.[69] The book's treatment of architectural sites went over some themes of paradox and folly familiar from *Los Angeles*, but in the end the Desert Freak was on a journey that was more about self than it was about the desert per se. What Banham did in *Scenes in America Deserta* pushed the object further than ever away from architecture, and towards (although he would not have said as much) a project of self-analysis. Whether there would have been a further development of this position is unclear: the final move of Banham's career saw a decisive snap back to architecture.

# 8  THE CONNOISSEUR OF RUINS

Banham's long association with the United States became permanent in mid-1976 when he took up the position of Chair of Design Studies at the State University of New York at Buffalo, having been courted by Harold Cohen, the ambitious Dean of Architecture. Cohen was anxious to establish an international reputation for the school and he paid above the odds to hire him.[1] It was partly a pension job for the Banhams, whose early careers had been insecure and poorly paid: America was a chance to make some money.[2] It was the end of a long period of near misses with the United States, including his participation in the International Design Conference, Aspen (IDCA), the visits to California since the mid-1960s, followed by regular teaching at UCLA and then USC from the early 1970s. What Banham had found in Los Angeles was a rich, sunny boomtown, its difficulties ameliorated by its wealth and the comfortable opportunities at well-supported institutions. Buffalo was something else. Banham arrived in the summer, along initially with his son Ben, while Mary continued to work on the Victoria & Albert Museum's exhibition about the 1951 Festival of Britain, *A Tonic to the Nation*.[3] The advance party quickly seems to have decided Buffalo was a mistake. Banham had been hired as a 'star turn', and despite his generally theatrical nature, didn't much feel like performing in the tough context of the American university.[4] And it quickly became clear that despite Cohen's excellent connections, for example with Buckminster Fuller, whom Banham admired, being at Buffalo was very different to being at UCL. He had moved, decisively, from the centre to the margins. Faculty commuted from New York or Chicago, and few had much invested in the city of Buffalo.[5] He had possibly not appreciated this in advance, insulated from the hierarchies of American academic life by the virtue of being an outsider. It was 'hugely difficult for him'.[6] He continued to write journalism for *New Society* for whom he became a de facto U.S. correspondent.[7] He never developed an equivalent presence in the U.S. media, however.[8] Buffalo itself compounded things. It had, Banham already knew, a great history of industrial architecture, although that had its limits. The architect Peter Cook thought it was a 'three day town'.[9] Since its peak in the 1950s, when it had 580,000 residents in the core city, it was down to less than 400,000, a decline of more than 30 per cent in 25 years (the figure is now 250,000, meaning a nearly 60 per cent decline from its peak).[10] The cause of the demographic decline was the collapse in the grain shipping business, which had made Buffalo the biggest and busiest such port in the world, and by 1976 had all but vanished.[11] Some vestiges of industry remained: in 1976 the sunset had a green glow from one of the last remaining steelworks in the city, although this would disappear by 1979.[12] The first four months in this city were extremely strange for the Banhams, a 'far more alien' environment than expected, and one that despite the defining presence of Polish and Italian immigrant families was unfamiliar to Europeans.[13] Then there was the winter, tougher than anything they had encountered previously in England and presenting serious challenges to Mary Banham's limited mobility. Buffalo was, on multiple levels, a challenge.

Without this salutary experience, however, Banham's last book, *A Concrete Atlantis* (1988), would never have emerged.[14] Safely removed to California, where the Banhams moved in 1980, he elected to write about Buffalo. In its choice of subject-matter it clearly alluded to some of the lived difficulties, for this more than any other book was about ruins. Here in Buffalo was a modern city in pieces, whose architectural pleasures consisted in picking over the debris, although in Banham's hands this was done with genuine love for the subject.[15] It was a straightforward piece of architectural history, unlike the hybrid form of *Scenes in America Deserta*, but like that book it contained some meditation on a civilization at its end point. Banham's interest in ruins stretched back further than that. There were hints of it in *Los Angeles: The Architecture of Four Ecologies*, where the elegiac treatment of late 1960s Venice Beach describes a failure: a mess of swampy canals and tacky approximations of the real Venice, with abandoned oil rigs and burned out piers, a resort town at the end of its days.[16] Banham's take on LA is often assumed to be relentlessly upbeat, but the book *Los Angeles* was shot through with images of decay. *Megastructure: Urban Futures of the Recent Past* (1976) most clearly located this elegiac tendency in Banham's writing.[17]

Megastructures were not ruins, but often alluded to them, whether it was in the unrefined nature of their surfaces (for example the widespread use of *béton brut*), or, in the case of the unbuilt schemes such as Archigram's Walking City, the sense of their occupying a near future in which the earth had been subject to some apocalypse; the future, in other words, might be ruined.[18] The fortified, defensive qualities of both Archigram's work and Paolo Soleri's at Arcosanti spoke to that apocalyptic imagery, without being very specific about an ethical position in relation to it (elsewhere, Banham described such imagery in terms of H. G. Wells's science fiction, suggesting an aesthetic rather than an ethical category).[19] And closely related to that impulse were the remnants of conflicts that littered the book, such as the Maunsell forts at Shivering Sands, a complex of offshore anti-aircraft gunnery platforms built off the Kent coast in 1943 and later abandoned, when they became an object of some architectural fascination.[20] The photograph Banham used

Cumbernauld Town Centre, 1967.
Cumbernauld Town Centre in 2017, after works to remove high-level access.

depicted the spectacular remnant of a country at war, an image of simultaneous advanced technology and brutality.

Precisely that quality also emerged in the images of Hans Hollein's fantasy megastructure of the USS *Enterprise* aircraft carrier stranded in the middle of generic European farmland. One of the most curious and enigmatic of all architectural images of the 1960s, it was nowhere adequately explained, least of all here, but if it could not easily be reduced to a single meaning, its imagery spoke inescapably of the ruin. Here was a great icon of military power beached, suggestive of both the ruins left behind by conflict and, albeit in some indeterminate future, the end of industrial civilization.[21]

That ruined quality was also strongly present in actual buildings in the book, such as the huge Marché Bonsecours grain elevator in Montreal, which, Banham wrote, had attracted almost as much interest as its EXPO '67 neighbours in the city.[22] It was not a ruin, but had some of the qualities of one in its indeterminate history and enigmatic state of completion/ destruction. The ruin was also present in the images of the town centre of Cumbernauld, Scotland, particularly its skeletal undercroft. Here was architecture stripped back to its most elemental forms, and neither this part of the complex nor, in the photography, the more public parts were any less ambiguous – this could have been a complex from some indeterminate time in the past.[23]

Banham was undoubtedly an enthusiast for the mega-structure.[24] But the book, although fascinated with the topic, was also depressive in tone, rather more so than the lecture he gave on the topic at Artnet in London in 1974.[25] Much of it was written in the past tense, which was to say unambig-uously that megastructures were over. Chapter One was titled 'Dinosaurs of the Modern Movement', a reference picked up later in the conclusion, which portrayed the megastructure as a fascinating and compelling folly but unambiguously a failure. 'Abandoned', collectively they were 'a whitening skeleton on the dark horizon of our recent architectural past'.[26] It was a striking image of extinction with which to begin the book, and one that recalled many of the images of decay and ruination from *Scenes in America Deserta*. Only a dozen or so true megastructures were ever built, Banham wrote, an astonishingly low number for such an allegedly important tendency. Why, he wondered, did they end up 'stranded like dinosaurs', implicitly ill-adapted and out of time, and, most importantly, extinct? Possibly, he went on,

> because the concept was faulted right through by an inner contradiction that could not be resolved. Some time around 1968 it seems to have been perceived that a city or a large part of a city designed by one man or any group unified enough to produce a comprehensible design would be a parlously thin, starved and impoverished environment both visually and in larger cultural terms . . . megastructure proved to be a self-cancelling concept.[27]

It was a tough assessment. The sometimes mournful text was full of paradoxes, pointing up megastructure's tendencies to self-sabotage and, by extension, the nature of human folly in general. Banham was writing in the aftermath of the 1973 oil crisis, which had put paid not only to his energy-intensive theory of modern design, but his equally energy-intensive vision of the western United States. Whatever Banham stood for in 1976 was, realistically, over.[28] The stranded dinosaur that appears in the conclusion of *Megastructure* was a melancholy but apt metaphor for the state of the modern movement, as well as perhaps for Banham himself.

To visit actually existing megastructures can confirm the sentiment of the book. Arcosanti, fifty years after its beginning, continues to rise into ruin (to borrow Robert Smithson's phrase) on the edge of the Arizona desert, still uncertain-looking, and as destroyed-looking as it is complete. In Scotland's central belt, Cumbernauld town centre, so prominent in *Megastructure*, is semi-abandoned now, its centre having been partially demolished at the start of the 2000s, the retail part semi-evacuated to more conventional units on its periphery. The residential parts of the town continue more or less as intended, but the monumental centre now only really exists in fragments, and one needs the photographs and plans of the original to reconstruct it in the imagination. Its now uncertain condition tends to confirm *Megastructure's* downbeat conclusion, a fact that might well have appealed to Banham. At the same time, plenty of megastructures have survived well (the Barbican Centre and South Bank in London, any number of university buildings), and the typology has arguably gained new life in China and Asia in general, although those places were beyond the scope of the book and the development happened later. From the perspective of 1976, however, the megastructure was finished, at least as a progressive idea; the mood had changed.

The elegiac mood in *Megastructure* found expression in *Scenes in America Deserta*, with its signal image of Zzyzx. What turned out to be Banham's last book, *A Concrete Atlantis*, took that mood further, exploring the city of Buffalo at the moment in its history when industry literally disappeared from its waterfront, which was also, coincidentally, the exact moment the Banhams arrived.[29] The book is also about the kind of industrial architecture in which Buffalo specialized: the grain elevator, a special kind of structure, usually concrete and often monumental, designed for storing and discharging grain by means of mechanical conveyor belts. Their distinctive forms, and the concrete from which they were made, were there to resist the immense pressures generated by grain under storage, as well as its tendency to catch fire.[30]

They had been an occasional subject in art, most popularly in the painting of the Philadelphia-born artist Charles Sheeler, who depicted them as the definitive American landscape icon.[31] Banham's first sight of them was as photographs in European architectural theory. The initial instance was an article by Walter Gropius, published in 1913 in the *Jahrbuch den Deutschen Werkbundes* (Yearbook of the German Werkbund), which famously reproduced photographs of fourteen American industrial buildings. Their fame has to do with their being reproduced again, or at least a selection of them, in Le Corbusier's articles for *L'Esprit nouveau* from 1921, later collected in a section of *Vers une architecture* in 1923.[32] At the time of their first appearance Gropius had not been to America, so what he was reproducing had something of the quality of myth about it: strange, distant architectural objects whose existence could not exactly be verified. That mythical quality was there in the book's title, the 'Atlantis' identifying a place whose existence was simultaneously believed and doubted. 'Dream analysis' is what Owen Hatherley would call these accounts, noting at the same time that the first Europeans to report on these peculiar objects were not architects but wealthy travellers, and their accounts appeared in the notoriously unreliable, myth-encrusted genre of travel writing.[33] It was a peculiar kind of European fantasy, a projection by travellers who, though fascinated, knew little of the objects that they saw and probably nothing of their inner workings.[34] Their exoticism had to do with their being characteristically American, and ubiquitous in that country. Invented in the 1820s in Buffalo, they could be found in all parts of the Americas where grain was grown.

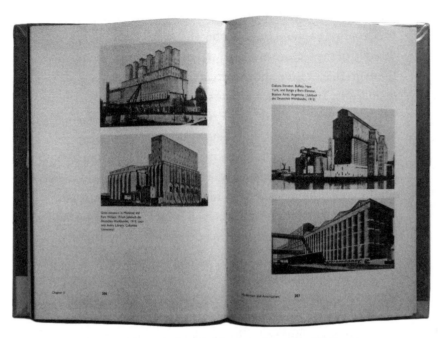

Walter Gropius, photographs from *Jahrbuch den Deutschen Werkbunde*.

The images themselves were mostly of poor quality too. Banham thought they had come from the offices of Albert Kahn, in the case of the handful of factory buildings, as well as the Atlas Portland Cement Company: 'They had obviously been rescreened from pictures that were already half-toned, and some parts may have been retouched as well.'[35] They had nevertheless fascinated Walter Gropius, who had apparently spent a year searching for them. They were 'compelling', not just to him, but to a generation of modernists on whom the effect was 'galvanic'. But the appeal seems to have been the picturesque one of the traveller, for neither Gropius nor any of the others said anything about the buildings' function. They were all about a yearning for idealized form. According to Banham's reading of a 1911 lecture by Gropius, they found in the monumental forms of the past, particularly ancient

Egypt, something adequate to the present.[36] There was
for Gropius (Banham inferred, because he did not refer
directly in the lecture to these images) something about
these grain elevators and factories that satisfied those
conditions. The *Jahrbuch* article wasn't much clearer,
Banham wrote, as it only made reference to American
architecture at the end, and then without any reference
to the enigmatic pictures (the same was true of Le Corbusier's
use of them). Their existence was therefore enigmatic, a
condition Banham resolved by reference to the art historian
Wilhelm Worringer's *Abstraction and Empathy*, first published
in 1908. Worringer's best-known book was an early argument
for abstraction as a spiritually evolved art, influential for
German avant-garde groups.[37] Worringer elaborated that
argument in his 1927 book on Egyptian art, which he thought
the ideal in terms of its purity of form; for him, Egyptian art
represented a primitive feeling awakening in modern man:
'only after the human spirit has passed, in thousands of years
of evolution along the whole course of rationalistic cognition
does the feeling for "the thing in itself" reawaken as the final
resolution of knowledge. That which was previously instinct
is now the ultimate product of cognition.'[38] In other words, the
grain elevator pictures represented, via Worringer and Gropius,
a kind of super-primitivism in which the modern had discarded
the superfluous, and in the process become spiritual.

For Gropius, the images represented the modern as noble
savage: primitive, instinctive, eternal. Le Corbusier reiterated
and considerably developed the theme, the rhetoric being
almost Futurist in its intensity, so Banham thought.[39] Here
the grain elevator was 'the guarantor of truth', architectural
truth that is; via its use of the simplest, Platonic forms, it
represented the authentic nature of modern architecture.
To make that point, Le Corbusier had not been averse to

retouching the images, in several cases erasing decoration
to make the forms simpler. It had been quite a journey from
Gropius to Le Corbusier, Banham wrote:

> what started out as high-principled but modest proposals
> for the reform of a once specialised branch of architecture
> – the design of better industrial buildings – has now become
> a presumptuous bid to possess the very soul of the Mother
> of the Arts, or at least to remind architects what the soul of
> their art could be in its most purified state.[40]

This was of course another example of Banham's scepticism
when it came to Le Corbusier, a position that had developed
in relation to two things: Le Corbusier's attitude to technology,
and the politics of his work in Britain. On the latter, Banham
was naturally sceptical about anything, or anybody with such
mainstream support, and here and elsewhere he was anxious
to puncture the myth.[41]

A *Concrete Atlantis* itself could claim to be about much
more than industrial ruins, to be in fact about a dream of
modern architecture buried in the movement's early rhetoric.
It was itself a fantasy, for neither Gropius nor Le Corbusier paid
much attention to what these industrial buildings were actually
for and how they worked. What mattered to both of them was
the form. In this, the poor quality of the pictures perversely
helped. Dark and grubby, the edges of the buildings indistinct,
they don't define any but the most basic forms (in retrospect
they look oddly like the architectural photographs of the artist-
architect Hiroshi Sugimoto, made with large-format cameras
fitted with lenses that were set intentionally beyond infinity to
suppress detail).[42] The *Jahrbuch* sequence had fourteen images:
grain elevators in Montreal and Fort William (Canada), Buenos
Aires and Bahia Blanca, Buffalo, Baltimore and Minneapolis,

factory buildings in Detroit and Cincinnati, and a Cincinnati warehouse too. You see each building typically from an angle, exaggerating both the perspective and the repetition of forms. This is especially true of the Buenos Aires building, with its forty or so silos along its frontage, like an immense Doric portico. Some of the forms suggested architectural modernism; many did not. The Montreal building was vaguely crenellated and castle-like, its stained surface suggestive of something unkempt and old. The Buenos Aires building looked similarly monumental and ancient, its columnar silos augmented by a cornice in the form of a repeated pediment, each one punctuated with an oracle. Meanwhile at the centre of the main facade there was what amounted to a portico. It wasn't one, because it gave on to no obvious opening to the building, but it was in the right place and gave the whole structure something of the look of a Greek temple. The grain elevator identified simply as South American was a blank, medieval castle in profile; adjacent to it, the twin elevators at Bahia Blanca are Gothic in profile. Both looked as if they had been abandoned. All signs of human life had been suppressed.

In Le Corbusier's treatment of the images there was a further abstraction, bringing the images closer to the way he had presented the ruins of Athens in *Vers une architecture*.[43] The Buenos Aires elevator was reproduced, but with the curious pediments removed – 'too obviously reminiscent of ancient styles', wrote Banham.[44] It made them less like historic monuments, certainly, less identifiable with a period, but also brought them into line with the way historic monuments like the Parthenon were used in the book, as exemplars of eternal forms. But overall these are strange images, neither clearly of the distant past nor the immediate present, mythical. Banham's project with regard to the images was to explore the creation and sustaining of that myth.

The idea of American industrial buildings as ruin ran all the way through A *Concrete Atlantis*, and especially in Chapter Three, by which time Banham had picked his way through the whole of the mournful landscape of contemporary Buffalo. He was certainly drawn to industrial ruin as the exemplar of some kind of new primitivism: early in the book he described 'works of engineering . . . happily co-opted as manifestations of a kind of modern "noble savagery" compatible with twentieth century styles of life' that 'could be held up as models for emulation'.[45] The industrial building was a primitive type, an authentic form that paradoxically held access to the pre-modern world. The understanding of the buildings as ruins was clear enough in relation to Buffalo, where there was no ambiguity that that was what they had become. The buildings of the river frontage, Banham wrote,

> do have an almost Egyptian monumentality in many cases and in abandonment and death they evoke the majesties of a departed civilization. Or so it used to seem to me looking downstream on the Buffalo river from the angle of South Street. On either side of the water, like an avenue of mighty tombs, were structures representing almost the whole history of the grain elevator . . . it was a privilege to know them in their ravaged antique grandeur.[46]

It is remarkable, in retrospect, for Banham to be describing the United States in this way, a measure, perhaps, of the shock of the transition to Buffalo at this moment, of its divergence from the U.S. of Banham's previous imagination. It was no longer, seen from Buffalo at least, a country representing a future, personal or political, but the reverse. And if Buffalo's industrial decline had continued unabated, it had also begun the process of capital-led transformation of its waterfront, and the ruin scenario was itself in decline.[47]

Banham nevertheless made a lot of it. The history of the Daylight Factory, the basis of Chapter One, described the United Shoe Machinery Company building in Beverly, Massachusetts, as wearing a 'Pompeian air of elegant and antique decay'.[48] The Pacific Coast Borax factory, an early concrete-framed structure, attracted his attention because it famously (in 1902) survived a catastrophic fire, and was used by its designers to promote the virtues of building in concrete: an image reproduced from the Atlas Portland Cement Company's *Reinforced Concrete in Factory Construction* (1915) makes the point, a surreal mass of melted steel, attesting to concrete's ability to withstand the ferocity of the fire. A sort of condensed apocalypse, it was a further illustration of the modern world containing the seeds of its

The Pacific Coast Borax factory showing fire damage.

own destruction. It was in the chapter on the grain elevator, however, that Banham gave full rein to his picturesque imagination, in an account of what was popularly known as Concrete Central:

> the first time I reached Concrete Central by land a series of incidents emphasized its abandonment and isolation. Shrubbery had already begun to grow out of its upper works, inviting a comparison with Roman ruins that was enhanced by the flight of a bird of prey from the head-house at the sound of my approach. That sound was amplified when my foot crashed through a rotted plywood cover that had been laid over an open culvert. As I extricated myself I reflected on my folly: had I sustained an incapacitating injury rather than mere scratches in that fall even those who knew approximately where I was would have had no idea how to reach me after they had finally decided they had waited too long for my return. I remembered the fate of the Chicago architectural photographer Richard Nickel, lying dead in the ruins of the Schiller theatre for weeks before his body was discovered. Yet the distance from help and civilization was exhilarating rather than depressing: the presence of the huge abandoned structure produced a mood more elegiac than otherwise . . . it was difficult not to see everything through eighteenth century picturesque visions of ancient sites or even Piranesi's views of the temples of Paestum. Longer study however suggested something more like the view that early Christian pilgrims might have taken of Rome: a double vision of something that was in itself ancient and therefore to be revered but was also to be respected for newer body of meanings laid over it by the beliefs of later peoples. I was looking at the great remains of a high and mighty period of constructive art in North America. But at a slight

cultural remove I was also – inevitably given my European
and Modernist education in architecture – looking at
a monument to a different civilisation that had been as
unknown to its builders as Christianity had been to the
builders of most of the monuments in Rome: the culture
of the European modern movement.[49]

Here was the architectural historian again as the Grand Tourist,
the detritus of the modern world standing in for ancient Rome.[50]
Robert Venturi and Denise Scott Brown were again a possible
point of comparison.[51] Banham returned to the conceit
repeatedly and it was a critical part of *Scenes in America Deserta*.
The book contains countless images of ruins, and in retrospect
it belongs to a tradition of criticism about industrial ruins that
was partly about their rising status in architecture at the time,
particularly when reused for cultural buildings.[52] It would go
on to preoccupy – frequently – journals of cultural criticism

Concrete Central, Buffalo, c. 1977. Photo by Reyner Banham.

Concrete Central, Buffalo, c. 1977. Photo by Reyner Banham.

such as *October*, in which Banham would have no place until years after his death – but the fact that he would be celebrated there is some indication that his work touched on some of the same concerns. For a journal like *October*, the ruin was an ambiguous object. In the right hands it was an allegorical device, a means of reading against industrial modernity and finding a way to critique its inherent positivism, to reveal it as myth.[53] At the same time, in architecture, the re-emergence of the ruin was as often as not understood as reactionary, certainly by those, such as Kenneth Frampton, who maintained a belief in the modern project. To deploy the imagery of the ruin in architecture in, for example, Charles Moore's work was to accept that architecture was little more than the play of surfaces, 'scenography', as Frampton had it, and the opposite of the supposed integrity of modernism.[54] Or the reuse of industrial ruins might be something actively hostile to the progressive version of the modern project: a means of occupying working-class space for the use of another class, the process generally

Concrete Central, Buffalo, c. 1977. Photo by Reyner Banham.

termed gentrification.[55] To associate oneself with ruins in the
1980s was not therefore straightforward; there were cultural
wars to fight, and as often as not, to align oneself with the ruin
was to align with the forces of reaction. The cult of the ruin
meant the abandonment of agency, of faith in the future, of
industry in general.

So where was Banham in all this? What were his ruin
politics? The question is a complex, and probably unresolvable,
one because Banham's own position changed according to
when he was writing, and in which context; there was at
various times and places an anti-picturesque Banham, that
found in the cult of the ruin a deadly reaction to the potential
of the modern movement. That was the Banham of 'The New
Brutalism', which as we saw earlier was an ethic of abrupt
and unresolvable contrasts and plain speaking. That position
was meant to needle the architectural establishment, and its
promotion of a stable, inclusive aesthetic in which the old could
be safely incorporated in the new and, implicitly, controlled.
This ameliorative and inclusive aesthetic supposed continuity
between past and present, and was the opposite of the Futurist-
oriented modern movement Banham had advocated in *Theory
and Design in the First Machine Age*, and then the New Brutalism.
The *Architectural Review*'s picturesque was meant to heal: in the
form of *The Bombed Buildings of Britain*, written by the journal's
editor, J. M. Richards, it argued that the recent destruction of
the Blitz could be recuperated for aesthetic pleasure, a position
that required, to say the least, a selective engagement with the
viewed subject.[56] In the words of the historian John Brewer on
the topic, the viewer of picturesque scenes is a 'spectator' rather
than a part of the viewed world. The inhabitants of that world,
be they Welsh peasant farmers or 'the sturdy husbandsmen
of Georgic poetry . . . were supposed to be self-sufficient, self-
contained, inhabiting a world that the tourist might admire but

never inhabit'.[57] The picturesque tourist, in other words, was never going to be the shepherd tending his flocks among the ruins of the Roman Forum, although he might fleetingly wish he was.

Banham's journalism for the *Architectural Review* was unequivocally anti-picturesque. He drew on his class background, his family's interests and his own training as an engineer to identify with the subjects of modernism. Unlike the picturesque tourists who kept their distance from the local peasants, Banham was with them, or their latter-day architectural equivalents, the engineers and builders.[58] But by the end of the 1960s and his visits to the United States he had constructed more of a touristic persona. The character in *Reyner Banham Loves Los Angeles* is in some respects a stereotypical Englishman Abroad, whose progress through the Californian metropolis is as full of comic incident as it is well informed. So it was with the ruins of Buffalo. As an ex-engineer, he had the confidence to explain the grain elevator's workings, but at the same time Banham was never going to work in a grain elevator, and his fascination for the form dated from the point at which they had fallen into disuse. They had not appeared in his writings before, and it was only as ruins that they did now, and his attitude to them in general with its allusions to Egyptian ruins was broadly ameliorative: the ruin as exemplar of a natural order that could not be changed, only accepted. Banham was arguably no longer the engineer, but the tourist.

Perhaps. It is a little too neat to argue that because the last part of the book brings the narrative right back to Futurism, and specifically the Fiat factory at Turin-Lingotto by the company's chief engineer Giacomo Matté-Trucco, built on a vast scale between 1914 and 1926. A single structure five storeys high, it is half a kilometre long and built with a banked test track on the roof, where cars were driven for the first time at the end of a production process that saw their construction rise vertically through the building. It was an important place for Banham to finish for several reasons, the first being the American design: Matté-Trucco designed the factory using existing American Daylight Factory principles, and Banham thought it looked most like Ernest Ransome's United Shoe Machinery Company plant (1903–6), which he had described much earlier. There was something melancholy about the Fiat factory, he wrote, because it was twenty years out of date, the Ransome design being from the turn of the century, the main body of the Fiat factory coming into use around 1920. To visit it is to visit a chapter in world history that is now closed: like the abandoned grain elevators of Buffalo, the Fiat factory was, Banham wrote, 'a kind of testament to a lost future'.[59]

That was not the whole story, however, because a large part of the account of the building has Banham driving (or more likely being driven) around the test track, which although flawed in both concept and execution was also a space of genuine wonder. The flaws were straightforward enough: apart from being on the roof, the most inconvenient place for the last part of the production process, the tightness of the track's curves made nonsense of its intention to test high-speed driving. But the wonder was real enough, the track 'magnificent', less a functional track than a symbolic crown for the factory and modern Italy in general – if that was what Banham was saying, he underlined it a few lines later by declaring it 'one of the sacred spaces of European modernism', along with a few words to the effect that it was, symbolically at least, still alive, looking exactly as it did in the first photographs.[60]

Then there were the images Banham used, especially those by Claudia Dapra, showing a building perfectly intact and, if not in actual use, in no sense a ruin as the Buffalo buildings were. The image of the test track is particularly striking, for example, a near-abstract composition of asphalt, banking and sky, pulling the factory away from history. On the opposite page is a smaller aerial view of the complex, supplied by Fiat themselves and dating from 1970, and looking from this angle rather like a megastructure (this in fact was the way Kenneth Frampton described it).[61] A megastructure – or perhaps a New Brutalist structure, with the frank, irresolvable juxtaposition of modernity and environment. In any case, however these images were meant, they did not exactly communicate a sense of ruination, but something else, something still capable of activation.

That implication, if it is not too much of a stretch, was certainly there in the closing six pages, which were given over entirely to a poetic description of the factory by a young designer and art critic, Edoardo Persico, briefly co-editor of the prestigious journal *Casabella* before his death in 1935. Persico's account ends the book, with no further comment from Banham; he eulogized the factory, in particular its test track, which he regarded as being in exactly the right place: 'Only the track is free beneath the heavens and before God.' The factory as a whole he saw as a means of producing a higher, modern order: the ramps' spirals, he wrote, 'are indeed a road to human liberty, where everything is elaborated in the individual, fused into the mass, and is integrated into a unity'.[62] This ecstatic, visionary account of the Fiat factory is anything but reactionary – it is Futurist in sensibility, and in placing it at the end of the book, Banham temporarily re-invoked the revolutionary potential of that moment. In doing that, leaving the reader in that place, he colours the previous accounts too, looping back to the New Brutalism. To return to Futurism in this way kept open the possibility, so clear in *Theory and Design in the First Machine Age*, of a technologically literate modern movement. This temporary

return to Futurism was a common theme in the reviews.[63] Nigel
Whiteley wrote,

> it reminds us that Banham's emotional home in the
> Modern Movement was Futurism and that his last major
> contribution to the revaluation and revision of the modern
> movement ends with a discussion – even a celebration – of
> a symbolically Futurist building which he had originally
> discussed nearly thirty years earlier without changing his
> mind about it.[64]

*A Concrete Atlantis* was therefore something of a hybrid
position: it revisited, if briefly, the techno-optimism of the
early work, but the mood was now predominantly elegiac, as
shown in a short, very late piece of writing in an exhibition
catalogue on the photography of the German duo Bernd and
Hilla Becher.[65] The Bechers had painstakingly documented
typologies of industrial architecture for decades, photographing
water towers, pit-head buildings and steelworks in monochrome
on a large-format camera with long exposures, a technique that
involved a great deal of technical skill and patience. The care
with which the work was done, and its superficial thoroughness,
was suggestive in the first instance of a Victorian taxonomy of
genres of birds or plants – but the Bechers never provided any
commentary on their images, and that fact, combined with the
anthropomorphic, portrait orientation of most the images and
their repetition, gave them a surreal quality that made them
incontrovertibly art. Banham was wise to that, writing how the
Bechers had helped produce a genuinely postmodern sensibility,
and had in fact become an 'essential part' of it; they had helped
'historicize' the monuments of modernism and render them
safely distant, making any return to the conditions of modernity
inconceivable. 'In the Postindustrial epoch', he wrote, 'we

believe we inhabit the common and ubiquitous monuments
of industry must be deprived of their power to inspire art
or – worse – progress.'[66] The Bechers achieved that through
the deadpan quality of their images, rendering the functional
a matter of aesthetics. That would seem to be a criticism
(Banham had, after all inveighed against postmodernism,
dismissing it as 'silly' at least ten times in a review of Charles
Jencks's book *The Language of Postmodern Architecture*).[67] If the
point of the modern movement was revolution, of harnessing
the transformative potential of technology, as he had argued
in *Theory and Design*, then these images of industrial ruins
were the reverse, making the industrial age seem remote
and a return to it largely inconceivable. All of which sounds
critical, but there was a softening of tone halfway through. The
Bechers' photographs represented something like the frailty
of the human condition, the persistence of folly (for example
in the half-timbered decoration Banham noticed on one of the
exhibition's water towers) and the inevitability of decay; nature
would inevitably take over and it was silly to pretend otherwise.
But while it stood, its 'teeming fecundity' was 'a standing
reproach to the frozen categories of official art'.[68] In other words,
the ruin had a purpose after all – to show up the limitations
of the category of art, revealing qualities of invention hidden
in plain sight. To recognize the ruin was on the one hand to
capitulate to the forces of reaction. On the other, it was to
recognize that invention might not be programmable; it might
be as much chance and indeterminacy as anything. It is a short,
commissioned piece that needs to affirm the Bechers' art, but
for all that it well represents Banham's changing thought.

Banham's later approach, sensitive to the traffic in images
and their mediatization, and the way these things picked at
narratives of progress, put him in the intellectual company
of others at the time whose work revisited the project of

modernism, such as the journal *October*, although there was
then no direct connection. Craig Owens's 1980 essay on postmodernism and allegory is one possible point of contact;[69] in
that essay Owens reclaimed allegory as a space of action for
contemporary art, and in so doing evolved a theory of postmodernism. Banham, a generation older and still ostensibly
clinging to modernism, is an unlikely comparison here in
some ways, but his understanding of the grain elevator as an
allegorical device put him in the same company, as well as
identifying the way images can trouble reality. Banham's
approach to the industrial ruins meant fascination with the
traffic of images, acceptance of the economic transformations
that had made it come about, and scepticism of their appropriation as sites for culture. Banham embodied that attitude
in practice and the work, as much as it is a piece of academic
research, was also the result of numerous informal urban
explorations that have a tradition all of their own. As Daniel
Campo described in an article about Buffalo that made much
of Banham, Buffalo's industrial architecture was the site of a
culture typical of what it termed 'weak market' cities, in other
words, places where the scope for the aggressive appropriation
of such buildings by the market was unlikely.[70] Instead, Buffalo's
remaining ruins (in this case a group of three unmodified silos
known locally as Silo City) were the site of various forms of
low-key cultural appropriation in which whimsy, chance and
the eccentric were much more important than any profit motive.
These practices celebrated the indeterminate present condition
of Buffalo's ruins, neither mourning the loss of the industrial
past, nor seeking to hasten their commercial redevelopment; in
a relatively sluggish economy such as Buffalo's, such a mediated
position was possible.

To use Banham's terminology from 1960, Buffalo's grain
elevators were a story about the First Machine Age. As it happens,

he could write about the Second Machine Age in exactly the same mode. In 1987 he wrote about Silicon Valley for the Italian architectural journal *Casabella*, arguing in a way that was both prescient and entirely mistaken that Silicon Valley had met its 'end'.[71] Banham's understanding of the place in 1987 was as a ruin: 'What can be seen along Stierlin Rd is in many senses the End of Silicon Valley, for the Days of Glory in the electronics industry are over.' His emblem was the Fairchild Instrument Corp's headquarters building on Ellis Street, Mountain View, built in 1967 and twenty years later abandoned and boarded up, along with much more recent buildings on Stierlin Road, many in a vaguely Michael Graves-postmodern style, a fact that no doubt pleased Banham, who had made his distaste for that style perfectly clear.[72] He also enjoyed the tendency of the nearby Bayshore Amphitheatre to self-combust due to its being built on a garbage dump, producing large quantities of methane, 'like some Old Testament vision of Divine Vengeance'.[73] He failed to anticipate Silicon Valley's extraordinary later resurgence (he was far from alone). No matter – what is important here is a shift in attitude from one early in the career straightforwardly celebratory of technology, to here a far more sceptical attitude in which technology contained the seeds of its own destruction. This image of Silicon Valley lying literally in ruins has a lot in common with the images of industrial Buffalo in *A Concrete Atlantis*. The encounter with the United States started as an encounter with the future, ending as an encounter with ruins, industrial or otherwise; Banham was their connoisseur.

# 9 REYNER BANHAM REVISITED

At the start of 1987 Banham was appointed Sheldon H. Solow
Professor of the History of Architecture at the Institute of Fine
Arts, New York University. He joked with Donald Posner of the
Institute about his age: 'you do realise how old I am, I trust . . .
Though I am currently in rude good health there must be an
increased actuarial risk of my suddenly slumping dead across
the seminar table.'[1] Nine months later he admitted to the
architect Dennis Sharp that he had undergone 'heavy surgery'
for colon cancer.[2] Six months after that, on 19 March, he was
dead, aged just 66, having never taken up the post. He spent
his last weeks in the oncology unit at the Royal Free Hospital,
in Hampstead, London, on one of the upper floors, with a view
of the Heath. The hospital, appropriately enough, was a late
flowering of Brutalism and one of the first buildings designed
with CAD.[3] He knew has was dying, but visitors reported his
fascination with the equipment that was keeping him alive, a
predictable if slightly morbid turn of attention, and one entirely
in line with his earlier technological rationalizations of difficult
life experience.[4] He wrote a story too that now only exists in the
memory of the family among whom it was circulated. 'The Wall'
was a fantasy of flying his hospital bed to New York to take up
the NYU appointment, only to be frustrated by the lead-lined
wall on one side of his hospital room. It was the last piece he
ever wrote, circulated among family only, and now lost.[5]

There were many obituaries on his death, most stressing
his role as a critic and the singular, sometimes eccentric nature
of his contribution to architecture and academic life.[6] The BBC
rebroadcast the Los Angeles film, introduced by Norman
Foster, as a tribute.[7] A series of lectures on design history was

inaugurated at the Victoria & Albert Museum in London in his memory, with contributions from global scholars, a book eventually resulting from the series.[8] In academic terms, the discipline of design history in Britain, through the Design History Society and its journal the *Journal of Design History*, took inspiration explicitly from Banham's career and life, developing a pragmatic, object-oriented approach to mass culture. It diverged markedly from the discipline of art history at this point, leaving implicit the debates about social class, gender and politics that had convulsed it from the mid-1980s onwards in the guise of the New Art-history; Banham provided a pragmatic model for doing design history, one whose politics were implied rather than made explicit.[9] Banham, however, played no major part in the disciplinary debates in art history in the 1980s.[10]

Banham's legacy is an uncertain one despite his familiarity. He might be inescapable if you are studying Brutalism, or the architecture of Los Angeles, and at the time of writing many still remember him as a journalist. But it is harder to identify a school of Banham, exactly, apart from perhaps among design historians, and even then they describe a set of interests in particular objects, rather than an intellectual approach.[11] The work is often at first sight tactical rather than strategic, and it is consequently sometimes hard to identify a consistent body of theory in Banham's writings. In this he is unlike the German-trained art historians from whose tradition he emerged in the 1950s, as well as the structuralist and poststructuralist writers' tradition with which he overlapped at least in terms of the interest in mass culture. His position can seem at times wholly pragmatic, contingent on his audience. This was broadly Nigel Whiteley's view of Banham.[12] It was also the view of the architectural critic Robert Maxwell, who wrote that Banham was not only a pragmatist but he thought that 'pragmatics are

or can be, independent of ideology. The pragmatic is his base for
criticism of architectural ideologies, and the fact that it is always
identified by a concrete instance obscures the critical role it
plays as a category.'[13] As the middle part of his career showed,
Banham's pragmatism, if that is what it was, could be seen as
allied to the architectural and political establishment. That
view was certainly what caused the conflict with the French
delegation at IDCA in 1970, and it certainly informs the view
of Banham who appears at the start of Felicity Scott's book on

History Faculty, West Road, Cambridge: Reyner Banham with his camera on
the catwalk.

architecture and technology during the Cold War, *Architecture or Techno-utopia.*[14]

Banham has been widely viewed as a pragmatist; he has also been seen as anti-academic, an idea he in part cultivated.[15] That might have been disingenuous given that an academic was what Banham precisely was, but it was there in 'The New Brutalism' with its attack on the New Art-history, and then again in the engagement with Los Angeles, which alighted on things calculated to offend academic sensibilities.[16] The pragmatism and anti-academicism could lead to a view that Banham was anti-theory, and from time to time Banham would elaborate an argument to that effect. The 1964 talk 'The Atavism of the Long-distance Mini-cyclist' was one such argument to that effect, staking out an anti-doctrinaire, pragmatic, theory-averse position in relation to mass culture that said one should be, broadly speaking, allowed to consume what one wanted.[17] In 1969's jointly authored 'Non-plan', there was a memorably apolitical conclusion: Marx, in the consumer world of children's toys, was known as the maker of brightly coloured plastic dumper trucks. 'Let's become that sort of Marxist.'[18] Banham's scepticism to theory cropped up too in the 1974 lecture on megastructures, with its digs at the Internationale Situationiste and 'dear old Guy Debord'; the IS were full of 'nuts', a view that Banham could no doubt equally have applied to the environmental protestors who disrupted the 1970 IDCA. Although Banham on occasion sided with student activism in the late 1960s, he was more often than not seemingly the voice of the establishment.

The pragmatism could on occasion seem cosy and self-regarding: that 1974 lecture was given to an audience of friends and supporters, some of whom (members of Archigram, for example) were cited in the lecture. And although in the beginning, through his embrace of Futurism and consumer

culture, Banham was an outsider, by the early 1970s he had in
some respects become the (architectural, at least) establishment.
It was hard to recognize challenges to the establishment from
wherever they came, hence the uncertain (but also interesting)
approach to environmentalism; ultimately this came down to
a matter of aesthetic preferences, hence also the distaste for
vernacular architecture. This may explain the difficulty with
postmodernism as an architectural style ('silly') because it
did not emerge looking like a challenge, or the reaction to
Modernism posed by David Watkin's deliberately provocative
book *Morality and Architecture*.[19] Banham excoriated Watkin
in a 1978 review of the book, but concentrated his fire on the
perceived misunderstanding of Modernism and Modernists,
rather than the visceral reaction that lay at the heart of Watkin's
argument. Watkin had deliberately misunderstood Pevsner,
but the argument had more of the character of a present-day
culture war in which Watkin, despite his apparent privilege,
was actually the insurgent. To disentangle that, Banham could
actually have used some of the structuralist theory he batted
away in an aside: 'the kind of epistemological seizure exhibited
by Levi-Straussians when someone uses the word "structural"
to describe the way a building, not a myth is put together'.[20]

Banham's last, unfinished, project was a history of High
Tech architecture commissioned by the German publisher
Axel Menges.[21] Banham referred to it in the draft NYU lecture
as *Making Architecture*, and notes towards it remain one of
the more extensive parts of the papers deposited in the Getty
archives. Banham's initial approach to High Tech architecture
had been ambivalent, at least on the evidence of his 1977
review of the Centre Georges Pompidou, which was sceptical
about the architectural programme of flexibility.[22] The new
project, although provisionally subtitled *The Paradoxes of High
Tech*, promised, on the evidence of the surviving draft of the

introduction, something more straightforwardly celebratory of a tendency that by 1987 was becoming the default style for capital (the Hong Kong and Shanghai Bank), global insurance (Lloyds) and luxury cars (Porsche). To write about it at this moment was quite different from writing about New Brutalism in 1955, or deserts in 1982: the project in this vestigial form lacked the same critical urgency.

## A Theory of Banham

It is easy enough to construct Banham as an anti-theorist, an object-oriented pragmatist, whose politics were those of the technological expert, not the barricade. He invites you to do this himself some of the time at least, in that earthy voice and straightforward prose, apparently a man of plain speech and ordinary tastes. This is the surface all readers of Banham have to deal with, and yet it is misleading because Banham's career was driven by theories as much as anything else. Those theories do not easily map onto what 'theories' have later come to mean in the humanities and social sciences, because Banham was effectively on the wrong side of the barricades in his own 1968 moment (IDCA 1970), and he also liked things – cars, aeroplanes, gadgets – that were in themselves suspect for left-leaning cultural theorists.

But Banham's theoretical world was certainly more complex than the pragmatist caricature, and it is important not to overlook, for example, both the title and the content of his first book. *Theory and Design in the First Machine Age* was a book of grand ideas and abstractions rather than concrete objects; the rhetoric of presence, of 'being there', that would later become so important is not there at all. Then there is 'The New Brutalism', with its manifesto-like abstractions, the environmental work and its probing of what 'environment' meant in terms of architecture, the rhetoric of 'ecologies' in *Los Angeles*, and the inquiry into vision in *Scenes in America Deserta*, and ruins in *A Concrete Atlantis*. All of these questions had a politics; the work was far from untheoretical, even if it did not always share the same preoccupations as what counted for theory elsewhere.

Two pieces from 1988 and (posthumously) 1990 indicate something of this theoretical complexity, and why Banham remains worth revisiting. The undelivered NYU inaugural address can be found in draft form in Banham's papers at the Getty.[23] It was subsequently republished in *Art in America* as 'Actual Monuments'.[24] The inauguration was set for 8 February 1988, the lecture titled slightly differently as a 'A Set of Actual Monuments'. Content-wise, it was, at least to begin with, seemingly the most pragmatic and most conventional statement of what it was to be an architectural historian, although it *was* also that rare thing in Banham, a statement of method. It dealt with the legacy of Henry-Russell Hitchcock, as the previous occupant of a professorial chair in architectural history at NYU's Institute of Fine Arts, Banham's most direct predecessor. Hitchcock had collaborated with Philip Johnson on the groundbreaking 1932 exhibition at MOMA *Modern Architecture*, and he was the chief author of the accompanying book *The International Style: Architecture since 1922*; together the book and the exhibition invented and popularized the term International Style, and Banham's talk partly had that project as a starting point.[25]

The talk, however, was less about the International Style than the manly business of doing architectural history. If architectural history was worth anything, Banham declared at the outset, it was about the direct experience of buildings in the world, which might well be physically gruelling or even risky. Pevsner, his PhD supervisor, he wrote, 'certainly *intended* to see every building of architectural note in the country and usually succeeded since he came back from the field trips completely exhausted' (Banham's emphasis).[26] He went on: 'the life of a hands-on historian can be rewarding but very tough – and actually dangerous if, like me, you have to explore ancient pipes and ducts or clamber about on the roofs of crumbling grain elevators,' referring of course to his recently published work on American industrial architecture, with its vivid account of his exploration of the more dilapidated parts of Buffalo.[27] Banham invoked Robert Maxwell about the 'Rhetoric of Presence' for the theory: 'I have been there and seen for myself and that is my license to speak.'[28] This ultra-pragmatic view of architectural history was the one espoused by Hitchcock, who, Banham wrote, avoided 'theory and ideology' in favour of the collection of evidence at first hand and the cataloguing and codification that goes along with that (he did not trouble himself with the idea, perfectly accessible by 1988, that the positivism of such activities might itself be evidence of theory and ideology (the point earlier made by Maxwell on his pragmatism).[29] Banham quoted Hitchcock approvingly from *The International Style*, 'architecture is always a set of actual monuments, not a vague corpus of theory.'[30] This was 'fighting talk', he went on, and would be still in the present day, admitting that now to deny theory would be the part that would have attracted attention ('there is no ideologue so ideological as the one who claims he isn't' – perhaps he had taken on Maxwell's aside after all).[31]

So far so clear: Banham was inheriting Hitchcock's chair, and the first half of the talk seemed to yearn for a return to his traditional architectural values, so much so that it is sometimes hard to disentangle Hitchcock from Banham. But it was misleading, deliberately so, because the second half of the lecture focused on what was not concrete: what was mediated, insecure and contingent, a radically expanded

view of architecture that can be identified in retrospect as
Banham's legacy. In the talk it was played out in the story of
*The International Style*, the book that accompanied the 1932
MOMA exhibition *Modern Architecture*.[32]

Banham elaborated its evolution from the 1932 edition
to the 1966 Norton paperback version, the one most widely
in circulation, from detailed changes to the title, to additions by
Hitchcock that quietly asserted his authorship over that of his
co-author Philip Johnson, to the rotation of the pictures
90 degrees so they would work in the smaller format:

> What had been an object of high impact architectural
> propaganda, every page opening clear and patent, has
> now become a text to be pored over. What had been an

Reyner Banham photographing a building in Sunnyvale, California,
c. 1983. Photo by Ben Banham.

object to be handled with pleasure is now just another academic paperback with the usual muddy illustrations on dull paper stock. And a travesty of the original.[33]

Architectural history, he went on, was not just a 'set of actual monuments', but it was also a 'set of actual books' and 'a set of actual historians', one of which was naturally Banham himself.[34] It was a rhetorically brilliant conclusion, turning what was otherwise a highly conventional essay in the 'rhetoric of presence' ('I was there') into something congruent with contemporary trends in theory. Here was an essay in what the architectural theorist Beatriz Colomina would later call the mediatization of architecture, which is to say the idea that architecture might be constituted in images, texts and other ephemera as much as buildings, the implication being that the real and the ephemeral were constantly in play, constantly conditioning each other, and always contingent.[35]

It was also implicitly an argument about institutional history and, through art practice, the idea of institutional critique. Banham did not use that concept, but he appeared to be working with the same ideas in that lecture: thinking about how a discipline (architectural history) makes its way in the world, with what tools and conventions, and what institutional frameworks. Institutional history was critical to art history at the time.[36] Banham challenged the architectural object here in a process that, although it might not have used the most fashionable vocabulary, was in other respects on trend. He merely described here what he had been doing all along throughout his career: his objects were in fact only sometimes those that could be visited, and in the case of a book like *Los Angeles*, they dissolved largely into representation. Setting himself up as a superficially traditional historian of architecture, Banham could also effectively oversee architecture's dissolution, increasingly the implication of the later work with its focus on landscapes and environments.[37]

Dissolution is too strong a word, perhaps, although there were certainly times when Banham did seem to want that. He certainly envisaged architecture as something inherently pluralistic: architecture was buildings, and the materials used to make them stand up, but it was also simultaneously its theory and history, its representation and apprehension by others, and architecture as an ineffable, contingent experience. If there is some theoretical consistency to be recovered from Banham, it is perhaps this radically expanded view of architecture, one that led in the later work towards an attempt to describe the whole environment, most vividly that of the high desert. The inaugural lecture did not describe all of that trajectory, but it was a powerful restatement of Banham's expanded understanding of architecture. The frustration with a conventional, object-oriented view of architecture surfaced again in what was to be the last of Banham's major articles to be published, eighteen months after his death. 'A Black Box: The Secret Profession of Architecture' appeared, appropriately, in the *New Statesman and Society* (Banham had contributed frequently to both magazines; they had recently merged).[38] It consisted in what seem now like valedictory reflections on the profession of architecture from the point of view of one who was intimately involved with it, but never wholly a part. Its startling opening paragraph divided the built world into architecture and non-architecture, based on recent visits to London to see the Lloyds Building under construction; Banham identified Nicholas Hawksmoor's interior of St Mary Woolnoth clearly as architecture, Christopher Wren, amazingly, not.[39] It didn't matter how striking St Paul's might be from Ludgate Hill, he thought; it wasn't architecture, but scenography. Similarly, whereas

Soane could do some 'pretty ugly stuff', thinking of the lantern of the mausoleum at Dulwich Picture Gallery, he continued, 'the result leaves us in no doubt that Sir John Soane was an absolute architect.'[40] Wren as a scene-maker, Hawksmoor as an architect: a strange, unexpected, counter-intuitive formulation, but one that makes more sense when one understands architecture as a three-dimensional spatial experience.

Confusingly for the non-initiate, Banham's thinking could include architecture and non-architecture in the same building. So at the recently completed AT&T headquarters in New York by Philip Johnson, the bottom of the building (he was thinking of the capacious and complex seven-storey lobby) was architecture in his view, but the upper levels not, and certainly not the controversial broken pediment at the top, which gave this 200-metre (660 ft) tower the look of a Chippendale chair.[41] Those upper parts, he wrote in an aside that would be inappropriate now, bore the same relation to architecture as 'female impersonation. It is not architecture but building in drag.'[42] It was a straightforward defence of modernism, in other words, and a moral position with a long pedigree.

But there was something both more complex and more personal about the piece, because it went on to attack the profession of architecture both for its opacity about what it did, and what it itself believes to be architecture. Banham relates an anecdote of being involved in a studio class, defending a piece of student work that had been criticized by colleagues. A design for a penthouse apartment, it appeared to satisfy all the criteria for the project, but it wasn't architecture, according to those colleagues, because it had been done in ballpoint pen, on 'what appeared to be institutional toilet paper'.[43] It revealed, Banham wrote, that the professional understanding of architecture was about something other than the design of buildings, and that the studio was in effect a 'tribal

longhouse' intent on perpetuating traditions for their own
sake. What architecture is, or was, was never clear to those
outside the longhouse; it was just understood by the initiates.
(The simile is an intriguing one, attacking in a single image
of a building Western architecture's sense of privilege and
sophistication.) But what was it that architects, as opposed
to engineers, or designers or builders, uniquely did? Banham
replied to his own rhetorical question: 'The answer, alas, is
that they do "architecture" and we are thus back at the black
box with which we began.' The conclusion was pessimistic.
What to do? Architecture could

> permit itself to be opened up to the understandings of the
> profane and the vulgar, at the risk of destroying itself as an
> art in the process. Or it could close ranks and continue as a
> conspiracy of secrecy, immune from scrutiny, but perpetually
> open to the suspicion, among the general public that there
> may be nothing at all inside the black box except a mystery
> for its own sake.[44]

They were effectively Banham's last published words,
and they described not only an intellectual position on the
profession of architecture but, you could say, a subject position.
Here was Banham himself, as close as it was possible to get to
architecture without being an architect, lacking – perhaps? – the
sorcery of class privilege to make the leap. Whatever Banham's
relation to architecture was exactly, a sense of its exclusiveness
endured for him. But that was exclusiveness defined on the
profession's terms; *his* architecture, as we have seen was open,
multiple, inclusive and many things besides buildings; and in
spite of his reputation for pragmatism, many of the things that
architecture might be in the end were theories. His architecture
was ideas as much as it was anything else.

## Reyner Banham Revisited

How do we revisit Banham, now? Given the volume of his production, its variety and its interdisciplinarity, there is an understandable tendency to wish to pin Banham down. But as this book has argued, there were probably more Banhams than even Todd Gannon has suggested, each project describing a new subject position.[45] There could be overlaps and contradictions; a seeming trajectory towards one thing could be diverted, or looped back upon, as arguably was the case with the last writings that seemed at some level to wish for a return to a straightforward form of architectural history, after a set of detours into the environment. It is also worth saying too that Banham's interests were not unique. He was a remarkable and singular individual, as posthumous assessments made clear: the astonishing volume of his output is one measure of that, as well as his unique public presence. But his concerns did not emerge from nowhere but were representative of, broadly speaking, group situations. He was unusually conscious of social class, as were those of his generation who were often the first to study at university level. His consciousness of mass-produced American popular culture was supported and encouraged by the involvement with the Independent Group in the first instance and *New Society* later on. The environmental thinking emerged when he found employment at UCL, whose school of architecture under Richard Llewelyn-Davies was reorganizing itself on those lines. The travelogue-like reportage of the Western United States came out of visits when Banham was, in the first instance, precisely what he described himself as: a tourist. And the reassertion of architectural history right at the end of his career had a great deal to do with his appointment at NYU precisely to do a job of architectural history. Banham was representative, as much as he was singular. The singularity comes in large part from his recognition of the contingency of his positions. He changed his mind, often, and was happy to admit it. His positions on anything were contingent and dynamic; he spoke in many different registers, more than academics usually do. Some of his most serious work – for example, *Scenes in America Deserta* – is the least academic. His 'Reyner' was an invention that allowed him the persona of an art critic in the first instance; elsewhere he was an engineer when he felt like it, especially when admonishing architects. He could be a technologically positivist advocate for good design, as he was at IDCA, or he could write about junk food. Threading all the way through this was a superbly trained, observant and meticulous historian.

So there is one story about complexity, and a taste for it. Part of Banham's cultivation of complexity had to do with the relative availability of opportunities, and an unusually supportive family to allow him to take advantage of those opportunities. But he was also able to make it into an approach to the world that was as open and expansive as possible. His most arresting work is therefore often that with the most expanded vision. That was first of all applied to architecture, and then to the later writings in which he made the whole environment open to critique. His *Los Angeles*, for example, describes a city of extraordinary pluralities, of multiple and unresolvable meanings. His journalism often explored these things first (that was certainly true in the case of LA). For some he was primarily a journalist rather than an intellectual, or to put it another way, he may have recycled himself as an intellectual, but he was a journalist at heart. In this arena, especially writing for *New Society*, the publication that gave him the freest rein, he expanded his range of interests to include anything that might be reasonably visual or material culture. Sometimes (like 'Vehicles of Desire', from 1955) his journalism would achieve something like iconic status; often it acted as research and development for the architectural historical work.

There was journalism; there was also the journalist. Banham very frequently wrote about himself; the journalism was in large part an account of life experiences: travel, driving, learning to consume new forms of culture, the encounter with the unexpected. It was a way of dealing with enthusiasms, which were many, especially aeroplanes and cars, Banham family obsessions. The journalism let Banham have more or less free rein with these things, so there could be reviews of Cadillacs and Ford Mustangs, and the products of the Douglas Aircraft Company, and Californian air shows. The architectural historian in Banham converted these enthusiasms to respectable ones: architecture, art, culture.

There is a revealing anecdote in Beatriz Colomina's lecture for the Victoria & Albert Banham series in which she recalls seeing Banham give three lectures sometime in the early 1980s at Columbia University, where Kenneth Frampton, the already venerable architectural theorist, was working. Each time Banham came to talk, Colomina wrote, 'Frampton left the building . . . Banham had changed in California, he said to me the next day when I enquired.'[46] Frampton's views, which he referred to obliquely in an interview for *October* in 2003, were partly about the trajectory away from what *he* was interested in, for Banham's *Theory and Design* had been essential to his own work.[47] It also indicated a divergent attitude to the United States; Frampton described being 'politicized' by the encounter with the U.S. in the middle of the 1960s, whereas Banham seemed simply to embrace it.[48] That divergence was clearest in the approach to California, which for Banham represented promise, for Frampton implicitly the exaggeration of the worst tendencies of the United States, tendencies that required resistance, not acquiescence. Banham's attraction to California by contrast saw him embrace those tendencies, consumerism in particular; in 'A Black Box' he thought Frampton's position 'self-righteous'.[49] Banham pulled away increasingly from architecture per se to urbanism (*Los Angeles*), desert landscapes, and, in *A Concrete Atlantis*, ruins, himself. For a theorist of architecture like Frampton, this could only be a disappointment. For others, Banham's career became more, not less, interesting as it pulled away from architecture.

I like the Californian Banham for precisely its pulling away from architecture, for its realization of the interdisciplinary promise of the early journalism ('Not Quite Architecture', 'Arts in Society').[50] He understood how consumer objects could, and often did, mock architecture; the observations about air conditioning and cars remain pertinent because their implications still arguably have to be fully acknowledged by architects, whose sphere of influence has arguably continued to shrink.[51] For Banham, that was not a cause for regret, as it was for architects of all stripes, but a challenge and something to embrace. The ability to imagine architecture beyond architecture remains usefully bracing, as does the take on cities, which allows that they may take almost any form as long as the infrastructure permits normal urban functions. At the start of the third decade of the twenty-first century, chastened by gentrification and pandemic, cities might well use such a routemap away from tradition. Banham's position was also one that not only accepted but celebrated pleasure, a still unusual, even unsettling idea in architecture schools.

Could there, in the end be a theory of Banham? Probably not, because in spite of his colossal and systemic knowledge of architecture, his approach was intuitive and gut-led, often reactive to and representative of the situations in which he found himself; it was a position not unlike that of the liberal journalist. He might not have done so well as an academic in the contemporary world, certainly not in the British system in which he started out. What often mattered most was the story; there was no overarching need for consistency, hence, the many apparent shifts of position, the inconsistencies and the many literal and metaphorical hats. He was simultaneously an aesthete and an enthusiast for mass culture, an historian of architecture, and an advocate of its dissolution, an academic who also claimed not to be one, a (cultural) Californian who was also still – just – an East Anglian. Technology was the thread that linked all of these things, however: less so technology as a theme, than an awareness of, and sometimes a cultivation of, its revolutionary potential. Technology was liable to turn everything upside down, not least architecture. Such a force made certainty a nonsense, and so one should, Banham's career demonstrated, be free to change one's mind. When consistency of identity has become so important, so defining, we need Banham's counter-example.

# REFERENCES

## 1 MULTIPLE BANHAMS

1 See Mark Howarth-Booth in *The Banham Lectures: Essays on Designing the Future*, ed. Jeremy Aynsley and Harriet Atkinson (Oxford, 2009), pp. 67–8.

2 Correspondence with Tim Street-Porter, 25 September 2020.

3 Interview with Ben and Mary Banham, London, 8 May 2017.

4 Debby Banham, funeral oration for Mary Banham, London, 25 January 2019. See also Debby Banham, 'Mary Banham Obituary', *The Guardian*, 4 March 2019.

5 Account of Banham's early life from Sutherland Lyall, 'Banham's Background', RIBA *Journal Conference Supplement* (October 1981), p. 3.

6 Reyner Banham, *Theory and Design in the First Machine Age* (London, 1960).

7 See Nigel Whiteley, *Reyner Banham: Historian of the Immediate Future* (Cambridge, MA, and London, 2002), p. 9. Numbers of art history PhDs in England grew through the influx of transplanted middle-European academics. Banham was part of a trend, although he was unusual in having a PhD in modern architecture.

8 The estimate of Banham's journalistic output is placed at 750 articles in Barbara Penner, 'The Man Who Wrote Too Well', *Places Journal* (September 2015), https://placesjournal.org. Adrian Forty thought it was as high as 775; see Forty, 'One Partially Americanised European', in *Twentieth Century Architecture and its Histories*, ed. Louise Campbell (London, 2000), p. 194. Gillian Naylor says 1,000 in *The Banham Lectures*, ed. Aynsley and Atkinson, p. 47.

9 Robert Maxwell, *Sweet Disorder and the Carefully Careless: Theory and Criticism in Architecture* (Princeton, NJ, 1993), p. 178.

10 Reyner Banham. 'La fine della Silicon Valley', *Casabella*, 539 (October 1987), pp. 42–3.

11 Interview with Debby Banham, Cambridge, 15 April 2019.

12 On this look, and the class implications, see Gillian Naylor in *The Banham Lectures*, ed. Aynsley and Atkinson, pp. 48–9. The cap was 'toffish', signifying Banham's upward trajectory. See also Lyall, 'Banham's Background', p. 4.

13 Banham, lecture at Artnet, London, 5 July 1976, available as 'The Rally – Part 1 – Reyner Banham', www.youtube.com, accessed 16 August 2020.

14  Todd Gannon, *Reyner Banham and the Paradoxes of High Tech* (Los Angeles, CA, 2018), p. 3.

15  See also Penner, 'The Man Who Wrote Too Well'.

16  Reyner Banham, 'The Writing on the Walls', *Times Literary Supplement* (17 November 1978), p. 1337. Jencks had been Banham's PhD student. On their difficult relationship, see Whiteley, *Reyner Banham*, pp. 373–7. For more on Banham's own postmodern tendencies, see Alan Colquhoun, 'Reyner Banham: A Reading for the 1980s', originally in Domus (1988). See *Collected Essays* (London, 2009), p. 251.

17  Reyner Banham, 'Vehicles of Desire', *Art* (1 September 1955), p. 3.

18  Roland Barthes, *Mythologies* (London, 1972), pp. 88–90.

19  Reyner Banham, 'The History of the Immediate Future', *Journal of the Royal Institute of British Architects*, LXVIII/7 (May 1961), pp. 252–60, 269.

20  It strongly features in Banham's posthumous 1990 article 'A Black Box: The Secret Profession of Architecture', *New Statesman and Society* (12 October 1990), pp. 22–5.

21  Transcript of 'The Atavism of the Short-distance Mini-cyclist', talk originally given in 1963, supplied by Ben Banham. Later published as Reyner Banham, 'The Atavism of the Short-distance Mini-cyclist', *Living Arts*, 3 (1964), pp. 91–7. On class and politics, see also Anne Massey, *The Independent Group: Modernism and Mass Culture in Britain* (Manchester, 1995), p. 33.

22  Terry Hamilton was killed in a car crash in 1962.

23  Massey, *The Independent Group*, p. 78.

24  For a public statement of this, see the Norwich sequence of *Reyner Banham Loves Los Angeles* (dir. Julian Cooper), BBC TV, 1972.

25  See, for example, Richard Hoggart, *The Uses of Literacy: Aspects of Working Class Life* (London, 1957).

26  For an elaboration of this myth in relation to contemporary architecture, see Reyner Banham, 'Coronation Street, Hoggartsborough', *New Statesman* (9 February 1962), pp. 200–201.

27  Banham, 'The Atavism of the Short-distance Mini-cyclist'.

28  Interview with Ben Banham, London, 31 October 2019. He was a lifelong subscriber to *Autosport*. He occasionally wrote directly about motor racing, as in Reyner Banham, 'Brands Hatch', *New Statesman* (17 July 1964), pp. 97–8.

29  Interview with Debby Banham.

30  Interview with Paul Barker, London, 24 May 2017.

31  Interview with Paul Barker.

32  Whiteley, *Reyner Banham*, pp. 4–5.

33  Her return precipitated a moment of genuine horror, confirmed by
    both children: the younger, Ben (aged one), ran to greet her as she
    stepped into the family home, running through the space where her
    leg used to be. Interview with Debby Banham; interview with Ben
    Banham, 31 October 2019.

34  Reyner Banham, *Scenes in America Deserta* (Layton, UT, 1982).

35  Reyner Banham, ed., *The Aspen Papers: Twenty Years of Design Theory
    from the International Design Conference in Aspen* (London, 1974),
    pp. 84–5.

36  Sigfried Giedion, *Mechanization Takes Command* (New York, 1948).

37  Rachel Carson, *Silent Spring* (Boston, MA, 1962).

38  Reyner Banham, *The Architecture of the Well-tempered Environment*,
    2nd edn (Chicago, IL, 1984), p. 13. For early reviews see, for example,
    Harry Faulkner-Brown, *RIBA Journal*, LXVII (May 1969), p. 208, and
    Banham's response, *RIBA Journal*, CXVII (July 1969), p. 263.

39  For an account of the radio talks, see Anthony Vidler, *Histories of the
    Immediate Present: Inventing Architectural Modernism* (Cambridge, MA,
    and London, 2008), pp. 140–56.

40  *Reyner Banham Loves Los Angeles*, 1972. For high-resolution extracts
    see also Richard J. Williams, 'City of Fantasies: Reyner Banham
    and the Architecture of LA', 2018, https://henitalks.com, accessed
    16 August 2020.

41  Peter Plagens, 'Los Angeles: The Ecology of Evil', *Artforum*, 11
    (December 1972), pp. 67–76.

42  Reyner Banham, *Megastructure: Urban Futures of the Recent Past*
    (London, 1976).

43  Reyner Banham, *A Concrete Atlantis: U.S. Industrial Building and
    European Modern Architecture, 1900–1925* (Cambridge, MA, and London,
    1986), pp. 166–7. Discussed further in Chapter Eight.

44  Interview with Ben and Mary Banham. This putative division of labour,
    between academic work and paid work, was a repeated theme in
    interviews with the Banhams.

45  Interview with Paul Barker. He joined *New Society* in 1964 as a writer,
    becoming deputy editor in 1965.

46  *A Critic Writes: Essays by Reyner Banham*, ed. Mary Banham, Paul
    Barker, Sutherland Lyall and Cedric Price (Berkeley and Los Angeles,
    CA, 1996).

47  Massey, *The Independent Group*, p. 84.

48  Reyner Banham, 'The Crisp at the Crossroads', *New Society* (9 July 1970),
    p. 77.

49  Interview with Paul Barker.

50  Banham, 'The Crisp at the Crossroads'.

51  Reyner Banham, *Los Angeles: The Architecture of Four Ecologies* (London, 1971), p. 111.

52  Ibid.

53  Ibid.

54  Barthes, *Mythologies*, pp. 88–90.

55  It was originally published in 1955 in *Les Lettres nouvelles*.

56  More on this in Chapter Six. Banham was not the only one to deploy this trope. See also Robert Venturi, Denise Scott Brown and Steven Izenour, *Learning from Las Vegas* (Cambridge, MA, and London, 1972).

57  Penner, 'The Man Who Wrote Too Well'.

58  Banham in *Design by Choice*, ed. Penny Sparke (London, 1981), p. 7. See also Lyall, 'Banham's Background', p. 5.

59  Banham, ed., *The Aspen Papers*, pp. 84–5.

60  Reyner Banham, Paul Barker, Peter Hall and Cedric Price, 'Non-plan: An Experiment in Freedom', *New Society* (20 March 1969), pp. 435–43.

61  Reyner Banham, 'Vehicles of Desire', *Art* (1 September 1955), p. 3.

62  For commentary on Banham's photography, including these images, see Mark Howarth-Booth, 'Reyner Banham and Photography', in *The Banham Lectures*, ed. Aynsley and Atkinson, pp. 59–72.

63  Gannon, *Reyner Banham and the Paradoxes of High Tech*.

64  Interview with Debby Banham.

65  Confirmed in various conversations with Ben Benham, 2017–19.

66  'The Independent Group' (Special Issue), *October*, 94 (Autumn 2000), pp. 1–128; 'New Brutalism' (Special Issue), *October*, 136 (Spring 2011), pp. 1–191. See commentary in Mark Crinson and Richard J. Williams, *The Architecture of Art History* (London, 2018), pp. 113–30. On Frampton's and Banham's politics, see Stan Allen and Hal Foster, 'A Conversation with Kenneth Frampton', *October*, 106 (Fall 2003), pp. 35–58.

67  Felicity D. Scott, *Architecture or Techno-utopia: Politics after Modernism* (Cambridge, MA, and London, 2007), pp. 3–4. For more, see Chapter Five.

68  Whiteley, *Reyner Banham*.

69  Penner, 'The Man Who Wrote Too Well'; Forty, 'One Partially Americanised European'.

70  Forty, 'One Partially Americanised European', p. 196. See also conversation with Forty (27 January 2017) and interview with Paul Barker.

71  *A Critic Writes*, ed. Mary Banham et al.

## 2 THE FUTURIST

1 David Robbins, *The Independent Group: Postwar Britain and the Aesthetics of Plenty* (Cambridge, MA, and London, 1990), p. 196.

2 Filippo Tommaso Marinetti, 'Manifeste de fondation du Futurisme', *Le Figaro* (20 February 1909).

3 Anne Massey, *The Independent Group: Modernism and Mass Culture in Britain, 1945–59* (Manchester, 1995), p. 2. See also p. 49 for the conceptual links Banham made between the IG and Futurism.

4 Reyner Banham, 'Primitives of a Mechanized Art', *The Listener* (3 December 1959), p. 974. The collection to which he refers was almost certainly F. T. Marinetti, ed., *I Manifesti del Futurismo, lanciati da Marinetti et al* (Milan, 1914).

5 John Maule McKean, 'The Last of England', *Building Design* (13 August 1976), p. 8.

6 Amici de Brera and the Italian Institute, *Modern Italian Art*, exh. cat., Tate Gallery, London, 1950.

7 *Modern Italian Art from the Estorick Collection*, Tate Gallery, London, 21 November–19 December 1956.

8 Reyner Banham, 'Sant'Elia', *Architectural Review*, 117 (May 1955), pp. 295–301.

9 For a detailed account of the literature, see Banham, 'Sant'Elia', p. 296.

10 Reyner Banham, 'The Theory of Modern Architecture, 1907–1927', PhD thesis, Courtauld Institute of Art, London, 1958; Reyner Banham, *Theory and Design in the First Machine Age* (London, 1960).

11 Reyner Banham, 'Primitives of a Mechanised Art', BBC Third Programme (21 November 1959). See discussion in Massey, *The Independent Group*, p. 49.

12 Anthony Vidler, *Histories of the Immediate Present: Inventing Architectural Modernism* (Cambridge, MA, and London, 2008), pp. 107–56.

13 Banham, 'Sant'Elia', p. 297. See also Reyner Banham, 'Futurism and Modern Architecture', *Architects' Journal*, 125 (17 January 1957), p. 119.

14 See, for example, Gillian Naylor, 'Theory and Design: The Banham Factor', in *The Banham Lectures: Essays on Designing the Future*, ed. Jeremy Aynsley and Harriet Atkinson (Oxford, 2009), p. 51.

15 Banham, 'Futurism and Modern Architecture', p. 119. See also Reyner Banham, 'Futurist Manifesto', *Architectural Review*, 126 (February 1959), pp. 77–80.

16 Ben and Mary Banham both described this tendency in an interview, 2017. He was a de facto 'war correspondent', inclined to 'throw a grenade if things were quiet'.

17   Banham, 'Futurism and Modern Architecture', p. 120. Banham used Pevsner against himself in this sentence; as a historian, Banham argued, Pevsner ought to have said more about Futurism, regardless of any uneasiness he may have had about it.

18   Banham, 'Sant'Elia', p. 301.

19   Ibid., p. 298.

20   S. Gooch, unpublished memoir of Banham family (2004), supplied by Ben Banham.

21   Ben Banham, interview with the author, London, 17 April 2017; Gooch, memoir.

22   Gooch, memoir.

23   Reyner Banham, 'Unlovable at Any Speed', *Architects' Journal* (21 December 1966), pp. 1527–9.

24   Ben Banham, interview with the author, London, 17 April 2017.

25   Ben Banham, correspondence with the author, 8 September 2017.

26   Mary Banham with Ben Banham, interview with the author, London, 8 May 2017.

27   Mary Banham in Gooch, memoir. Banham himself widely refers to repeated 24-hour shifts. See Martin Pawley, 'Last of the Piston Engine Men', *Building Design* (1 October 1971), p. 6.

28   Debby Banham, interview with the author, 15 April 2019.

29   Gooch, memoir.

30   Ibid. Whatever the details, it was traumatic. Story confirmed by Mary Banham again in 2017. Interview with Ben and Mary Banham, London, 8 May 2017.

31   Quoted in Nigel Whiteley, *Reyner Banham: Historian of the Immediate Future* (Cambridge, MA, and London, 2002), p. 5.

32   Reyner Banham, 'Big Doug, Small Piece', CXXXVI (1 August 1962), pp. 251–3

33   Banham, *Theory and Design*, p. 328.

34   Interview with Ben Banham, London, 31 October 2019.

35   Whiteley, *Reyner Banham*, p. 65.

36   Stan Allen and Hal Foster, 'A Conversation with Kenneth Frampton', *October*, 103 (Fall 2003), pp. 38–9.

37   See Nikolaus Pevsner, *Pioneers of Modern Design* (London, 1936); Sigfried Giedion, *Space, Time and Architecture* (Cambridge, MA, and London, 1941).

38   P. Goodman, review of *Theory and Design in the First Machine Age*, *Arts* (January 1961), p. 20.

39   See Whiteley, *Reyner Banham*; also review of Whiteley in Hal Foster, 'Expendabilia', *London Review of Books*, XXIV/9 (9 May 2002).

40  Ben Banham, correspondence with the author, 27 September 2019.

41  See Harry H. Hilberry, 'Review: Theory and Design in the First Machine Age by Reyner Banham', *Journal of the Society of Architectural Historians*, XXII/4 (December 1963), p. 241.

42  Banham, 'The Theory of Modern Architecture, 1907–1927'.

43  Reyner Banham, introduction to paperback edition of *Theory and Design in the First Machine Age* (Oxford, 1980), p. 12.

44  Debby Banham, correspondence with the author, 27 September 2019. While there is no evidence Banham himself was ever in analysis, Ben Banham (son) was in psychoanalysis for several years as a child. Interview with Ben Banham, London, 31 October 2019.

45  Sexuality and gender in Futurist theory is the subject of Cinzia Sartini Blum, *The Other Modernism: F. T. Marinetti's Futurist Fiction of Power* (Berkeley and Los Angeles, CA, 1996). See also Gunter Berghaus, 'The Other Modernism: F. T. Marinetti's Futurist Fiction of Power by Cinzia Sartini Blum', *Modern Language Review*, XCIII/1 (1998), pp. 244–6.

46  Reyner Banham, 'History and Psychiatry', *Architectural Review*, 127 (May 1960), pp. 324–32.

47  Banham, *Theory and Design*, p. 14.

48  Philip Johnson, 'Where Are We At?', *Architectural Review*, 127 (September 1960), p. 175.

49  Banham, *Theory and Design*, p. 89. See also Banham's preview of the Loos argument in 'The Decisive Contribution of Adolf Loos', *Architectural Review*, 121 (February 1957), pp. 85–8.

50  Banham, *Theory and Design*, pp. 93–4.

51  Ibid., p. 97.

52  For more on Mario Sironi, *The Syphon* (1916), see www.tate.org.uk.

53  Barbara Pezzini, 'The 1912 Futurist Exhibition at the Sackville Gallery, London: An Avant-garde Show within the Old-master Trade', *Burlington Magazine*, CLV (July 2013), pp. 471–9; V. Gioè, 'Futurism in England: A Bibliography', *Bulletin of Bibliography*, XLIV/3 (1987), pp. 175–6.

54  Banham did move towards revising that view in 1957, although it did not make it into the PhD or the book. See Banham, 'Futurism and Modern Architecture', p. 119.

55  On Johnson and fascism, see Mark Lamster, *The Man in the Glass House: Philip Johnson, Architect of the Modern Century* (New York, 2018).

56  Johnson, 'Where Are We At?', p. 175.

57  Banham, *Theory and Design*, pp. 99–105.

58  Marie-Aude Bonniel, '*Le Figaro* publie en Une le manifeste du Futurisme le 20 février 1909', *Le Figaro*, 20 February 2019.

59  Banham, *Theory and Design*, p. 99.

60  Ibid., p. 101.

61  Ibid., p. 104.

62  Ibid., p. 102.

63  Banham doesn't seem to have thought much of Ballard, despite attempts by academics to associate the two: Ben Banham, correspondence with the author, 27 September 2017. One recent attempt to align them is Mark Dorrian, 'Banham avec Ballard: On Style and Violence', *Cabinet*, 66 (Spring 2018–Winter 2019), www.cabinetmagazine.org, accessed 13 August 2020.

64  Banham, *Theory and Design*, p. 104.

65  Ibid., pp. 104–5.

66  Ibid., p. 123. The reference to Ruskin comes from a talk by Marinetti at the Lyceum Club in London, March 1912.

67  Banham, 'Futurism and Modern Architecture', pp. 120–22.

68  Banham, *Theory and Design*, p. 129.

69  Banham, 'Futurism and Modern Architecture', p. 126. This Harvard graduate school project, with its elevated freeway cutting through the square, 'would have delighted any Futurist'.

70  Banham, *Theory and Design*, p. 129.

71  Banham said of the spectacular urban images from Boccioni's manifesto of Futurist painting and sculpture that they 'describe the London scene into which we stepped as we left the ICA those evenings of 1953 and 1954'. See Massey, *The Independent Group*, p. 49. See also Banham, 'Futurism and Modern Architecture', which makes several connections of this kind. For a more sceptical take on the elevation of Futurism, see Alan Colquhoun's review of *Theory and Design*, originally in the *British Journal of Aesthetics* (1962), republished in *Collected Essays* (London, 2009), pp. 18–22.

72  'This study of the architectural theory of the second and third decades of the present century rests upon the assumption that the main repository of such theory is to be found in the writings of Le Corbusier and the books published by the Bauhaus.' Banham, 'The Theory of Modern Architecture, 1907–1927', abstract, unpaginated.

73  Banham, 'The Bauhaus', *Theory and Design*, p. 278.

74  Banham, *Theory and Design*, p. 216.

75  Ibid., pp. 223–4.

76  Ibid.

77  Ibid., p. 243.

78  Debby Banham, interview with the author, 15 April 2019. The Primrose Hill flat came after a period lodging with grandparents in south London. The Banhams' bedroom doubled as a living room.

79  Banham, *Theory and Design*, p. 246.

80  Lionel Brett, 'The Space Machine', *Architectural Review* (November 1947), pp. 147–50. For a comprehensive anthology of British views of Le Corbusier, see Irena Murray and Julian Osley, eds, *Le Corbusier and Britain: An Anthology* (Abingdon, 2010).

81  Published in English as *The City of Tomorrow and Its Planning* (London, 1929).

82  Banham, *Theory and Design*, p. 247.

83  Ibid., p. 255.

84  Ibid.

85  Ibid., p. 324.

86  Bernard Tschumi, *Architecture and Disjunction* (Cambridge, MA, and London, 1996).

87  This is a strikingly different reading of the Villa Savoye to Colin Rowe, 'The Mathematics of the Ideal Villa', *Architectural Review* (March 1947), pp. 101–4. Rowe's essay is all about continuity between the past and the present. See also Colquhoun's 1962 review in *Collected Essays*, p. 21.

88  Banham, *Theory and Design*, p. 328.

89  Ibid., p. 323.

90  Ibid., p. 330.

91  Vidler, *Histories of the Immediate Present*, p. 121.

## 3 THE NEW BRUTALIST

1  Reyner Banham, *The New Brutalism: Ethic or Aesthetic* (London, 1966), p. 134.

2  Peter Smithson and Alison Smithson, 'House in Soho, London', *Architectural Design* (December 1953), p. 342; this was the first time the term New Brutalism appears to have been used in English. For a later piece, also very short, see 'The New Brutalism', *Architectural Design*, 27 (April 1957), p. 1. Both pieces are reprinted in *October*, 136 (Spring 2011).

3  Letter to Eric de Maré, originally in the *Architectural Review* (August 1956); repr. in Banham, *The New Brutalism*, p. 10. See also Kenneth Frampton, *Modern Architecture: A Critical History* (London, 1992), p. 262.

4  Banham, *The New Brutalism: Ethic or Aesthetic*, p. 10.

5  Ibid.

6  Mark Crinson, *Alison and Peter Smithson* (London, 2018), p. 13. Recovering Brutalism as a form of (cultural) activism is the subject of Ben Highmore, *The Art of Brutalism: Rescuing Hope from Catastrophe in 1950s Britain* (New Haven, CT, 2017).

7   These concerns have arguably made his work more durable than
    Lawrence Alloway's on the same topic. For this argument see Anne
    Massey, *The Independent Group: Modernism and Mass Culture in Britain,
    1945–59* (Manchester, 1995), pp. 119, 124.

8   Crinson, *Alison and Peter Smithson*, pp. 22–3.

9   Alison Smithson and Peter Smithson, 'The New Brutalism',
    *Architectural Design* (April 1955), discussed in Crinson, *Alison and Peter
    Smithson*.

10  Frampton, *Modern Architecture*, p. 265.

11  Alan Powers, ed., *Robin Hood Gardens: Re-visions* (London, 2010), p. 58.
    The film was shown on 10 July 1970. The Smithsons' words betray an
    unquestionable exoticization of their subject now.

12  On the formation of this group, see Massey, *The Independent Group*, p. 57;
    on p. 99 she describes it as a 'clique'.

13  Crinson, *Alison and Peter Smithson*, pp. 23–4.

14  Reyner Banham, 'The New Brutalism', *Architectural Review* (December
    1955), pp. 355–61.

15  Smithson and Smithson, 'House in Soho'.

16  Discussed at length in Dirk van den Heuvel, 'Between Brutalists: The
    Banham Hypothesis and the Smithson Way of Life', *Journal
    of Architecture*, xx/2 (2015), pp. 293–308, esp. p. 297.

17  Alex Potts, 'New Brutalism and Pop', in *Neo-Avant Garde and
    Postmodern: Postwar Architecture in Britain and Beyond*, ed. Mark
    Crinson and Claire Zimmerman (New Haven, CT, 2010), p. 32.

18  Wilson quoted in David Robbins, *The Independent Group: Postwar Britain
    and the Aesthetics of Plenty* (Cambridge, MA, and London), p. 196.

19  In Banham's usage, here and elsewhere, the New Art-History always
    has a hyphen, as does 'art-history'. In the later, art historical usage, it
    does not. For more on the term, and its relation to architecture, see
    Mark Crinson and Richard J. Williams, *The Architecture of Art History*
    (London, 2018), pp. 95–112.

20  'Oedipal' is Hal Foster's term for their relationship in 'Expendabilia',
    *London Review of Books*, xxiv/9 (9 May 2002), pp. 14–15. The most
    oedipal of Banham's writings is arguably Reyner Banham, 'Futurism
    and Modern Architecture', *Architects' Journal*, 125 (17 January 1957),
    pp. 119–26.

21  Banham, 'The New Brutalism', p. 355.

22  Ibid., p. 361.

23  Potts, 'New Brutalism and Pop', p. 35.

24  Crinson, *Alison and Peter Smithson*, p. 7.

25  Banham, 'The New Brutalism', p. 357.

26 Ibid.

27 Ibid., p. 356.

28 Barnabas Calder, *Raw Concrete: The Beauty of Brutalism* (London, 2016), p. 12.

29 On the picturesque, see also Anthony Vidler, *Histories of the Immediate Present: Inventing Architectural Modernism* (Cambridge, MA, and London, 2008), pp. 108–13.

30 Massey, *The Independent Group*, p. 59.

31 Charles Jencks, *Modern Movements in Architecture* (London, 1973), p. 256.

32 Frampton, *Modern Architecture*, p. 264.

33 Jencks, *Modern Movements in Architecture*, p. 256.

34 It was reconstructed more than once, one copy (now in the collections of the University of Edinburgh) was made for an exhibition of Nigel Henderson's work at the Scottish National Gallery of Modern Art in 2001, curated by Victoria Walsh. For catalogue, see Victoria Walsh, *Nigel Henderson: Parallel of Life and Art* (London, 2001).

35 This part is widely quoted. My source is Frampton, *Modern Architecture*, p. 265.

36 Banham, *The New Brutalism: Ethic or Aesthetic*.

37 Frampton, *Modern Architecture*, p. 265.

38 Reyner Banham, 'This Is Tomorrow', *Architectural Review*, 120 (September 1956), pp. 186–8.

39 Banham subsequently made a radio programme on Park Hill, 'Sheffield after Womersley', BBC Third Programme, 18 March 1964; for details see https://genome.ch.bbc.co.uk.

40 Banham would only have known of these South American projects in photographs.

41 Reyner Banham, 'Park Hill Housing, Sheffield', *Architectural Review*, 130 (December 1961), p. 410.

42 Ibid., p. 409.

43 Ibid.

44 R. Banham, 'The Style for the Job', *New Statesman*, 67 (14 February 1964), p. 261.

45 Banham, *The New Brutalism: Ethic or Aesthetic*.

46 Reyner Banham, *Guide to Modern Architecture* (London, 1962).

47 It was averaging more than £300 at the time of writing.

48 Banham, *The New Brutalism: Ethic or Aesthetic*, p. 134.

49 Ibid., p. 16.

50 Ibid., p. 134.

51 See 'The Atavism of the Short-distance Mini-cyclist', discussed in Chapter One.

52  For a brief account of factionalism in the LCC department, see Elain Harwood, 'London County Council Architects', *Oxford Dictionary of National Biography*, 21 May 2009, www.oxforddnb.com, accessed 19 August 2020. See also Diana Rowntree, 'Kenneth Campbell', *The Guardian*, 11 July 2002.

53  Owen Hatherley, 'Strange, Angry Objects', *London Review of Books* (17 November 2016), pp. 11–16.

54  Banham, *The New Brutalism: Ethic or Aesthetic*, p. 11.

55  Ibid. See the account of the de-Stalinization moment in Soviet architecture in Richard Anderson, *Russia, Modern Architectures in History* (London, 2015), p. 216.

56  He did not mean the defiantly Corbusian – and later – Alton West estate.

57  Banham, *The New Brutalism: Ethic or Aesthetic*, p. 13.

58  John Piper, *The Bombed Buildings of Britain* (London, 1942). See also discussion in Richard J. Williams, *The Anxious City* (London, 2004), pp. 25ff.

59  Banham, *The New Brutalism: Ethic or Aesthetic*, p. 13.

60  Ibid., p. 19.

61  Ibid., p. 135.

62  Hatherley, 'Strange, Angry Objects'.

63  Alex Kitnick, 'Introduction', *October*, 136 (Spring 2011), p. 3. For more on *October* and its attitude to architecture, see Crinson and Williams, *The Architecture of Art History*, pp. 75–94.

64  Kitnick, 'Introduction', p. 6.

65  See Powers, ed., *Robin Hood Gardens: Re-visions*.

66  Calder, *Raw Concrete*, p. 3. Hatherley, in 'Strange, Angry Objects', notes a tendency towards *Bildungsroman* in many accounts of Brutalism.

## 4 THE AUTOPHILE

1  Description based on the account of the mechanically similar 1953 Eldorado. See Steve Cropley, 'Giant Test: 1953 Cadillac Eldorado Biarritz Convertible v 1960 Lincoln Continental Mk v Convertible', *Car* (November 1988), p. 190.

2  Dagmar, born Virginia Ruth Egnor (1921–2001).

3  Reyner Banham, 'Detroit Tin Revisited', in *Design, 1900–1960: Studies in Design and Popular Culture of the Twentieth Century*, ed. Thomas Faulkner (Newcastle, 1976), pp. 139–40.

4  *Fathers of Pop* (dir. Julian Cooper), BBC TV, 1979. Cooper also worked with Banham on *Reyner Banham Loves Los Angeles* (1972) and *The Road to Eldorado* (1979).

5   Ben Banham, correspondence with the author, 10 October 2019.

6   Reyner Banham, 'The Atavism of the Short-distance Mini-cyclist',
    *Living Arts*, 3 (1964), pp. 91–7.

7   Penny Sparke in *The Banham Lectures: Essays on Designing the Future*,
    ed. Jeremy Aynsley and Harriet Atkinson (Oxford, 2009), p. 132.

8   Penny Sparke, ed., *Design by Choice* (London, 1981).

9   'People were kind of cracking jokes which I had no possibility of
    entering into. Everybody seemed to have known each other for so
    long.' Richard Smith, quoted in David Robbins, *The Independent Group:
    Postwar Britain and the Aesthetics of Plenty* (Cambridge, MA, and
    London, 1990), p. 43.

10  The key history of the IG is Anne Massey, *The Independent Group:
    Modernism and Mass Culture in Britain, 1949–1959* (Manchester, 1995).
    See also Lawrence Alloway and Toni diRenzio, quoted in Robbins,
    *The Independent Group*, pp. 169, 193.

11  'His real muse was Marinetti and his polemical motorcars vied with
    buildings even more than they did in *Vers une architecture*. When I
    bought a car (£70 for a Lancia, the one that appears in the photographs
    of Terrangni's Casa del Fascio) I was co-opted as family chauffeur for
    windblown visits to car racing at Silverstone to see Fangio, Gonzales,
    Moss and Hawthorne in action.' Wilson, quoted in Robbins, *The
    Independent Group*, p. 196.

12  Massey, *The Independent Group*, pp. 82–4.

13  Robbins, *The Independent Group*, p. 30. See also Massey, *The Independent
    Group*, p. 82.

14  S. Gooch, unpublished memoir of Banham family (2004), supplied by
    Ben Banham.

15  Recounted by Tim Benton in *The Banham Lectures: Essays on Designing
    the Future*, ed. Aynsley and Atkinson, p. 13.

16  Mark Girouard, *Big Jim: The Life and Work of James Stirling* (London,
    1998), pp. 116–36.

17  Banham recalled the first experience of American cars in the film
    *Fathers of Pop*: 'In 1951 and 1952 none of us really knew how to read the
    forms and symbols of the car; that was to come later when John McHale
    and Lawrence Alloway took over the running of the IG. But even then
    we could hardly fail to be impressed by the sheer size of the thing, which
    in those days of austerity was a kind of effrontery. And at the same
    time we could hardly help being amused by the claims to aristocratic
    good breeding of this heraldry on the front here. Or the implications
    of supernatural speed given by the moderne angel. Impressed by the
    sense of jet power or is it sex in these chromium bulges here? Certainly

we were impressed by the sculptural skill with which this cascade of chromium round the front here is managed and the neat and dramatic way in which the headlamps have been included in the design. And by the sheer mastery of the line and curve in this kind of detailing; and the vast Cinemascope screen in front of the driver and all the science fiction imagery in front of him on either side of the wheel.'

18  Reyner Banham, 'Vehicles of Desire', *Art* (1 September 1955), p. 3.

19  Massey, *The Independent Group*, pp. 92–3.

20  See, for example, Antonio Amado, *Voiture Minimum: Le Corbusier and the Automobile* (Cambridge, MA, and London, 2011).

21  'The End of Insolence', first published in 1960. See *Design by Choice*, ed. Sparke, p. 121. The Beetle placed most of its weight over the rear axle, possibly the worst place for it. It is very unstable by comparison with modern cars.

22  Banham, 'Vehicles of Desire'.

23  Ibid. See also later commentary from *Fathers of Pop*, n.17 above.

24  It seems a major oversight now not to have mentioned Allen by name, but in later writings on car design, Banham discussed her importance at length. See, for example, Banham, 'Detroit Tin Revisited'.

25  The substance of the argument about Le Corbusier in *Theory and Design in the First Machine Age*.

26  Alice Twemlow, '"A Throw-away Esthetic": New Measures and Metaphors in Product Design Criticism', in *Sifting the Trash: A History of Design Criticism* (Cambridge, MA, and London, 2017), available at https://alicetwemlow.com, accessed 20 August 2020.

27  For a recent commentary, see Hal Foster, 'Madder Men', *London Review of Books* (24 October 2019), pp. 29–30. Like many, Foster attributes the phrase 'a lush situation' to advertising, rather than Allen. This would take away some of its appeal for the IG members: Allen wasn't in the business, but one of them. She provided a model to follow, as well as some of the subject matter.

28  Banham, 'Vehicles of Desire'.

29  Berenson's ecstatic description of the young Titian would be a good comparison. See Bernard Berenson, *The Venetian Painters of the Renaissance* (London and New York, 1894), section x.

30  For more on Earl, see Anne Massey, *Out of the Ivory Tower: The Independent Group and Popular Culture* (Manchester, 2013), pp. 126–7.

31  Alloway, quoted in Robbins, *The Independent Group*, p. 50.

32  Banham, 'Vehicles of Desire'.

33  Roland Barthes, 'The New Citroën', *Mythologies* (London, 1972), pp. 88–90.

34  See Massey, *Out of the Ivory Tower*, p. 124. Banham's position could be interpreted variously. See Cheryl Buckley, cited ibid., p. 26. Banham's interest in cars was a stereotypical obsession with 'boys' toys'.

35  See discussion of the left and anti-Americanism in Chapter One.

36  See Robbins, *The Independent Group*. An epidiascope is a projector for books and other flat items.

37  The limber holes opened up spaces between inner (pressure) and outer (hydrodynamic) hulls; without them there was a tendency for the submarine to refuse to dive.

38  Hamilton, commercially successful by that stage, also owned expensive cars. Interview with Ben Banham, London, 19 March 2018.

39  Foster, 'Madder Men', p. 29.

40  Forge's career oddly paralleled Banham's. Born in Kent, and London-based for the first half of his career, he emigrated to the U.S. in 1973 and spent the remainder of his life there.

41  Andrew Forge, 'We Dream of Motor-cars', *Encounter*, 6 (January 1956), pp. 65–8.

42  Reyner Banham, 'We Dream of Motor Cars', *Encounter* (March 1956), pp. 70–72.

43  Erwin Panofsky, 'The Ideological Antecedents of the Rolls-Royce Radiator', *Proceedings of the American Philosophical Society*, CVII/4 (15 August 1963), pp. 273–88.

44  Banham, 'We Dream of Motor Cars'.

45  Forge reply to Banham, 'We Dream of Motor Cars', p. 72.

46  Sublimation of that kind was a frequent reference in the so-called Kinsey Report, in which cars were a regular figure: see A. C. Kinsey, *Sexual Behaviour in the Human Male* (Philadelphia, PA, 1948), p. 607.

47  Most obviously in *Los Angeles: The Architecture of Four Ecologies* (London, 1971).

48  Reyner Banham, 'Night Mrs Jagbag', *Architects' Journal* (29 November 1961); repr. in *Design by Choice*, ed. Sparke, pp. 124–6.

49  Reyner Banham, 'Horse of a Different Colour', *New Society* (3 November 1967), pp. 436–7.

50  For Banham on *Playboy*, see 'I'd Crawl a Mile for . . . *Playboy*', *Architects' Journal* (7 April 1960), pp. 527–9.

51  Banham, 'Horse of a Different Colour', p. 437.

52  Reyner Banham, 'Roadscape with Rusting Nails', *The Listener* (29 August 1968), p. 267.

53  Banham, 'Detroit Tin Revisited'. The conference, and Banham's contribution to it, are described by Tim Benton in *The Banham Lectures*, ed. Aynsley and Atkinson, pp. 27–9.

54  Banham, 'Detroit Tin Revisited', p. 120.

55  R. Barthes, 'The New Citroën'.

56  Banham, 'Detroit Tin Revisited', p. 127.

57  Ibid., p. 139.

58  Ibid., p. 140.

59  J. G. Ballard, *Crash* (London, 1973). Ballard got to know Paolozzi and the Smithsons after the dissolution of the Independent Group, and wrote favourably of the 1956 exhibition *This Is Tomorrow*, but there was no formal connection. See Roger Luckhurst, 'J. G. Ballard and Modern Art', British Library, 25 May 2016, www.bl.uk, accessed 20 August 2010.

60  Reyner Banham, *Scenes in America Deserta* (Layton, UT, 1982), p. 150. Otherwise references to Ballard are very rare.

61  'In Ballard's version, however, "styling" – the phenomenon so effusively celebrated in Banham's earlier text – now became problematized as the means by which design occludes the violence immanent to the device. Stylization and the death of affect turn out to be intimately related.' Mark Dorrian, 'Banham avec Ballard: On Style and Violence', *Cabinet*, 66 (Spring 2018–Winter 2019), www.cabinetmagazine.org.

62  A view often stated by both Ben and Debby Banham in interviews with the author, 2017–19.

63  Ben Banham, correspondence with the author, 31 May 2019.

### 5 THE ENVIRONMENTALIST

1  Rachel Carson, *Silent Spring* (Boston, MA, 1962). By the time of the publication of the second edition of the book, the popular literature on the environment had become vast. E. F. Schumacher's *Small Is Beautiful* appeared in 1973.

2  Ibid., p. 5.

3  Reyner Banham, *The Architecture of the Well-tempered Environment*, 2nd edn (Chicago, IL, 1984), p. 13.

4  Ibid.

5  On boffins and technological optimism in Banham, see Todd Gannon, *Reyner Banham and the Paradoxes of High Tech* (Los Angeles, CA, 2018), pp. 100–101.

6  Tim Benton in *The Banham Lectures: Essays on Designing the Future*, ed. Jeremy Aynsley and Harriet Atkinson (Oxford, 2009), pp. 12–13: 'RB was a kind of godfather to the OU course A305 The History of Architecture and Design 1890–1939 which I helped to design and write in 1975. He contributed Unit 21 on Mechanical Services derived in part

from *The Architecture of the Well-tempered Environment*, whose second edition came out in 1973.'

7   Reyner Banham, 'A Home Is Not a House', *Art in America* (April 1965), pp. 75–9. It is one of the key texts reproduced in *Design by Choice*, ed. Penny Sparke (London, 1981).

8   The MOMA exhibition closed in February 1965, two months before the publication of 'A Home Is Not a House'. See B. Rudofsky, *Architecture without Architects: An Introduction to Non-pedigreed Architecture*, exh. cat., Museum of Modern Art, New York (1964).

9   Banham, 'A Home Is Not a House', p. 79.

10  Ibid., p. 75.

11  Ibid., p. 78.

12  Banham, *Architecture of the Well-tempered Environment*. On the connection between 'A Home Is Not a House' and the book, see Gannon, *Reyner Banham and the Paradoxes of High Tech*, p. 102.

13  Banham, *Architecture of the Well-tempered Environment*.

14  Ibid., p. 80.

15  There are some additional handwritten notes in the Getty papers. The total cubic capacity of the system was 703,000 cubic ft; seven changes of atmosphere were possible daily in winter, ten in summer; the velocity of the system was 85ft/second; the steam-powered Lancashire boilers were 7ft 6in in diameter, and 28ft long. Banham papers, Getty Research Institute, Box 2, File F5.

16  Banham, *Architecture of the Well-tempered Environment*, p. 81.

17  See letter from Tony Noakes, DHSS architect, to Mr Maritz Vandenberg of Architectural Press, 2 July 1980, Banham papers, Getty Research Institute, Box 6, File 5. Noakes provides more detail on the RVH's history in a letter to the *Journal of the Royal Institute of British Architects* (27 October 1981).

18  Banham, *Architecture of the Well-tempered Environment*, p. 75.

19  Ibid., p. 84.

20  Reyner Banham, *The New Brutalism: Ethic or Aesthetic* (London, 1966). p. 134.

21  Interview with Ben and Mary Banham, London, 8 May 2017.

22  James Marston Fitch, review of 'The Architecture of the Well-tempered Environment by Reyner Banham', *Journal of the Society of Architectural Historians*, XXIX/3 (October 1970), pp. 282–4.

23  Nigel Whiteley, *Reyner Banham: Historian of the Immediate Future* (Cambridge, MA, and London, 2002), p. 199.

24  Ben Banham, correspondence with the author, 19 November 2019.

25  Banham, *Architecture of the Well-tempered Environment*, p. 3.

26  Banham, quoted in S. Gooch, unpublished memoir of Banham family, 2004, supplied by Ben Banham.

27  Banham, *Architecture of the Well-tempered Environment*, p. 11.

28  See discussion in Whiteley, *Reyner Banham*, p. 199.

29  This was Robert Maxwell's view. 'While Banham propagandized for Archigram, Archigram became propaganda for his own point of view.' See *Sweet Disorder and the Carefully Careless: Theory and Criticism in Architecture* (Princeton, NI, 1993), p. 181.

30  Reyner Banham, 'Centre Georges Pompidou', *Architectural Review*, 161 (May 1977), pp. 272–94.

31  Reyner Banham, 'High Tech and Advanced Engineering', in Gannon, *Reyner Banham*, p. 239. See also p. 233 for a list of High Tech consumer items: 'proprietary medicines to running shoes and skiing equipment, to almost anything controlled by a microprocessor chip . . . round-cornered (portable radios, or if made from white wire mesh, cosmetic trays) to horizontally ribbed (travel goods) to matte black (light fittings) to "industrial blue" (also light fittings) to dead white (certain sports cars) or black and perforated (furniture) and almost anything at all that even faintly resembles a space vehicle or a toy robot from Japan.'

32  Whiteley, *Reyner Banham*, pp. 199–200.

33  Ibid., p. 200.

34  Banham, *Architecture of the Well-tempered Environment*, p. 41.

35  Banham, handwritten memoir, (undated, probably 1973), Banham papers, Getty Research Institute, Box 18, File 3.

36  On the IG's production of a U.S.-focused modernism, see Anne Massey, *The Independent Group: Modernism and Mass Culture in Britain, 1945–59* (Manchester, 1995), p. 2.

37  Banham, *Architecture of the Well-tempered Environment*, p. 160. See also discussion in Whiteley, *Reyner Banham*, p. 206.

38  Le Corbusier, *Quand les cathédrales étaient blanches* [1937] (Paris, 2012), pp. 39–40.

39  Ibid., p. 40.

40  Reyner Banham, 'History Faculty, Cambridge', *Architectural Review*, 144 (November 1968), p. 329.

41  Banham, *Architecture of the Well-tempered Environment*, p. 148.

42  Ibid., p. 130.

43  For a development of this argument see Mark Crinson and Richard J. Williams, *The Architecture of Art History* (London, 2018).

44  Or boffins, see Gannon, *Reyner Banham*, pp. 100–101.

45  Banham, *Architecture of the Well-tempered Environment*, pp. 191–2.

46  See complete list of programmes and speakers for 1951–73 in
    *The Aspen Papers: Twenty Years of Design Theory from the International
    Design Conference in Aspen*, ed. Reyner Banham (London, 1974),
    pp. 4–9.

47  Repeated in Maxwell, *Sweet Disorder and the Carefully Careless*,
    p. 181.

48  *The Aspen Papers*, ed. Banham, p. 207.

49  Banham papers, Getty Research Institute, Box 18, File 3.

50  Ibid.

51  Ibid.

52  Letter to Mary Banham, quoted in Alice Twemlow, *Sifting the Trash:
    A History of Design Criticism* (Cambridge, MA, and London, 2017).

53  Banham, *Architecture of the Well-tempered Environment*, p. 274.

54  'The Environmental Witch-Hunt', in *The Aspen Papers*, ed. Banham,
    pp. 208–10.

55  Twemlow, *Sifting the Trash*.

56  See also 1963 talk, discussed in Chapter Four.

57  *The Aspen Papers*, ed. Banham.

58  Interview with Ben Banham, London, 17 April 2017.

59  Felicity D. Scott, *Architecture or Techno-utopia: Politics after Modernism*
    (Cambridge, MA, and London, 2007), pp. 3–4.

60  Alexander Gordon, 'Designing for Survival: The President Introduces
    His Long Life/Loose Fit/Low Energy Study', *Journal of the Royal
    Institute of British Architects*, LXXIX/9 (1972), pp. 374–6. See also Craig
    Langston, 'Measuring Good Architecture: Long Life, Loose Fit, Low
    Energy', *European Journal of Sustainable Development*, III/4 (2014),
    pp. 163–74.

61  Reyner Banham, 'Long Life/Loose Fit/Low Energy vs Foster', *New
    Society*, 22 (9 November 1972), pp. 344–5.

62  Ibid.

63  Ibid., p. 345.

64  Whiteley, *Reyner Banham*, p. 199.

65  Banham, *Architecture of the Well-tempered Environment*, p. 14.

66  Walter Segal, 'The Fruits of Originality', *Architects' Journal* (6 March
    1969), pp. 622–3. Segal's work is prominent at the Centre for Alternative
    Technology at Machynlleth, Wales. His approval indicates that
    Banham's problem with environmentalism was with mainstream
    architecture's appropriation of it.

67  Banham, *Architecture of the Well-tempered Environment*, p. 13.

## 6 THE ANGELENO

1 *Reyner Banham Loves Los Angeles* (dir. Julian Cooper), BBC TV, 1972.
2 Reyner Banham, *Los Angeles: The Architecture of Four Ecologies* (London, 1971).
3 Ibid., p. 244.
4 Anthony Vidler, *Histories of the Immediate Present: Inventing Architectural Modernism* (Cambridge, MA, and London, 2008), p. 143. For another essay in the environmental mode represented by *Los Angeles*, see Reyner Banham, 'Flatscape with Containers', *Architectural Design*, 38 (November 1968), pp. 1378–9.
5 United States Census Bureau, *Statistical Abstract of the United States: 1968 (89th Edition)* (Washington, DC, 1968), p. 19.
6 P. Hall, *London 2000* (London, 1971).
7 Melvin Webber, ed., *Explorations into Urban Structure* (Philadelphia, PA, 1964).
8 *Reyner Banham Loves Los Angeles*.
9 Ibid.
10 Ibid.
11 Interview with Ben and Mary Banham, London, 8 May 2017.
12 Nigel Whiteley, *Reyner Banham: Historian of the Immediate Future* (Cambridge, MA, and London, 2002), p. 28.
13 Reyner Banham, 'Unlovable at Any Speed', *Architects' Journal*, 144 (21 December 1966), pp. 1527–9.
14 Ibid.
15 Ralph Nader, *Unsafe at Any Speed* (New York, 1965).
16 Banham, 'Unlovable at Any Speed'.
17 Reyner Banham, 'Encounter with Sunset Boulevard', *The Listener* (22 August 1968), pp. 235–6. See also discussion in Vidler, *Histories of the Immediate Present*, p. 144.
18 Banham, 'Encounter with Sunset Boulevard'.
19 Reyner Banham, 'Roadscape with Rusting Nails', *The Listener* (29 August 1968), pp. 267–8. The original radio programme was broadcast on 19 August 1968; repr. in *A Critic Writes: Essays by Reyner Banham*, ed. Mary Banham, Paul Barker, Sutherland Lyall and Cedric Price (Berkeley and Los Angeles, CA, 1996), pp. 124–8.
20 Banham, 'Roadscape', p. 267.
21 Banham, 'Unlovable at Any Speed'.
22 Banham, 'Roadscape', p. 268.
23 Ibid.

24 Samuel Wagstaff Jr, 'Talking with Tony Smith', *Artforum* (December 1966), pp. 14–19. It is likely Banham saw it. A copy of Robert Smithson's 1968 essay, 'A Sedimentation of the Mind', which discusses Smith, can be found in the Getty papers along with materials for *Scenes in America Deserta*, but Smith's story was very widely cited in American contemporary art circles. Banham papers, Getty Research Institute, Box 1, File 1.

25 On the *flâneur* in this context, see Brian Morris, 'Screening Los Angeles: Architecture, Migrancy and Mobility', in *Drifting: Architecture and Migrancy*, ed. Stephen Cairns (Abingdon, 2003), pp. 252–70; also Steven Jacobs, 'Leafing Through Los Angeles: Edward Ruscha's Photographic Books', in *Camera Constructs: Photography, Architecture and the Modern City*, ed. Andrew Higgott and Timothy Wray (Abingdon, 2016), pp. 211–22.

26 Correspondence with Ben Banham, 17 May 2020. 'Mary baulked at becoming a taxi service for us kids. The head of school at UCLA moved on to a senior Federal post in early '68 & his replacement was less enthusiastic, so nothing came of the offer.'

27 Reyner Banham, Paul Barker, Peter Hall and Cedric Price, 'Non-plan: An Experiment in Freedom', *New Society* (20 March 1969), pp. 435–43.

28 Interview with Paul Barker, 24 May 2017. See also the account in Paul Barker, 'Non-plan Revisited', in *The Banham Lectures: Essays on Designing the Future*, ed. Jeremy Aynsley and Harriet Atkinson (Oxford, 2009), pp. 177–9.

29 Banham et al., 'Non-plan', p. 436.

30 Peter Hall, one of the authors of 'Non-plan', later provided the definitive popular account of planning history including the 1947 Act in *Cities of Tomorrow: An Intellectual History of Urban Planning and Design since 1880* (Oxford, 1988).

31 Banham et al., 'Non-plan', p. 436.

32 Ibid. On the same topic, see Reyner Banham, 'Disservice Areas', *New Society* (23 May 1968), pp. 762–3. Commentary in Richard J. Williams, 'Pleasure and the Motorway', in *Autopia: Cars and Culture*, ed. Joe Kerr and Peter Wollen (London, 2002), pp. 281–7.

33 Robert Venturi, Denise Scott Brown and Steven Izenour, *Learning from Las Vegas* (Cambridge, MA, and London, 1972).

34 Graham Percy Obituary, *Independent*, 10 January 2008, www.independent.co.uk.

35 See special issue edited by Iain Nairn, 'Outrage', *Architectural Review* (June 1955).

36 Banham, 'Encounter with Sunset Boulevard', p. 235.

37  Reyner Banham, *A City Crowned with Green*, BBC TV, 12 June 1964, available at www.bbc.co.uk, accessed 24 August 2020.

38  Interview with Mary and Ben Banham, London, 8 May 2017. There was typically academic work and work 'to pay the bills'.

39  Interview with Paul Barker.

40  Venturi, Scott Brown and Izenour, *Learning from Las Vegas*.

41  See account of Banham's photography, especially of Los Angeles, in Mark Howarth-Booth, 'Reyner Banham and Photography', in *The Banham Lectures*, ed. Aynsley and Atkinson, pp. 63–5. Around 2,000 of Banham's photographs can be found in the archives of the Architectural Association, London.

42  A key concept later in Reyner Banham, *Scenes in America Deserta* (Layton, UT, 1982).

43  Vidler, *Histories of the Immediate Present*, p. 154.

44  For a study of the phenomenon, see Arnaud Maillet, *The Claude Glass: Use and Meaning of the Black Mirror in Western Art* (Cambridge, MA, and London, 2004).

45  Banham, *Los Angeles*, p. 23.

46  Banham, 'Unlovable at Any Speed', p. 1527. The 'woman' was Mary.

47  Banham, *Los Angeles*, pp. 23–4.

48  Ibid., p. 37.

49  Ibid., p. 38.

50  Ibid., p. 49.

51  Ibid., p. 88.

52  Ibid., p. 91.

53  Ibid., p. 213.

54  Ibid. The story was 'now known to be a jesting fabrication'.

55  Jane Jacobs, *The Death and Life of Great American Cities* (New York, 1961).

56  Banham, *Los Angeles*, p. 216.

57  Thomas S. Hines, 'Reyner Banham, *Los Angeles: The Architecture of Four Ecologies*', *Journal of the Society of Architectural Historians*, XXXI/1 (March 1972), p. 76. For a similar conclusion, see Mark Girouard, 'Banham's Utopia', *The Listener* (3 June 1971), p. 726.

58  Banham, *Los Angeles*, p. 121.

59  It was rebroadcast in 1988 as a posthumous tribute, with an introduction from the architect Norman Foster.

60  Peter Plagens, 'Los Angeles: The Ecology of Evil', *Artforum*, 11 (December 1972), pp. 67–76.

61  Ibid., p. 76.

62  Ibid.

63  Ibid.

64 Banham, *Los Angeles*, pp. 23-4. Also noted in the otherwise positive review by Mark Girouard; see Girouard, 'Banham's Utopia'.

65 Plagens, 'Los Angeles'.

66 The mainstream press response was generally welcoming. See, for example, Philip French, *The Times*, 5 April 1971, p. 11.

67 Banham, *Los Angeles*, pp. 16-17.

68 Mike Davis, *City of Quartz: Excavating the Future in Los Angeles* (London, 1990).

69 Ibid., pp. 73-4. See also Mike Davis, *Ecology of Fear: Los Angeles and the Imagination of Disaster* (New York, 1998).

70 Edward W. Soja, *My Los Angeles* (Berkeley and Los Angeles, CA, 2014), p. 15.

71 For a more extended discussion on Banham and postmodernism, see Whiteley, *Reyner Banham*, pp. 268-74. See also Alan Colquhoun, 'Reyner Banham: A Reading for the 1980s', *Collected Essays* (London, 2009), pp. 248-52.

72 Hines, 'Reyner Banham, *Los Angeles*', p. 76. 'Voyeur' perfectly describes the anecdote at the start of 'Autopia'.

73 See also Colin Marshall, 'A 'radical alternative': how one man changed the perception of Los Angeles', *The Guardian*, 24 August 2016.

74 Reyner Banham, *The Architecture of the Well-tempered Environment* (Chicago, IL, 1984), p. 16.

75 Erika D. Smith, 'In 2019, homelessness truly felt like a crisis in every corner of L.A.', *Los Angeles Times*, 20 December 2019.

## 7 THE DESERT FREAK

1 Reyner Banham, *Scenes in America Deserta* (Layton, UT, 1982). It only gets a few lines in Nigel Whiteley's otherwise comprehensive *Reyner Banham: Historian of the Immediate Future* (Cambridge, MA, and London, 2002), pp. 404-9. Vidler cites it briefly as an extension of his analysis of *Los Angeles*: see Anthony Vidler, *Histories of the Immediate Present: Inventing Architectural Modernism* (Cambridge, MA, and London, 2008), p. 154.

2 Interview with Ben and Debby Banham, London, 12 December 2019.

3 Tim Heald, 'Desert Lover', *Radio Times* (31 May 1978), p. 35: 'Roads to El Dorado' was broadcast on BBC 2, Sunday, 3 June 1979 in the series *The World About Us.*

4 Banham, *Scenes in America Deserta*, pp. 60-61.

5 Banham papers, Getty Research Institute, Box 1, Folder 2.

6 Vidler, *Histories of the Immediate Present*, p. 154.

7  Banham papers, Getty Research Institute, Box 1, Folder 2, undated proposal typescript for *Scenes in America Deserta*, *c*. 1979.

8  Interview with Ben and Debby Banham.

9  C. M. Doughty, *Travels in Arabia Deserta* (Cambridge, 1888).

10  Banham papers, Getty Research Institute, Box 13, Folder 2. Also interview with Tracey Schuster, Los Angeles, 2 February 2017. Schuster, a student of Banhams at UC Santa Cruz, recalled him teaching anything from Italian Renaissance architecture to Pop art.

11  T. E. Lawrence, *The Seven Pillars of Wisdom* (London, 1935). Lawrence describes adopting Arab dress on p. 129.

12  Doughty, *Travels in Arabia Deserta*, esp. chapters 1–3.

13  Ibid., p. xxix.

14  First reported in Heald, 'Desert Lover'. See also Banham, *Scenes in America Deserta*, pp. 153–4.

15  J. C. Van Dyke, *The Desert: Further Studies in Natural Appearances* (New York, 1901).

16  Ibid., pp. 111–14, esp. p. 114.

17  Banham, *Scenes in America Deserta*, p. 154.

18  Ibid., p. 156.

19  Ibid.

20  It was recorded for Hyperion Records by the King's Singers in 2006 and performed by them at the late-night BBC Prom on 5 August 2008.

21  Broadcast on Sunday, 3 June 1979.

22  First draft running order of BBC TV programme, probably Julian Cooper to Banham (undated, probably 1978). Banham papers, Getty Research Institute, Box 1, Folder 2.

23  Heald, 'Desert Lover'.

24  Ibid.

25  Correspondence with Stangos, Banham papers, Getty Research Institute, Box 13, Folder 2; interview with Ben and Debby Banham, London, 12 December 2019.

26  Assorted correspondence, Banham papers, Getty Research Institute, Box 1, Folder 2.

27  Letter from Gibbs M. Smith to Banham, 6 February 1979, Banham papers, Getty Research Institute, Box 1, Folder 2.

28  Banham Papers, Getty Research Institute, Box 12, File 4. Banham was invited to speak, possibly more than once, at a NEH-funded conference on the literature of the American Southwest, held at Tucson Public Library. The title, *The Writers of the Purple Sage*, referred to the *Riders of the Purple Sage*, the 1912 Western novel by Zane Grey, as well as perhaps obliquely to a musical offshoot of the Grateful Dead.

Two volumes of essays from the conferences were published, edited by Judy Nolte Temple.

29 Banham, *Scenes in America Deserta*, p. 5.
30 Ibid., p. 13.
31 Ibid., p. 16.
32 Ibid., p. 17.
33 Ibid., p. 18.
34 Ibid.
35 Heald, 'Desert Lover'.
36 Interview with Ben and Debby Banham; also interview with Mary and Ben Banham, London, 8 May 2017. All have described *Scenes in America Deserta* as hard to read for this reason.
37 Letter from Dennis Casebier to Banham, 26 June 1978, Banham papers, Getty Research Institute, Box 1, File 1.
38 Banham, *Scenes in America Deserta*, p. 37.
39 Ray Bradbury, *The Martian Chronicles* (New York, 1950). For commentary on Bradbury and the desert, see for example Lauren Weiner, 'The Dark and Starry Eyes of Ray Bradbury', *New Atlantis*, 36 (2012), pp. 79–91.
40 Banham, *Scenes in America Deserta*, p. 188.
41 Robert Smithson, 'A Sedimentation of the Mind: Earth Proposals', *Artforum*, 7/1 (September 1968), pp. 44–50. See also Smithson's 'The Monuments of Passaic', *Artforum*, 6/4 (December 1967), pp. 48–51. This is not mentioned by Banham, but its concept of 'ruins in reverse' is apposite. 'Sedimentation', plus assorted notes on Smithson, can be found in the Banham papers, Getty Research Institute, Box 1, File 1.
42 Banham's account here is heavily reliant on Frank Lloyd Wright's own legendary self-mythologization, for example in his *An Autobiography* (New York, 1943).
43 Banham, *Scenes in America Deserta*, p. 69.
44 Ibid., p. 71.
45 Reyner Banham, *The Architecture of the Well-tempered Environment*, 2nd edn (Chicago, IL, 1984), p. 111.
46 For the mythification of Wright, see for example, Philip Johnson, 'The Frontiersman', *Architectural Review*, 106 (August 1949), p. 105: 'Frank Lloyd Wright is the greatest living architect and for many reasons.' The formalist understanding of Wright persisted alongside this. See a late example by Frampton, first published in 1980, which focused on the 'myth of the prairie': Kenneth Frampton, *Modern Architecture: A Critical History* (London, 1992), pp. 57–63.
47 Banham, *Scenes in America Deserta*, p. 76.

48  Ibid., p. 74.

49  Ibid., p. 80. This continues, on the evidence of a visit in December 2019.

50  Ibid., p. 78. This story is very much part of the Wright myth, repeated by the Taliesin West tour guides.

51  Reyner Banham, *Megastructure: Urban Futures of the Recent Past* (London and New York, 1976), p. 202.

52  Edwin Heathcote, 'Arcosanti: Dreamer in the Dust', *Icon*, 175 (January 2018), pp. 92–102, available at www.iconeye.com, accessed 25 August 2020. It was rarely covered in detail in the international architectural press. An exception was 'Arcosanti: Architect P. Soleri', *L'Architecture d'aujourd'hui*, 167 (May–June 1973), pp. 84–7.

53  Interview with Ben and Debby Banham. See also the confrontation with youthful activists at IDCA 1970, described in Chapter Five.

54  Banham, *Megastructure*, p. 202.

55  Reyner Banham, 'Mesa Messiah', *New Society* (6 May 1976), p. 306.

56  Ibid.

57  Ibid.

58  Banham, *Scenes in America Deserta*, p. 85.

59  Ibid., p. 86.

60  This is also Whiteley's conclusion, although the book does not feature strongly in his account. See Whiteley, *Reyner Banham*, p. 408.

61  For a more recent example, a diary-like account of Clark's encounter with two paintings by Poussin in 2000, see T. J. Clark, *The Sight of Death: An Experiment in Art Writing* (New Haven, CT, 2006).

62  Banham, *Scenes in America Deserta*, p. 209.

63  Vidler, *Histories of the Immediate Present*, p. 154.

64  Banham, *Scenes in America Deserta*, p. 220.

65  Ibid., p. 221.

66  Ibid., p. 228.

67  Ibid., p. 17.

68  Reyner Banham, letter to Gibbs Smith, 13 February 1979, Banham papers, Getty Research Institute, Box 1, File 2.

69  Banham papers, Getty Research Institute, Box 1, File 1.

## 8  THE CONNOISSEUR OF RUINS

1  Hadas A. Steiner, 'Cropping the View: Reyner Banham and the Image of Buffalo', in *Buffalo at the Crossroads: The Past, Present and Future of American Urbanism*, ed. Peter H. Christensen (Ithaca, NY, 2020), p. 297 n. 1. See also conversation with Ben Banham, London, November 2019.

2  Interview with Ben and Mary Banham, London, 4 April 2017.

3 See *A Tonic to the Nation: The Festival of Britain, 1951*, ed. Mary Banham and Bevis Hillier, exh. cat., Victoria & Albert Museum, London (London, 1976).

4 Interview with Ben and Mary Banham.

5 Steiner, 'Cropping the View', p. 245. Steiner stretches a point here, arguing that 'displacement from the center' was Banham's comfort zone. The decision was more pragmatic.

6 Interview with Ben and Mary Banham.

7 Barker thought Banham's contributions lost focus once he moved to the U.S.: in London everything was tested through conversation before it made it into writing. In Buffalo there were far fewer people to have a conversation with. Interview with Paul Barker, London, 24 May 2017.

8 Ibid.

9 Interview with Ben and Mary Banham.

10 Data from https://data.census.gov, 29 May 2020. For an architectural overview of Buffalo's history, see Christensen, ed., *Buffalo at the Crossroads*.

11 Reyner Banham, *A Concrete Atlantis: U.S. Industrial Building and European Modern Architecture, 1900–1925* (Cambridge, MA, and London, 1986), p. 154.

12 Interview with Ben and Mary Banham.

13 Ben has also liked to suggest that Buffalo's waterfront was in the hands of the Sicilian mafia. Interview with Ben and Mary Banham.

14 Banham, *A Concrete Atlantis*.

15 Bernard Tschumi wrote about the pleasure of exploring the ruined Villa Savoye in a well- known article published in 1976. The speculation about the erotics of ruins would have left Banham unmoved, as would the style, but there are otherwise some similarities in approach with the more subjective parts of *A Concrete Atlantis*. Bernard Tschumi, 'Architecture and Transgression', in *Architecture and Disjunction* (Cambridge, MA, and London, 1996), pp. 70–76.

16 Reyner Banham, *Los Angeles: The Architecture of Four Ecologies* (London, 1971), pp. 37–56.

17 Reyner Banham, *Megastructure: Urban Futures of the Recent Past* (London, 1976).

18 The *Walking City* was 'clearly projected as stalking across a ruined world in the aftermath of a nuclear war'. Kenneth Frampton, *Modern Architecture: A Critical History* (London, 1992), p. 281.

19 See lecture by Banham on megastructures at Artnet, London, 15 October 1974, available at www.youtube.com, accessed

27 August 2020. The lecture mainly concerns the definition of the term 'megastructure', taking on Tomás Maldonado's work.

20 Banham, *Megastructure*, especially p. 22.

21 Ibid., p. 21. The nuclear-powered USS *Enterprise*, commissioned in 1961, was the largest aircraft carrier ever built, a showcase of contemporary U.S. military technology.

22 Ibid., pp. 118–19.

23 Ibid., p. 105.

24 Nigel Whiteley, *Reyner Banham: Historian of the Immediate Future* (Cambridge, MA, and London, 2002), p. 290. See also 1974 lecture on the topic (n. 19).

25 Banham, lecture at Artnet.

26 Banham, *Megastructure*, p. 11.

27 Ibid., p. 216.

28 For more on this moment in American architectural history and Banham's place in it, see Felicity D. Scott, *Architecture or Techno-utopia: Politics after Modernism* (Cambridge, MA, and London, 2007).

29 Conversation with Ben Banham.

30 Steiner, 'Cropping the View', p. 257.

31 See, for example, *American Landscape* (1930), in MOMA's collection; the scene includes a grain elevator alongside Ford's River Rouge plant.

32 Le Corbusier, *Vers une architecture* (Paris, 1923).

33 Owen Hatherley, 'Silo Dreams: Metamorphoses of the Grain Elevator', *Journal of Architecture*, XX/3 (2015), pp. 474–88.

34 Whiteley, *Reyner Banham*.

35 Banham, *A Concrete Atlantis*, p. 196.

36 Ibid., p. 199.

37 The edition to which Banham referred was an English translation by Michael Bullock from 1953. Ibid., p. 258, n. 51.

38 Ibid., p. 205. He refers to Wilhelm Worringer, *Egyptian Art*, trans. B. Rackham (London, 1928), p. 258, n. 7.

39 Banham, *A Concrete Atlantis*, p. 215.

40 Ibid., p. 205.

41 On Le Corbusier's reception in Britain, see *Le Corbusier and Britain: An Anthology*, ed. Irena Murray and Julian Osley (Abingdon, 2010); also Adrian Forty, 'Le Corbusier's British Reputation', in *Le Corbusier: Architect of the Century*, ed. Michael Raeburn and Victoria Wilson (London, 1987), and Graham Livesey and Antony Moulis, 'From Impact to Legacy: Interpreting Critical Writing on Le Corbusier from the 1920s to the Present', in *Le Corbusier 50 Years Later: Universitat Politècnica de València, 18–20 November 2015*), DOI: http://dx.doi.org/10.4995/LC2015.2015.712

42  The photographs of modernist icons were made from 1997,
    commissioned by Chicago's Museum of Contemporary Art.
    See www.sugimotohiroshi.com.

43  See illustrations in Le Corbusier, *Towards a New Architecture* (London,
    1931), pp. 134–5.

44  Banham, *A Concrete Atlantis*, p. 222.

45  Ibid., p. 15.

46  Ibid., pp. 19–20.

47  See Christensen, *Buffalo at the Crossroads*.

48  Banham, *A Concrete Atlantis*, p. 70.

49  Ibid., pp. 166–7.

50  Another view: he was the 'Hunter Thompson' of architectural history,
    alluding to the performative craziness of the author of *Fear and
    Loathing in Las Vegas*. See S. Hall Kaplan, review of *A Concrete Atlantis*,
    *Los Angeles Times*, 14 September 1986, p. 12.

51  Robert Venturi, Denise Scott Brown and Steven Izenour, *Learning
    from Las Vegas* (Cambridge, MA, and London, 1972). See also Robert
    Smithson, 'The Monuments of Passaic', *Artforum*, VI/4 (December
    1967), pp. 48–51.

52  It was a key theme in reviews of the book too. See P. Campbell,
    'The New Lloyds', *London Review of Books* (24 July 1986), pp. 22–3.

53  See, for example, Craig Owens, 'The Allegorical Impulse: Toward
    a Theory of Postmodernism', *October*, 12 (Spring 1980), pp. 67–86.
    Banham's own (posthumous) appearance in *October*, via the excavation
    and republication of 'The New Brutalism', did not happen until 2011.

54  Kenneth Frampton, *Modern Architecture: A Critical History* (London,
    1992), pp. 292–3.

55  The process as manifest in New York is best documented in Sharon
    Zukin's *Loft Living: Culture and Capital in Urban Change* (Baltimore, MD,
    1982).

56  J. M. Richards, ed., *The Bombed Buildings of Britain* (Cheam, Surrey,
    1943).

57  John Brewer, *The Pleasures of the Imagination* (London, 1997), p. 654.

58  'His esthetic judgment is disciplined by a comprehension of structural
    fact that few American critics can match.' James Marston Fitch, review
    of *A Concrete Atlantis*, *AIA Journal* (March 1987). From Banham papers,
    Getty Research Institute, Box 10, File 9.

59  Banham, *A Concrete Atlantis*, p. 70.

60  Ibid., pp. 242–3.

61  Frampton, *Modern Architecture*, p. 39.

62  Persico in Banham, *A Concrete Atlantis*, pp. 252–3.

63 For more on the book's residual Futurism, see Joseph Mascheck, 'Temples to the Dynamo: The "Daylight" Factory and the Grain Elevator', *Art in America* (January 1987), pp. 13–14. See also Sutherland Lyall, 'Modern Icons', *New Statesman* (1 August 1986), p. 27.

64 Whiteley, *Reyner Banham*, p. 79.

65 Reyner Banham, 'The Becher Vision', in Bernd Becher and Hilla Becher, *Water Towers* (Cambridge, MA, and London, 1988), pp. 7–8.

66 Ibid., p. 7.

67 Reyner Banham, 'The Writing on the Walls', *Times Literary Supplement* (17 November 1978), p. 1337.

68 Banham, 'The Becher Vision', p. 8.

69 Owens, 'The Allegorical Impulse'.

70 Daniel Campo, 'Historic Preservation in an Economic Void: Reviving Buffalo's Concrete Atlantis', *Journal of Planning History*, XV/4 (2016), pp. 314–45.

71 Reyner Banham, 'La fine della Silicon Valley', *Casabella*, 539 (October 1987), pp. 42–3. See also notes in Banham Papers, Getty Research Institute, Box 10, F19. Banham had earlier written on Silicon Valley's style in 'Silicon Style', *Architectural Review*, 169 (May 1981), pp. 283–90. On p. 284, he noted that all was not well as early as 1981: 'There are a lot of For Lease signs in the Vale of Chips right now.'

72 Banham, 'The Writing on the Walls'.

73 Banham, 'La fine della Silicon Valley', p. 42.

## 9 REYNER BANHAM, REVISITED

1 Reyner Banham, Letter to Donald Posner, 1 January 1987, Reyner Banham papers, Getty Research Institute, Box 16 File 3.

2 Reyner Banham, Letter to Dennis Sharp, 14 September 1987, Reyner Banham papers, Getty Research Institute, Box 16 File 7.

3 By the firm Llewelyn-Davies Weeks Forestier-Walker & Bor, completed in 1974. Richard Llewelyn-Davies was Banham's head of department at UCL.

4 Peter Hall, 'Foreword', in *A Critic Writes: Essays by Reyner Banham*, ed. Mary Banham, Paul Barker, Sutherland Lyall and Cedric Price (Berkeley and Los Angeles, CA, 1996), pp. xi–xii. Also interview with Banham's grandson, Oli Arditi, 7 March 2020.

5 Interview with Ben and Mary Banham, London, 8 May 2017; interview with Arditi.

6 See for example, 'Obituary of Professor Reyner Banham', *The Times*, 22 March 1988; Paul Goldberger, 'Reyner Banham, Architectural

Critic Dies at 66', *New York Times*, 22 March 1988; 'British Critic Reyner Banham', *Los Angeles Times*, 23 March 1988.

7 Sunday, 1 May 1988. Source https://genome.ch.bbc.co.uk.

8 *The Banham Lectures: Essays on Designing the Future*, ed. Jeremy Aynsley and Harriet Atkinson (Oxford, 2009).

9 For more on this question, see Mark Crinson and Richard J. Williams, *The Architecture of Art History* (London, 2018), esp. chapters 4 and 5.

10 Interview with Tracey Schuster, Getty Research Institute, 7 February 2017.

11 Aynsley and Atkinson, ed., *The Banham Lectures*.

12 Nigel Whiteley, *Reyner Banham: Historian of the Immediate Future* (Cambridge, MA, and London, 2002).

13 Robert Maxwell, 'The Plenitude of Presence', *Architectural Design*, LI/6 (1981), pp. 52–7. See discussion in Whiteley, *Reyner Banham*, pp. 409–10.

14 See Felicity D. Scott, *Architecture or Techno-utopia: Politics after Modernism* (Cambridge, MA, and London, 2007), pp. 3–4. Banham appears briefly here to signify a rearguard position as regards technology; he is a representative of an earlier, more innocent time.

15 For example, the discussion about the New Art-history in 'The New Brutalism'.

16 On anti-academicism, see Whiteley, *Reyner Banham*, p. 395; also Anne Massey, *The Independent Group: Modernism and Mass Culture in Britain, 1945–59* (Manchester, 1995), p. 74.

17 Reyner Banham, 'The Atavism of the Short-distance Mini-cyclist', *Living Arts*, 3 (1964), pp. 91–7.

18 Reyner Banham, Paul Barker, Peter Hall and Cedric Price, 'Non-plan: An Experiment in Freedom', *New Society* (20 March 1969), p. 443.

19 David Watkin, *Morality and Architecture* (Oxford, 1977).

20 Reyner Banham, 'Pevsner's Progress', *Times Literary Supplement* (17 February 1978), p. 191. For more on this episode, see Whiteley, *Reyner Banham*, pp. 368–72.

21 See Banham papers, Getty Research Institute, Box 8, File 2. Also discussion in Todd Gannon, *Reyner Banham and the Paradoxes of High Tech* (Los Angeles, CA, 2018), pp. 2–3.

22 Reyner Banham, 'Centre Georges Pompidou', *Architectural Review*, 161 (May 1977), pp. 272–94.

23 Preparations for the IFA inaugural lecture were well advanced at Banham's death; the guest list had been finalized and included Robert Maxwell, Alan Colquhoun, Robert Gutman, Kenneth Frampton, Robin Middleton, Christiane Collins and others. Correspondence, n.d., Banham papers, Getty Research Institute, Box 16, File 3.

24  First published in *Art in America*, 76 (October 1988), pp. 172–7. My
version is from *A Critic Writes*, ed. Mary Banham et al., pp. 281–91.
Related material in Banham Papers, Getty Research Institute, Box 16,
file 3.

25  Henry-Russell Hitchcock and P. Johnson, *The International Style:
Architecture since 1922*, exh. cat., Museum of Modern Art, New York
(New York, 1932).

26  Banham, 'Actual Monuments', p. 283.

27  Ibid., p. 283. See Reyner Banham, *A Concrete Atlantis: U.S. Industrial
Building and European Modern Architecture, 1900–1925* (Cambridge, MA,
and London, 1986), p. 154.

28  Banham, 'Actual Monuments', p. 283.

29  Maxwell, 'The Plenitude of Presence'.

30  Banham, 'Actual Monuments', p. 284.

31  Ibid., p. 284.

32  Hitchcock and Johnson, *The International Style*.

33  Banham, 'Actual Monuments', p. 290.

34  Ibid., p. 291.

35  See Beatriz Colomina, *Privacy and Publicity: Modern Architecture as Mass
Media* (Cambridge, MA, and London, 1995), Also Colomina, 'Enclosed
by Images', in *The Banham Lectures*, ed. Aynsley and Atkinson, pp. 197–9.

36  The New York-based journal *October* was a leader in this process at the
same time Banham was considering these ideas. See, for example, its
special issue on the Belgian artist Marcel Broodthaers (vol. XLII, 1987),
or articles on the Musée d'Orsay or the concept of the Panopticon
(vol. XLI, also 1987).

37  There is a queer subtext to the production of *The International Style*,
namely the research trip Hitchcock and Johnson took to Europe in
1929, and their tense relationship on it, exacerbated by Johnson's
numerous sexual conquests. It could have been used to support
Banham's argument about the definition of architectural history being
located in architectural historians as much as buildings, although
Banham never showed much inclination for this kind of speculation.
See Johnson's correspondence home, Johnson papers, Getty Research
Institute, Box 25, File 4.

38  Reyner Banham, 'A Black Box: The Secret Profession of Architecture',
*New Statesman and Society* (12 October 1990), pp. 22–5. I refer to the
version in *A Critic Writes*, ed. M. Banham et al., pp. 292–9.

39  Visits done sometimes in the company of Oli Arditi in full Western
regalia. Arditi interview.

40  Banham, 'A Black Box', p. 292.

41 For his review of the AT&T, see Reyner Banham, 'AT&T: The Post-Deco Skyscraper', *Architectural Review*, 176 (August 1984), pp. 22–9.

42 Banham, 'A Black Box', p. 293.

43 Ibid., pp. 294–5.

44 Ibid., p. 299.

45 Gannon, *Reyner Banham*, p. 3.

46 Colomina, 'Enclosed by Images', p. 198. Banham and Frampton's differing reactions to the United States are discussed briefly in Stan Allen and Hal Foster, 'A Conversation with Kenneth Frampton', *October*, 106 (Fall 2003), p. 39.

47 It was the model for Frampton's *Modern Architecture: A Critical History* (London, 1992). Frampton was generous about Banham in person to me, despite their differences. Conversation with Frampton, Glasgow, 17 March 2017.

48 Allen and Foster, 'A Conversation with Kenneth Frampton', p. 39.

49 Banham, 'A Black Box', p. 298. Discussed in Whiteley, *Reyner Banham*, p. 395.

50 The bylines used for his work by the *Architects' Journal* and *New Society* respectively.

51 Resulting in the embattled 'resistance' in Frampton. Banham, 'A Black Box', p. 294; Frampton, *Modern Architecture: A Critical History*, p. 343. Frampton's conclusion pits architecture and technology against each other.

# SELECT BIBLIOGRAPHY

WRITINGS BY BANHAM

**Books and anthologies**

*Theory and Design in the First Machine Age* (London, 1960)

*Guide to Modern Architecture* (London, 1962)

*The New Brutalism: Ethic or Aesthetic* (London, 1966)

*The Architecture of the Well-tempered Environment* (London, 1969; 2nd edn, Chicago, IL, 1984)

*Los Angeles: The Architecture of Four Ecologies* (London, 1971)

ed., *The Aspen Papers: Twenty Years of Design Theory from the International Design Conference in Aspen* (London, 1974)

*Age of the Masters: A Personal View of Modern Architecture* (London, 1975)

*Megastructure: Urban Futures of the Recent Past* (London, 1976)

*Design by Choice*, ed. Penny Sparke (London, 1981)

—, Charles Beveridge and Henry-Russell Hitchcock, *Buffalo Architecture: A Guide* (Cambridge, MA, and London, 1981)

*Scenes in America Deserta* (Layton, UT, 1982)

*A Concrete Atlantis: U.S. Industrial Building and European Modern Architecture, 1900–1925* (Cambridge, MA, and London, 1986)

*Visions of Ron Herron* (London, 1994)

*A Critic Writes: Essays by Reyner Banham*, ed. Mary Banham, Paul Barker, Sutherland Lyall and Cedric Price (Berkeley and Los Angeles, CA, 1996)

**Selected articles**

'Vehicles of Desire', *Art* (1 September 1955), p. 3

'Sant'Elia', *Architectural Review*, 117 (May 1955), pp. 295–301

'The New Brutalism', *Architectural Review*, 118 (December 1955), pp. 355–61

'Footnotes to Sant'Elia', *Architectural Review*, 119 (December 1955), pp. 343–4

'This Is Tomorrow', *Architectural Review*, 120 (September 1956), pp. 186–8

'Futurism and Modern Architecture', *Architects' Journal*, 125 (17 January 1957), pp. 119–26

'The Decisive Contribution of Adolf Loos', *Architectural Review*, 121 (February 1957), pp. 85–8

'Futurist Manifesto', *Architectural Review*, 126 (February 1959), pp. 77–80

'I'd Crawl a Mile for . . . *Playboy*', *Architects' Journal* (7 April 1960), pp. 527–9

'History and Psychiatry', *Architectural Review*, 127 (May 1960), pp. 324–32

'The History of the Immediate Future', *Journal of the Royal Institute of British Architects*, LXVIII/7 (May 1961), pp. 252–60, 269

'Night Mrs Jagbag', *Architects' Journal* (29 November 1961), pp. 1020-22

'Park Hill Housing, Sheffield', *Architectural Review*, 130 (December 1961), p. 409

'Coronation Street, Hoggartsborough', *New Statesman* (9 February 1962), pp. 200-201

'Big Doug, Small Piece', *Architects' Journal*, cxxxvi (1 August 1962), pp. 251-3

'The Style for the Job', *New Statesman* (14 February 1964), p. 261

'The Atavism of the Short-distance Mini-cyclist', *Living Arts*, 3 (1964), pp. 91-7

'Brands Hatch', *New Statesman* (17 July 1964), pp. 97-8

'A Home Is Not a House', *Art in America* (April 1965), pp. 75-9

'Unlovable at Any Speed', *Architects' Journal* (21 December 1966), pp. 1527-9

'Horse of a Different Colour', *New Society* (3 November 1967), pp. 436-7

'Disservice Areas', *New Society* (23 May 1968), pp. 762-3

'Encounter with Sunset Boulevard', *The Listener* (22 August 1968), pp. 235-6

'Roadscape with Rusting Nails', *The Listener* (29 August 1968), pp. 267-8

'Beverly Hills, Too, Is a Ghetto', *The Listener* (5 September 1968), pp. 296-8

'The Art of Doing Your Thing', *The Listener* (12 September 1968), pp. 330-31

'Flatscape with Containers', *Architectural Design*, 38 (November 1968), pp. 1378-9

'History Faculty, Cambridge', *Architectural Review*, 144 (November 1968), pp. 328-41

—, Paul Barker, Peter Hall and Cedric Price, 'Non-plan: An Experiment in Freedom', *New Society* (20 March 1969), pp. 435-43

'The Crisp at the Crossroads', *New Society* (9 July 1970), p. 77

'Long Life/Loose Fit/Low Energy vs Foster', *New Society* (9 November 1972), pp. 344-5

'Detroit Tin Revisited', in *Design, 1900-1960: Studies in Design and Popular Culture of the Twentieth Century*, ed. T. Faulkner (Newcastle, 1976), pp. 120-40

'Mesa Messiah', *New Society* (6 May 1976), pp. 306-7

'Centre Georges Pompidou', *Architectural Review*, 161 (May 1977), pp. 272-94

'Pevsner's Progress', *Times Literary Supplement* (17 February 1978), pp. 191-2

'The Writing on the Walls', *Times Literary Supplement* (17 November 1978), p. 1337.

'Silicon Style', *Architectural Review*, 169 (May 1981), pp. 283-90

'AT&T: The Post-Deco Skyscraper', *Architectural Review*, 176 (August 1984), pp. 22-9

'La fine della Silicon Valley', *Casabella*, 539 (October 1987), pp. 42-3

'Actual Monuments', *Art in America*, 76 (October 1988), pp. 172–7. See also
  'A Set of Actual Monuments', *Architectural Review*, 185 (April 1989),
  pp. 89–92
'The Becher Vision', in Bernd Becher and Hilla Becher, *Water Towers*
  (Cambridge, MA, and London, 1988), pp. 7–8.
'A Black Box: The Secret Profession of Architecture', *New Statesman and
  Society* (12 October 1990), pp. 22–5


UNPUBLISHED SOURCES

'The Theory of Modern Architecture, 1907–1927', PhD thesis, Courtauld
  Institute of Art, 1958
Reyner Banham Papers, 1877–1988, Special Collections, Getty Research
  Institute, Los Angeles


OTHER SOURCES

Allen, Stan, and Hal Foster, 'A Conversation with Kenneth Frampton',
  *October*, 106 (Fall 2003), pp. 35–58.
Aynsley, Jeremy, and Harriet Atkinson, eds, *The Banham Lectures:
  Essays on Designing the Future* (Oxford, 2009)
Banham, Debby, 'Mary Banham Obituary', *The Guardian*, 4 March 2019
Campbell, P., 'The New Lloyds', *London Review of Books* (24 July 1986),
  pp. 22–3
Campo, Daniel, 'Historic Preservation in an Economic Void: Reviving
  Buffalo's Concrete Atlantis', *Journal of Planning History*, XV/4 (2016),
  pp. 314–45
Christensen, Peter H., ed., *Buffalo at the Crossroads: The Past, Present and
  Future of American Urbanism* (Ithaca, NY, 2020)
Colquhoun, A., *Collected Essays in Architectural Criticism* (London, 2009)
Crinson, Mark, and Claire Zimmerman, eds, *Neo-avant-garde and
  Postmodern: Postwar Architecture in Britain and Beyond* (New Haven, CT,
  2010)
Crinson, Mark, *Alison and Peter Smithson* (London, 2018)
—, and Richard J. Williams, *The Architecture of Art History: A Historiography*
  (London, 2018)
Davis, Mike, *City of Quartz: Excavating the Future in Los Angeles* (London,
  1990)
Dorrian, Mark, 'Banham avec Ballard: On Style and Violence', *Cabinet*, 66
  (Spring 2018–Winter 2019), www.cabinetmagazine.org, accessed
  13 August 2020

Forge, Andrew, 'We Dream of Motor-cars', *Encounter*, 6 (January 1956),
pp. 65–8

Forty, Adrian, 'One Partially Americanised European', in *Twentieth Century
Architecture and its Histories*, ed. Louise Campbell (London, 2000),
pp. 195–206

Foster, Hal, 'Expendabilia', *London Review of Books* (9 May 2002), pp. 14–15

—, 'Madder Men', *London Review of Books* (24 October 2019), pp. 29–30

Frampton, Kenneth, *Modern Architecture: A Critical History* (London, 1992)

French, Philip, review of Reyner Banham, *Los Angeles: The Architecture of
Four Ecologies*, *The Times*, 5 April 1971

Gannon, Todd, *Reyner Banham and the Paradoxes of High Tech* (Los Angeles,
CA, 2018)

Girouard, Mark, *Big Jim: The Life and Work of James Stirling* (London, 1998)

Goldberger, Paul, 'Reyner Banham, Architectural Critic Dies at 66', *New York
Times*, 22 March 1988

Hatherley, Owen, 'Silo Dreams: Metamorphoses of the Grain Elevator',
*Journal of Architecture*, XX/3 (2015), pp. 474–88

—, 'Strange, Angry Objects', *London Review of Books* (17 November 2016),
pp. 11–16

Highmore, Ben, *The Art of Brutalism: Rescuing Hope from Catastrophe in 1950s
Britain* (New Haven, CT, 2017)

Hilberry, Harry H., '*Theory and Design in the First Machine Age* by Reyner
Banham', *Journal of the Society of Architectural Historians*, XXII/4
(December 1963), p. 241

Hines, Thomas S., 'Reyner Banham, *Los Angeles: The Architecture of Four
Ecologies*', *Journal of the Society of Architectural Historians*, XXXI/1
(March 1972), p. 76

Hitchcock, Henry-Russell, and Philip Johnson, *The International Style:
Architecture since 1922*, exh. cat., Museum of Modern Art, New York
(New York, 1932)

'The Independent Group', *October* (Special Issue), 94 (Autumn 2000),
pp. 1–128

Johnson, Philip, 'Where Are We At?', *Architectural Review*, 127 (September
1960), pp. 173–5

Kaplan, S. Hall, review of *A Concrete Atlantis*, *Los Angeles Times*,
14 September 1986, p. 12

Lyall, Sutherland, 'Modern Icons', *New Statesman* (1 August 1986), p. 27

McKean, John Maule, 'The Last of England', *Building Design* (13 August
1976), p. 8

Marshall, Colin, 'A "Radical Alternative": How One Man Changed the
Perception of Los Angeles', *The Guardian*, 24 August 2016

Masheck, Joseph, 'Temples to the Dynamo: The "Daylight" Factory and
the Grain Elevator', *Art in America* (January 1987), pp. 13–14

Massey, Anne, *The Independent Group: Modernism and Mass Culture in Britain,
1945–59* (Manchester, 1995)

—, *Out of the Ivory Tower: The Independent Group and Popular Culture*
(Manchester, 2013)

Maxwell, Robert, 'The Plenitude of Presence', *Architectural Design*, LI/6
(1981), pp. 52–7

—, *Sweet Disorder and the Carefully Careless: Theory and Criticism in
Architecture* (Princeton, NJ, 1993)

'The New Brutalism', *October* (Special Issue), 136 (Spring 2011), pp. 1–191

Pawley, Martin, 'Last of the Piston Engine Men', *Building Design* (1 October
1971), p. 6

Penner, Barbara, 'The Man Who Wrote Too Well', *Places Journal*,
September 2015, https://placesjournal.org

Plagens, Peter, 'Los Angeles: The Ecology of Evil', *Artforum*, 11 (December
1972), pp. 67–76.

Robbins, David, ed., *The Independent Group: Postwar Britain and the
Aesthetics of Plenty* (Cambridge, MA, and London, 1990)

Scott, Felicity D., *Architecture or Techno-utopia: Politics after Modernism*
(Cambridge, MA, and London, 2007)

Smithson, Alison, and Peter Smithson, 'The New Brutalism', *Architectural
Design*, 27 (April 1955)

Soja, Edward W., *My Los Angeles* (Berkeley and Los Angeles, CA, 2014)

Vidler, Anthony, *Histories of the Immediate Present: Inventing Architectural
Modernism* (Cambridge, MA, and London, 2008)

Walsh, Victoria, *Nigel Henderson: Parallel of Life and Art* (London, 2001)

Watkin, David, *Morality and Architecture* (Oxford, 1977)

Whiteley, Nigel, *Reyner Banham: Historian of the Immediate Future*
(Cambridge, MA, and London, 2002)

Williams, Richard J., 'Pleasure and the Motorway', in *Autopia: Cars and
Culture*, ed. Joe Kerr and Peter Wollen (London, 2002), pp. 281–7

—, 'The City on the Highway, Revisited', in *The Routledge Companion to
Urban Imaginaries*, ed. Christoph Lindner and Miriam Meissner
(Abingdon, 2018), pp. 262–74

# ACKNOWLEDGEMENTS

This book emerged from two things: an extended visit to the Getty Research Institute, Los Angeles, at the beginning of 2017 and, not for the first time, a series of conversations with Vivian Constantinopoulos at Reaktion Books. Getty provided generous funding for me to explore the Banham papers, which I had only glimpsed on previous visits. Their support allowed me the time and space to work up a book proposal, and Vivian was again open-minded enough to take it on. Throughout the writing process, the University of Edinburgh provided invaluable support for travel, images and research time.

I am enormously grateful to the Banham family, not least Mary Banham, whom I was fortunate to interview twice before her death in early 2019. Ben and Debby Banham were particularly generous with interviews and advice, as was Oli Arditi. Adrian Forty, Kenneth Frampton, Tracey Schuster and Cathy Soussloff were among those who had vivid memories of Banham as a colleague and teacher. Paul Barker, Banham's erstwhile editor at *New Society*, provided the most generous interview and commentary on Banham, and I feel very fortunate to have met him before his death in 2019. His essay 'Non-plan', which he drafted with Banham, was as formative to me as anything else cited here. Other friends and colleagues provided all kinds of ideas and support, above all Mark Crinson, who in fact pointed me to 'Non-plan' in the first place, long ago, and here provided a robust commentary on a first draft. The book is very much better for his advice. I also want to thank Neil Cox, Peter France, Rose France, Simon Gooch, Penny Lewis, Christoph Lindner, Rosalind McKever, Munira Mirza, Tim Street-Porter, Sarah Thacker, Tamara Trodd, Marcus Verhagen, Vicky Walsh and Iain Boyd Whyte for commentary, help and advice at different times.

# PHOTO ACKNOWLEDGEMENTS

The author and publishers wish to express their thanks to the below sources of illustrative material and/or permission to reproduce it.

Architectural Association Archives, London (photos Reyner Banham): pp. 220, 221, 222; Architectural Press Archive/RIBA Collections: pp. 20, 87 (photo Bill Toomey), 233; from Architectural Review (December 1955): p. 68; from Art in America (April 1965): p. 121; photo Ben Banham: p. 239; courtesy Debby Banham: pp. 16, 19 (photo James Stirling); from Reyner Banham, 'Park Hill Housing, Sheffield', Architectural Review (December 1961): p. 85; from Reyner Banham, 'Sant'Elia', Architectural Review (May 1955): p. 44; from Reyner Banham, The Architecture of the Well-tempered Environment (London and Chicago, IL, 1969): pp. 124, 131; from Reyner Banham, A Concrete Atlantis: U.S. Industrial Building and European Modern Architecture, 1900–1925 (Cambridge, MA, and London, 1986): pp. 213, 218; from Reyner Banham, Los Angeles: The Architecture of Four Ecologies (Berkeley and Los Angeles, CA, and London, 1971): pp. 33, 153; from Reyner Banham, Megastructure: Urban Futures of the Recent Past (London and New York, 1976): p. 208 (above); from Thomas Faulkner, ed., Design 1900–1960: Studies in Design and Popular Culture of the Twentieth Century (Newcastle, 1976): p. 96; courtesy Simon Gooch: pp. 14, 15, 46; GTHO (CC BY-SA 3.0): p. 105; © R. Hamilton, all rights reserved/DACS 2021 (photo: Pallant House Gallery, Chichester): p. 111; courtesy Louis Hellman: pp 170, 171; Iantomferry (CC BY-SA 4.0): p. 134; from New Society (20 March 1969): pp. 158, 159; © The Paolozzi Foundation/DACS 2021 (photo © Tate): p. 101; RIBA Collections: pp. 23 (photo John McCann), 77 (photo John Maltby); San Diego Air & Space Museum Archives: p. 47; © Smithson Family Collection (photo © Centre Pompidou, MNAM-CCI, Dist. RMN-Grand Palais/Philippe Migeat): p. 82; photos © Tim Street-Porter: pp. 12, 178; sv1ambo (CC BY 2.0): p. 103; photo © Tate: p. 72; Richard J. Williams: pp. 63, 65, 78, 84, 87, 174, 175, 188, 189, 195, 196, 198, 208 (below).

# INDEX

Page numbers in *italics* indicate illustrations